STECK-VAUGHN

# AMERICA'S HISTORY
## LAND OF LIBERTY
### BOOK TWO: SINCE 1865

by VIVIAN BERNSTEIN

**Reviewers**

**Dr. John L. Esposito**
Georgetown University
Washington, D.C.

**Mel Miller**
Social Studies Consultant
Macomb County Intermediate School District
Clinton Township, Michigan

**Harcourt Achieve**

Rigby • Saxon • Steck-Vaughn

www.HarcourtAchieve.com
1.800.531.5015

## About the Author

Vivian Bernstein is the author of *World History and You, America's Story, World Geography and You, American Government, Decisions for Health,* and *Life Skills for Today.* Bernstein is active with professional organizations in social studies, education, and reading. She gives presentations to school faculties and professional groups about content area reading. She received her Master of Arts degree from New York University and was a teacher in the New York City Public School System for a number of years.

## Staff Credits

*Executive Editor:* Tina Posner
*Supervising Editor*: Donna Townsend
*Editor*: Linda Doehne

*Design Staff:* Stephanie Arsenault, Donna Cunningham, Joan Cunningham, Deborah Diver, John-Paxton Gremillion, Scott Huber, Heather Jernt, Alan Klemp, Joyce Spicer

## Acknowledgments

**Text Credits:** p. 109 Excerpt from The Grapes of Wrath by John Steinbeck. Copyright 1939, renewed © 1967 by John Steinbeck Viking Penguin. p. 134 From IN SEARCH OF LIGHT by Edward R. Murrow, edited by E. Bliss, Jr., copyright © 1967 by the Estate of Edward R. Murrow. Used by permission of Random House, Inc. p. 135 Reprinted with the permission of Simon & Schuster Adult Publishing Group, from JOURNEY TO WASHINGTON by Daniel K. Inouye with Lawrence Elliot. Copyright © 1967 by Prentice-Hall, Inc.; copyright renewed ©1995 by Senator Daniel K. Inouye. p. 162 Excerpts from the June 2, 1995 interview with Rosa Parks, as found on www.achievement.org. Copyright © 2004 Academy of Achievement. Reprinted with permission. p. 163 Abridged, with slight changes, from WARRIORS DON'T CRY by Melba Pattillo Beals. Copyright © 1994, 1995 by Melba Beals. Used by permission of Arria Books, an imprint of Simon & Schuster Adult Publishing Group. p. 238 Excerpt from "Statement by the President in His Address to the Nation," by George W. Bush, September 11, 2001. p. 239 Excerpt from Never Forget: An Oral History of September 11, 2001 by Mitchell Fink and Lois Mathias, pp. 166–169. Copyright © 2002 by Mitchell Fink and Lois Mathias. HarperCollins. Reprinted with permission.

**Cartography:** GeoSystems, Inc., Ortelius Design, Inc.

**Charts, Graphs, and Tables:** Chuck Mackey

**Illustration Credits:** 238 ©D&G Limited, LLC

**Photo Credits:** Cover (a) ©Joe Rosenthal/Corbis; (b) ©Bettmann/Corbis; (c) ©Najlah Feanny/Corbis.

Additional Photography By Comstock Royalty Free and Getty Images Royalty Free.

2–3 ©Smithsonian American Art Museum, Washington, DC/Art Resource, NY; 4 ©Library of Congress; 5 ©The Library of Congress; 5–6 ©The Granger Collection; 8, 9 ©The Granger Collection; 10 ©Bern Keating/Black Star/Stock Photo; 11 ©The Granger Collection; 14 ©Grant Heilman Photography; 15 ©Nebraska State Historical Society; 17 ©The Granger Collection; 19 ©The Granger Collection; 20 ©Robb De Wall/Crazy Horse Memorial; 24 ©Bettmann/CORBIS; 25 ©The Granger Collection; 27 (a, b) ©The Granger Collection; 29–30 ©The Granger Collection; 34 ©Culver Pictures; 35–36 ©Bettmann/CORBIS; 38 ©Culver Pictures; 40 ©Bettmann/CORBIS; 41 ©The Granger Collection; 45–49 ©The Granger Collection; 51–52 (a) ©The Granger Collection; 58–59 ©Courtesy Frederic Remington Art Museum, Ogdensburg, NY; 60 ©Bettmann/CORBIS; 61 ©Culver Pictures; 62 ©Alaska State Library; 63–64 ©The Granger Collection; 66 ©The Granger Collection; 70 ©Culver Pictures; 72 ©Miami Herald/Angel Valentin; 73 (a, b) ©Bettmann/CORBIS; 74–75 ©The Granger Collection; 76 ©Culver Pictures; 80 ©The Granger Collection; 82 ©The Granger Collection; 83 ©Bettmann/CORBIS; 85 ©The Granger Collection; 87 ©The Granger Collection; 88 ©Bettmann/CORBIS; 93 ©The Granger Collection; 94 ©Culver Pictures; 95 ©Archive Photos/Getty Images; 96–97 ©The Granger Collection; 98 (a–d) ©The Granger Collection; 98 (e) ©Bettmann/CORBIS; 99 ©The Granger Collection; 104–105 ©Superstock; 106 ©HA Collection; 107 ©Bettmann/CORBIS; 109 ©Bettmann/CORBIS; 110 ©AP Wide World Photos; 112 (a) ©Archive Photos/Getty Images; 112 (b) ©Bettmann/CORBIS; 113 ©Bettmann/CORBIS; 118 ©Bettmann/CORBIS; 119 (a) ©The Granger Collection; 119 (b) ©Bettmann/CORBIS; 119 (c) ©AP Wide World Photos; 120 ©Culver Pictures; 121 ©Topham/The Image Works; 122 ©Hulton Archive/Getty Images; 124–125 ©Bettmann/CORBIS; 128–129 ©Bettmann/CORBIS; 131 (a) ©Michel Semeniako/Gamma-Liaison; 131 (b) ©Piotr Malecki/Getty Images; 134 (a) ©AP Wide World Photos; 136 ©Bettmann/CORBIS; 142–143 ©1996 Norman Rockwell Family Trust, reprinted by permission. Collection of the Norman Rockwell Museum at Stockbridge, Massachusetts; 144 ©Quinn Stewart; 145 ©CORBIS; 146–147 ©UPI/Bettmann/CORBIS; 150 ©CORBIS; 151 ©National Portrait Gallery/Smithsonian Institution/Art Resource; 154 ©Carl Iwasaki/Time & Life Pictures/Getty Images; 155 ©Bettmann/CORBIS; 156–157 ©UPI/Bettmann/CORBIS; 158 ©AP Wide World Photos; 159–160 ©CORBIS; 161 ©CNP Archive Photos/Hulton Archive/Getty Images; 163 ©UPI/Bettmann/CORBIS; 167 ©HA Collection; 168 ©CORBIS; 170–171 ©CORBIS; 172 (a) ©Howard Ruffner/Black Star/Stock Photo; 172 (b) ©CORBIS; 173 ©CORBIS; 174 ©AP Wide World Photos; 178 ©HA Collection; 179 ©CORBIS; 180 ©Bettmann/CORBIS; 181 ©Najlah Feanny/Corbis; 182 ©CORBIS; 183 ©AP Wide World Photos; 184 ©Bettmann/CORBIS; 187 (a, b) ©The Granger Collection; 190–191 ©Joe Sohm/Chromosohm/The Stock Connection; 192 ©Alan Mingam/Gamma-Liaison; 193 ©Sygma/CORBIS; 194 ©Alan Mingam/Gamma-Liaison; 195 ©Martin Jager/Gamma-Liaison; 196 ©Geoff Donen/Gamma-Liaison; 197 ©UPI/Bettmann/CORBIS; 198 (a) ©Eric Bouvet/Gamma-Liaison; 198 (b) ©Chip Hires/Gamma-Liaison; 199 ©Wally McNamee/Corbis; 202 ©Reuters/Bettmann/CORBIS; 203 (a) ©Peter Turnley/Corbis; 203 (b) ©Dennis Brack/Black Star/Stock Photo; 207 ©Chip Hires/Gamma-Liaison; 209 ©Larry Downing/Sygma/CORBIS; 213 ©Jeff Stahler reprinted by permission of United Feature Syndicate, Inc.; 214 ©Robert Schuster; 215 ©Courtesy Texas Highways; 216 ©P.F. Bentley Photography; 217 ©Gilles Mingasson/Gamma-Liaison; 218 (a) ©Porter Gifford/Gamma-Liaison; 218 (b) ©AP Wide World Photos; 220 ©Wally McNamee/Corbis; 223 ©Lucidio Studio, Inc./Superstock; 224 ©Bonnie Kamin/PhotoEdit; 225 ©AP Wide World Photos; 226 ©Jeff Greenberg/Photo Edit; 227 ©Jonathan Nourok/PhotoEdit; 228 ©Lynn Goldsmith/Corbis; 232 © AP Wide World Photos; 233 ©Bill Ross/Corbis; 235 ©AP Wide World Photos; 237 ©Jason Reed/Reuters/Corbis; 238 ©AP Wide World Photos; 239 ©Ricky Flores/The Journal News/Corbis; 240 ©Alex Wong/Getty Images; 243 (a) ©AP Wide World Photos; 244 ©Mirrorpix/Getty Images; 245 ©AP Wide World Photos; 248 ©AP Wide World Photos; 267–272 ©National Portrait Gallery/Smithsonian Institution/Art Resource

# CONTENTS

# To the Reader

You are about to read the exciting story of the United States after the Civil War. As you read *America's History: Land of Liberty*, you will learn how the North and the South were reunited after the Civil War and how the South was rebuilt. The United States changed from a nation of farmers to a nation of big business and industry. Learn how Alaska and Hawaii became part of the United States. Explore the ways that millions of immigrants from many nations have changed and improved the United States. Learn how the United States became a world power and succeeded in defeating its enemies during two world wars. Understand how progress in science and technology has allowed Americans to walk on the moon and explore space. Discover how the United States has become the most important nation in the world today.

As you explore your nation's past, use *America's History: Land of Liberty* to become a stronger social studies student. You will need a social studies notebook for assignments and writing activities. Begin by mastering new vocabulary words for each chapter and reviewing vocabulary from earlier chapters. Locate new places on a map and understand the ways geography can affect history. Read each chapter carefully. A second reading will improve your comprehension and recall. By working carefully on end of chapter activities, you will improve your vocabulary, critical thinking, writing, and social studies skills.

As you study American history, you will learn how many kinds of Americans built your nation. Think about the ways events of the past have created the nation that you are a part of today. An understanding of America's triumphs and mistakes in the past can help you work for a better future. As you journey through American history, remember that the story of the United States is your story, too!

*Vivian Bernstein*

# The Five Themes of Geography

Geographers divide geography into five themes, or main ideas. The themes are a way to organize the study of geography.

## Movement
Huge ships transport goods in and out of the Port of Los Angeles, one of the busiest ports in the United States.

## Human-Environment Interaction
In Las Vegas, one of the fastest growing cities in the United States, new neighborhoods are being built on desert land. Desert animals have a smaller area in which to live. Building also hurts the area's limited water supplies.

**Location**
Chicago, Illinois, is located on the shores of Lake Michigan.

**Place**
Marshy wetlands and the plants and animals that live there make the Florida Everglades a special place.

**egion**
the United States, the Rocky Mountains form e backbone of the Mountain region.

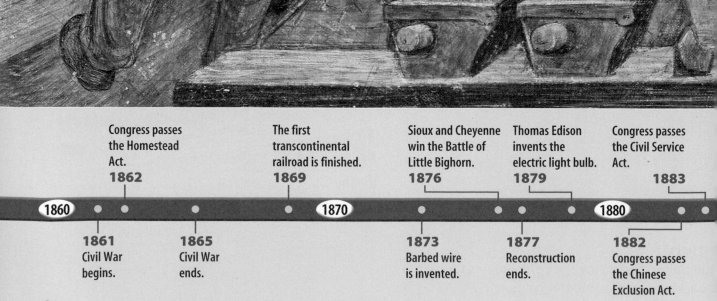

| | | | | | |
|---|---|---|---|---|---|
| Congress passes the Homestead Act. **1862** | | The first transcontinental railroad is finished. **1869** | Sioux and Cheyenne win the Battle of Little Bighorn. **1876** | Thomas Edison invents the electric light bulb. **1879** | Congress passes the Civil Service Act. **1883** |

**1860**  •  •  •  **1870**  •  •  •  **1880**  •  •

| **1861** Civil War begins. | **1865** Civil War ends. | | **1873** Barbed wire is invented. | **1877** Reconstruction ends. | **1882** Congress passes the Chinese Exclusion Act. |
|---|---|---|---|---|---|

2

# an Industrial Nation

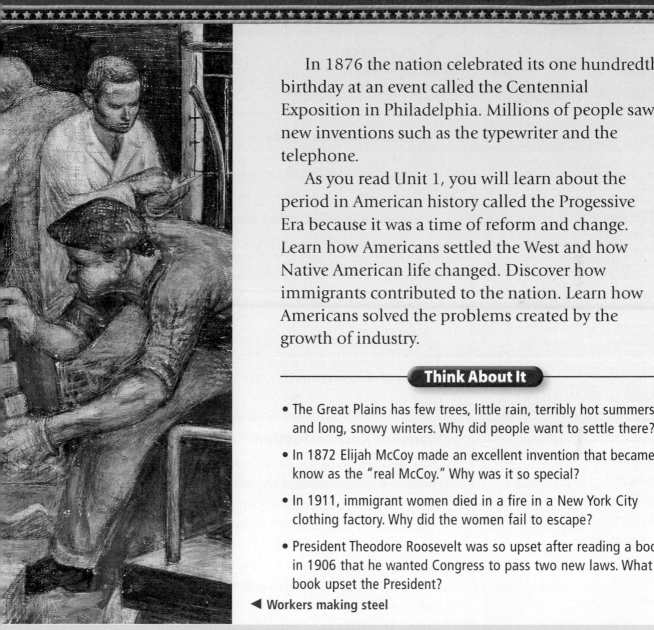

In 1876 the nation celebrated its one hundredth birthday at an event called the Centennial Exposition in Philadelphia. Millions of people saw new inventions such as the typewriter and the telephone.

As you read Unit 1, you will learn about the period in American history called the Progessive Era because it was a time of reform and change. Learn how Americans settled the West and how Native American life changed. Discover how immigrants contributed to the nation. Learn how Americans solved the problems created by the growth of industry.

## Think About It

- The Great Plains has few trees, little rain, terribly hot summers, and long, snowy winters. Why did people want to settle there?

- In 1872 Elijah McCoy made an excellent invention that became know as the "real McCoy." Why was it so special?

- In 1911, immigrant women died in a fire in a New York City clothing factory. Why did the women fail to escape?

- President Theodore Roosevelt was so upset after reading a book in 1906 that he wanted Congress to pass two new laws. What book upset the President?

◄ Workers making steel

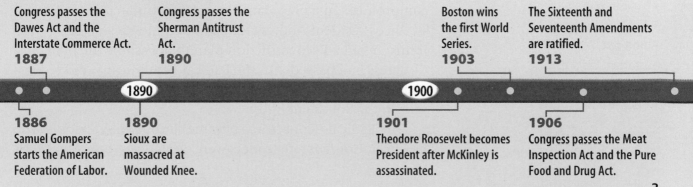

| Congress passes the Dawes Act and the Interstate Commerce Act. **1887** | Congress passes the Sherman Antitrust Act. **1890** | | Boston wins the first World Series. **1903** | The Sixteenth and Seventeenth Amendments are ratified. **1913** |

**1890**   **1900**

**1886**
Samuel Gompers starts the American Federation of Labor.

**1890**
Sioux are massacred at Wounded Knee.

**1901**
Theodore Roosevelt becomes President after McKinley is assassinated.

**1906**
Congress passes the Meat Inspection Act and the Pure Food and Drug Act.

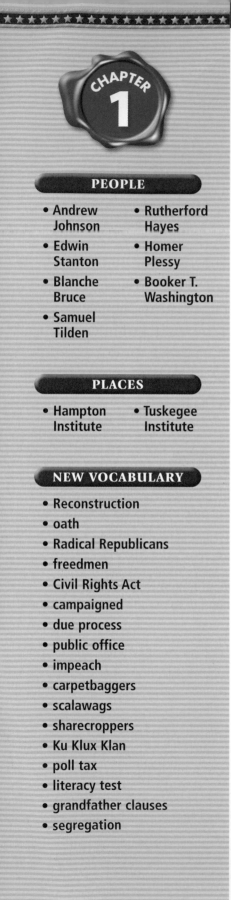
# The Reconstruction Years

## Focus on Main Ideas

1. How did the Republicans help African Americans during Reconstruction?

2. Why were the Fourteenth and Fifteenth Amendments added to the Constitution?

3. What changes took place in the South after Reconstruction?

▲ Freedmen learned to read with this spelling book.

The United States faced serious problems after the Civil War. Much of the South had been destroyed. During the years known as **Reconstruction**, Southern states would rebuild their economies and become part of the United States again.

## Plans for Reconstruction

Lincoln's goals for Reconstruction were to reunite all of the states and to rebuild the country. Lincoln planned to allow Southern states to rejoin the Union if one tenth of their voters would take an **oath** to be loyal to the Union. One group in Congress, which became known as the **Radical Republicans**, disagreed with Lincoln's plan. They believed that the South was to blame for the war and should be punished. Lincoln vetoed the harsh Reconstruction plan passed by Congress. Before Lincoln and the Congress could compromise on a plan, Lincoln was assassinated.

Vice President Andrew Johnson became President. Johnson had a Reconstruction plan that was like the plan Congress had passed, but the Radical Republicans rejected it. The Radical Republicans believed that Johnson's plan did not punish the South enough.

The Radical Republicans became furious when people who had been Confederate leaders were elected to Congress and to state governments. They were also furious when Southern states passed laws called Black Codes. These laws treated African Americans as if they were still enslaved. Congress created an agency called the Freedmen's Bureau to help the **freedmen**, enslaved African Americans who became free after the Civil War. The Black Codes in the South said freedmen could only work as farmers or house servants. Freedmen had to carry special passes when they traveled. They could not serve on juries or vote. Since the Republicans controlled Congress, they decided to use their power to change what was happening in the South.

## Congress and Reconstruction

The Radical Republicans created their own Reconstruction plan. Their first action was to pass a **Civil Rights Act** in 1866. This law said that African Americans were American citizens and had equal rights under the law. Next the Republicans wanted to add the Fourteenth Amendment to the Constitution. President Johnson **campaigned** against the amendment and the Radical Republicans. Despite Johnson's efforts, Republicans won control of Congress in the election of 1866. The Fourteenth Amendment was ratified in 1868.

▼ By the end of the Civil War, much of the the South looked like the photograph below of Richmond, Virginia. Many soldiers returned to their homes to find that they had been destroyed. Throughout the South many farms, factories, railroads, bridges, and buildings would have to be rebuilt.

The Fourteenth Amendment has been called the Equal Rights Amendment. The amendment said that all people born in the United States were citizens of their state and the nation. This included African Americans. The amendment also said that states could not make laws that took away the rights of citizens. States had to give all people **due process** under the law.

In 1867 the Republicans passed the Reconstruction Act. The act had five parts. First, any state governments in the South that had been created under Lincoln's plan or Johnson's plan were not recognized by Congress. Instead federal troops would be sent to rule the South. Second, people who had been Confederate soldiers or leaders could not vote or hold **public office**. Third, all other white men and all African American men could vote and be elected to public office. Fourth, Southern states had to write new state constitutions that guaranteed African American men the right to vote. Fifth, all Southern states had to ratify the Fourteenth Amendment before they could rejoin the Union.

Johnson vetoed Congress's plan for Reconstruction, but Congress passed it again and the Reconstruction Act became law. By 1870 all Southern states had ratified the Fourteenth Amendment and had rejoined the Union.

## The Impeachment of Johnson

The Radical Republicans disliked Andrew Johnson because he opposed their Reconstruction plans. They wanted to remove Johnson from the job of President. According to the Constitution, the House of Representatives can **impeach** a President

▲ After the Civil War, African Americans had the right to vote. Their votes helped to elect African American leaders during the years of Reconstruction.

who commits crimes. Then the President is put on trial in the Senate. If two thirds of the senators find the President guilty, the President loses his job.

In 1868 the House of Representatives voted to impeach Johnson. Congress had never before voted to impeach a President. Johnson was accused of not carrying out the Reconstruction plan of Congress and of breaking the Tenure in Office Act. Congress had passed the Tenure of Office Act to have power over the President. This law said that he could not fire anyone without the Senate's approval. When the President fired Edwin Stanton, the secretary of war and a supporter of the Radical Republicans, Johnson had broken the Tenure of Office Act.

After Johnson was impeached, he had a trial in the Senate that lasted three months. The Senate needed 36 votes to find Johnson guilty. Only 35 senators voted against him. The other senators correctly believed that Johnson was a poor leader and a poor President, but he had not committed crimes. Johnson finished his term as President.

In November 1868 the popular Union war hero General Ulysses S. Grant was elected President. For the first time, African Americans were able to vote in an election for President. They helped Grant win. Grant did a poor job as President. Many of the people that he appointed stole money from the government. Still, in 1872, Grant was reelected to a second term.

Under President Grant, the Fifteenth Amendment became part of the Constitution in 1870. This amendment said citizens cannot be denied the right to vote because of their race. Therefore, African American men had the right to vote. Women were not yet allowed to vote in any state, but they could vote in the Territory of Wyoming.

## The South During Reconstruction

During Reconstruction the South was controlled by three groups—**carpetbaggers**, **scalawags**, and African American Republicans. Carpetbaggers came from the North. They were called carpetbaggers because travelers carried their clothing in bags made of carpet material. Some carpetbaggers really tried

▲ Most African Americans who had been slaves remained in the South as farmers. They started small farms on land that they rented from the plantation owners. They paid for the use of the land by giving the owner part of the crops they raised.

to help the South, but many used their power to get rich. Scalawags were white Republican Southerners. They became the largest group in Reconstruction governments. Before the war, most scalawags had been small farmers. After the war they wanted the power that had belonged to rich plantation owners. Most former Confederates hated the scalawags.

African Americans had a small role in government while the Union Army controlled the South. During Reconstruction many African Americans were elected to public office in state governments. Also, 22 African Americans were elected to Congress before 1900, including 2 senators and 20 representatives. One of the two senators was Blanche Bruce from Mississippi. In the Senate, Bruce worked to help African Americans, Native Americans, and Chinese immigrants win equal rights. Bruce was respected as an honest senator who cared about helping different groups of Americans.

## African Americans in the South After the Civil War

After the Civil War, there were four million freedmen who had no money, no land, no jobs, and no education. The Freedmen's Bureau gave African Americans and poor whites food, clothing, and medical care. It started new hospitals and more than 4,000 public

▲ Hiram Revels of Mississippi, seated at left, was the first African American elected to the United States Senate. The other men were the first African Americans elected to the House of Representatives. All seven men were in Congress during the 1870s.

▲ Members of the Ku Klux Klan threatened, attacked, and killed African Americans. The Klan wanted to control African Americans who had won voting rights and other rights after the Civil War. In 1871, Congress passed a law giving the President the power to use troops to stop the Klan.

schools. The Bureau also started several universities for African Americans.

Freedmen needed jobs after the war, but there were few kinds of work besides farming that they knew how to do. Since they did not have money to buy land, seeds, tools, and farm animals, they were forced to become **sharecroppers**. They rented farm land by giving landowners a share of their crops. They paid for the use of their tools, seeds, and farm animals with another share of their crops. This system forced sharecroppers to give more than half of their crops to the landowners. They had few crops left to sell or to use for themselves, so sharecroppers remained very poor year after year.

In 1866 white Southerners started a secret organization called the **Ku Klux Klan**. Members wore white hoods and white robes. Their goal was to stop freedmen from using the new rights they had won. Many freedmen were beaten and many others were killed by the Klan.

## The End of Reconstruction

In 1872, while Grant was President, Congress passed a law that allowed most Confederates to vote and hold public office. Once that happened, Democrats slowly won control of the South just as they had before the Civil War.

During the election of 1876, Democratic Governor Samuel Tilden of New York ran against Republican Governor Rutherford Hayes of Ohio. To win the election, one candidate needed a majority of electoral votes. Each side said it had won a majority of electoral votes. Each side also said there had been cheating during the election. Since it was

9

▲ The decision of the Supreme Court in the 1896 case of *Plessy* v. *Ferguson* kept segregation in the United States until the 1950s.

hard to decide which candidate was the real winner, Congress created a special committee to choose the President. That committee chose Hayes as the winner of the election after Democrats and Republicans worked out a compromise.

Under this Compromise of 1877, Hayes promised to remove all federal troops from the South. He also promised that federal money would be used to build railroads in the South. The Democrats accepted this compromise. In March 1877, Hayes became the new President. He ordered federal troops to leave the South. Reconstruction had ended.

## The South After Reconstruction

The Fifteenth Amendment was supposed to protect the right of African Americans to vote. When federal troops left, Southern governments passed laws that took away that right. One law required voters to pay a special **poll tax** in order to vote. Most African Americans were too poor to pay the tax. Another law required people to pass a difficult **literacy test**. These laws also had **grandfather clauses**. These clauses said that people whose grandfather had voted in 1867 did not have to pay poll taxes or pass literacy tests to vote. These laws allowed poor whites to vote but made it impossible for most African Americans to vote.

Governments throughout the South also began to pass **segregation** laws called Jim Crow laws. These laws kept African Americans and whites apart in public places such as schools, hotels, beaches, churches, and restaurants.

In 1896 the Supreme Court protected segregation in a case called Plessy v. Ferguson. Homer Plessy, an African American, wanted to ride in the same railroad cars as white people. The Court ruled against Plessy and said that states could pass segregation laws to keep African Americans and white people apart. However, the public places for African Americans had to be equal to those for whites. Whites used this "separate but equal" decision to carry out segregation until the 1950s.

In 1776 the United States had started with the goal that this nation would allow all people to have freedom and equality. The years after Reconstruction proved that this goal had not been reached. But the Thirteenth, Fourteenth, and Fifteenth Amendments gave the nation better tools for reaching its goal. Many years later, those amendments would finally allow all Americans to have equal rights.

# Booker T. Washington 1856–1915

Booker T. Washington was born into slavery, but he became an important African American leader. He advised governors, Congressmen, and two Presidents on how to help African Americans.

Washington became free when he was nine years old. He wanted an education very badly, so he went to school at the Hampton Institute, a school for African American students. He became a teacher.

In 1881 Washington started the Tuskegee Institute in Alabama. Washington's goal was to teach African Americans different trades at the school so they could get better jobs. Many students at Tuskegee became teachers who later started their own schools for African Americans. Washington was the principal at Tuskegee for 33 years.

While Washington worked at Tuskegee, he often thought about the problems African Americans had in the South. Washington wanted to help African Americans have a better life even though they were not treated fairly. He believed that African Americans needed good jobs so they could earn more money and then buy their own land. By doing this, they would slowly have more power to improve their civil rights.

Washington said these ideas in a famous speech, the Atlanta Compromise. He asked other Americans to be fair and to give African Americans better jobs. He said that African Americans must accept segregation and not ask for equal rights. As they earned more money, they would receive better treatment. Not all African Americans agreed with Washington's ideas. Some believed African Americans should demand equal rights.

Booker T. Washington succeeded in helping many African Americans get a good education. Today Washington is remembered as one of the most important African American leaders during the years after Reconstruction.

## In Your Own Words

Write a paragraph in your notebook that tells how Booker T. Washington tried to help African Americans.

★★★★★★★★★★★★★★★★★★★★★★★★★★★★★★★★★★★★★★★★★★★★★★★★★★★★★★★

## CHAPTER 1 MAIN IDEAS

- The years after the Civil War were called Reconstruction.

- After Abraham Lincoln was assassinated, Andrew Johnson became President.

- Radical Republicans, members of Congress who blamed the South for the war and felt the South should be punished, opposed President Johnson's Reconstruction plan.

- President Johnson was impeached.

- Reconstruction came to an end in March 1877 when President Hayes ordered federal troops to leave the South.

- After Reconstruction, Southern states passed laws that took many rights away from African Americans. Segregation laws separated African Americans and whites in many public places.

## VOCABULARY

**Choose the Meaning** ■ Write the letter of the word or phrase that best completes each sentence.

1. An **oath** is a _____ .

   a. promise to be loyal
   b. proposed law
   c. plan

2. **Freedmen** were people who _____ .

   a. passed the Black Codes
   b. wanted to stop enslaved African Americans from gaining their freedom
   c. became free after the Civil War

3. The **Civil Rights Act** said that African Americans _____ .

   a. were American citizens
   b. had to pay for their freedom
   c. could not hold any public offices

4. To **impeach** means to _____ .

   a. be elected to a public office
   b. be charged with a crime in order to be removed from public office
   c. be chosen to run for political office

5. **Sharecroppers** rented land from landowners in return for _____ .

   a. money
   b. labor
   c. crops

6. A **poll tax** had to be paid so that a person could _____ .

   a. own land
   b. move to another place
   c. vote

## USING GRAPHIC ORGANIZERS

**Concept Web** ■ Complete the graphic organizer with information about Reconstruction.

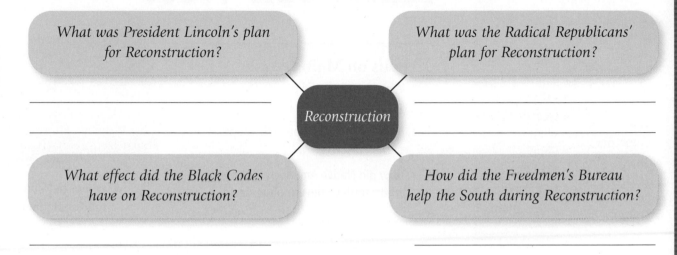

What was President Lincoln's plan for Reconstruction?

_____

_____

What was the Radical Republicans' plan for Reconstruction?

_____

_____

Reconstruction

What effect did the Black Codes have on Reconstruction?

_____

_____

How did the Freedmen's Bureau help the South during Reconstruction?

_____

_____

## CRITICAL THINKING

**Distinguishing Relevant Information** ■ Imagine you are telling a friend about Reconstruction in the South after the Civil War. Read each sentence below. Decide which sentences are relevant to what you will say. Put a check in front of the relevant sentences. There are four relevant sentences.

_____ 1. President Lincoln cared about Southerners.

_____ 2. President Johnson and the Radical Republicans disagreed over Reconstruction plans.

_____ 3. The Fourteenth and Fifteenth amendments were added to the Constitution.

_____ 4. Radical Republicans tried to impeach President Johnson.

_____ 5. Carpetbaggers, scalawags, and African American Republicans controlled the South during Reconstruction.

_____ 6. Samuel Tilden ran for President in 1876.

## USING INFORMATION

**Writing an Opinion** ■ After the Civil War, there were different ideas about rebuilding the South and bringing the Southern states back into the Union. Write a paragraph explaining which plan of Reconstruction you would have supported.

## PEOPLE

- Cyrus McCormick
- Leland Stanford
- Henry Comstock
- Chief Seattle
- Cheyenne
- Arapaho
- Colonel John Chivington
- Sioux
- Sitting Bull
- Crazy Horse
- George Custer
- Chief Joseph
- Nez Percé
- Helen Hunt Jackson
- Red Cloud
- Korczak Ziolkowski

## PLACES

- Omaha
- Sacramento
- Promontory Point
- Abilene
- Chicago
- Black Hills

## NEW VOCABULARY

- technology
- reaper
- transcontinental
- spike
- open range
- barbed wire
- reservations
- poverty

# Growth in the American West

## Focus on Main Ideas

1. What problems did people face as they settled on the Great Plains?

2. How did railroads cause the population of the West to grow?

3. How did Native American life change as white settlers moved to the Great Plains?

▲ Wheat field on the Great Plains

Would you want to settle on the Great Plains, where there is little rain and very few trees? The summers are blazing hot and the winters are freezing cold. Dust storms, windstorms, snowstorms, and tornadoes are common. Despite these hardships, during the 1860s many Americans began to make the Great Plains their home.

## The Homestead Act

Throughout the nation's history, there had been a frontier, land that had few settlers. After the American Revolution, the frontier was the land between the original 13 states and the Mississippi River. As Americans settled that land and moved west, the Great Plains became the frontier.

The Great Plains is the flat region between the Mississippi River and the Rocky Mountains. Because this region received little rain and had few forests, it was called the Great American Desert. Few people wanted to settle there. To encourage people to settle on the Great Plains, Congress passed the Homestead Act in 1862. This law gave settlers 160 acres of free land on the Great Plains. The law required a settler to live on the land, build a house, and farm the land for five years. About two million people moved to the Great Plains because of the Homestead Act.

Life was difficult for the new settlers. People were lonely because they lived far apart and had few neighbors. There were few stores where settlers could shop.

Farming was difficult on the Great Plains, but new **technology** helped the farmers. At first farmers found it difficult to turn over the soil to plant seeds because the thick grass of the Great Plains had very long, strong roots. This problem was solved with the invention of the steel plow, which worked better than iron plows. The lack of rain made it difficult to grow crops. So farmers used windmills to pump water up from deep underground. They also planted special kinds of wheat that needed less water. To harvest large fields of wheat and corn, farmers used a machine called the **reaper**. It had been invented by Cyrus McCormick in 1831.

By the 1890s huge amounts of wheat and corn were being grown on the Great Plains. The region became known as "America's breadbasket."

## Railroads Opened the West

In 1860 there were no railroads west of the Missouri River. Building a **transcontinental** railroad would allow people to travel from the Atlantic Ocean to the Pacific Ocean. To reach this goal, Congress passed the Pacific Railway Act in 1862. This act allowed the Union Pacific

▲ Life was difficult for settlers on the Great Plains. Because there were few trees, homes were built from sod, or squares of grass. The family pictured above might have lived there for some time because they have had time to add glass windows and a new section to the original house.

Railroad Company to build a railroad that started in Omaha, Nebraska, and went west. The Central Pacific Railroad Company would build a railroad that would move east from Sacramento, California.

Both companies worked fast to lay as many miles of railroad tracks as possible. It was hard work to build railroads across rivers and mountains. The work was so dangerous that many men died while working on the railroads.

Thousands of immigrants were hired to build the railroads. The Central Pacific hired Chinese immigrants, and the Union Pacific hired Irish immigrants. Immigrants from other European countries, as well as many African Americans, also helped to build these railroads.

On May 10, 1869, the tracks of the Central Pacific and Union Pacific railroads met at a place called Promontory Point in Utah. Leland Stanford, the owner of the Central Pacific, used a silver hammer to drive a golden **spike** into the ground. The spike joined the two railroads together. The nation's first transcontinental railroad was finished. People could travel by train from New York to California in a week. By covered wagon the trip took six months. Soon more transcontinental railroad routes were built.

## Mining on the Last Frontier

The 1849 California gold rush was the first of many gold rushes in the West. Throughout Colorado, Nevada, Idaho, Montana, and the Dakotas, the search for gold, silver, and other metals continued.

In 1859 miners found small amounts of gold and large amounts of silver in Nevada. The place became known as the Comstock Lode, after Henry Comstock. Comstock did not find the gold and silver, but he took credit for finding it.

Mining towns developed near mines. Most people in mining towns were men. However, some women moved to mining towns and ran restaurants and laundries. Others ran boarding houses, or places for miners to eat and sleep. Once all the gold and silver from these mines was removed, people often left. Busy mining towns turned into empty towns called "ghost towns."

## Raising Cattle on the Great Plains

Early Spanish settlers were the first to raise cattle in the American Southwest. The Spanish taught the Mexicans how to raise cattle. After the United States won control of the Mexican Cession, American cowboys, or cowhands, learned their skills from Mexican cowboys called vaqueros. Many cowhands were Mexican Americans or African Americans.

The longhorn cattle raised by the Spanish now lived in large herds in Mexico and in Texas. Texas became the cattle-raising center of the United States. Much of the land in Texas and other parts of the Great Plains was called the **open range**. The open range was grassy land that belonged to the federal government. Cattle were allowed to graze, or feed, freely on this land.

Each spring the cowhands would begin the long drive, or trip, to move their cattle to Abilene, Kansas. It would take two months of hard work for the cowhands, riding horses, to move thousands of cattle from Texas to Abilene.

In Abilene the cattle were shipped to Chicago, Illinois, by railroad. Chicago became the meat-packing center of the United States.

As more farmers settled on the Great Plains, there were fights between farmers and ranchers, or cattle raisers. Farmers did not want cattle moving freely through their crops and destroying their farms.

The open range came to an end with the invention of **barbed wire** in 1873. Barbed wire made it easy to put fences around large areas of land. Farmers used barbed wire to keep cattle off their farms. That forced ranchers to raise cattle on their own land. Since cattle could no longer eat free grass on the open range, ranchers had to buy corn, hay, and grain from the farmers to feed the cattle.

## Native Americans of the Great Plains

Before the Civil War, the federal government had said that the West would belong to the Native Americans "as long as the rivers shall run and the grass shall grow." This promise was broken when whites tried to take control of Native American lands.

The people of the Great Plains depended on buffalo to survive. Before 1860 there were about 12 million buffalo on the Great Plains. The Native Americans of the Plains ate buffalo meat and made clothes and homes from buffalo skins. They moved from place to place to follow the herds of buffalo.

It was almost impossible for white settlers and Native Americans to live together on the Great Plains. Native Americans wanted to move from place to place as they hunted buffalo. White settlers wanted the land for farming and ranching. Settlers killed millions of buffalo. By 1903 there were only 34 buffalo left in the entire country. As the buffalo disappeared, Native Americans often starved and died.

From 1850 to 1890, the United States Army fought against the Plains Indians. During these wars thousands of Indians were killed. As a result of the wars, Native Americans were forced to move onto **reservations**, land set aside for them. These reservations usually had such poor-quality land that settlers did not want to live there. As early as 1854, an important Native American leader in the Northwest, Chief Seattle, warned his people that they would be forced to live and suffer on reservations:

"Day and night cannot dwell together. The Red Man [Native American] has ever fled the approach of the White Man. . . . It matters little where we pass the remnant of our days. They will not be many. The Indians' night promises to be dark."

◄ Cowboys, or cowhands, first learned their skills from Mexican cowhands called vaqueros. American cowboys even wore clothing similar to that worn by vaqueros.

When gold was discovered in Colorado in 1859, people looking for gold settled on land that belonged to the Cheyenne and the Arapaho. After Native Americans attacked these settlers, Colonel John Chivington attacked a peaceful group of Cheyenne, and about 450 Cheyenne were killed. The Cheyenne and Arapaho were forced to move to reservations in Oklahoma and in the Black Hills of Dakota.

In 1868 the federal government signed a treaty with the Sioux nation. This treaty gave the Sioux a reservation that included all the land in what is now South Dakota west of the Missouri River. The Black Hills were part of the land promised to the Sioux. After gold was found in the Black Hills of South Dakota in 1874, the army ordered the Sioux to stay on a reservation. The Sioux leaders Sitting Bull and Crazy Horse refused. So in 1876 General George Custer led about 200 soldiers in an attack against the Sioux at the Battle of Little Bighorn. Thousands of Sioux and Cheyenne led by Sitting Bull and Crazy Horse defeated Custer. Custer and all of his soldiers were killed, and the battle became known as "Custer's Last Stand." It was one of the greatest Native American victories. Although the Sioux and Cheyenne won this battle, they lost other

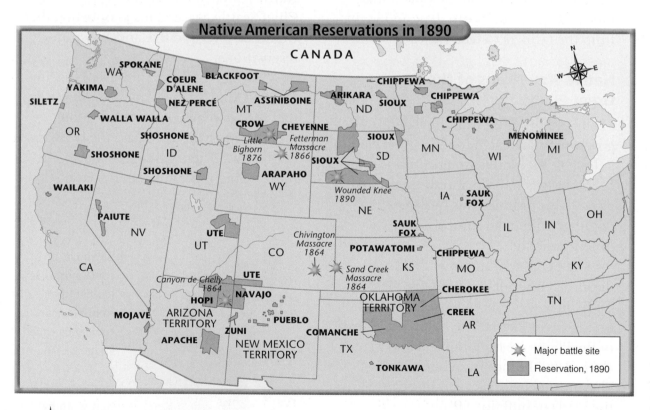

Native American Reservations in 1890

## ☀ MAP STUDY

There were many reservations set aside for Native Americans west of the Mississippi River in 1890. There were also many battles fought for control of the land in the West. What battle took place in Montana in 1876?

(Geography Theme: place)

battles to the army. In 1881 Sitting Bull and his followers surrendered.

Chief Joseph, the leader of the peaceful Nez Percé tribe, wanted to save his people from being forced onto a reservation. He tried to escape to Canada with tribe members. They had almost reached Canada when they were captured by the army. Eventually Chief Joseph agreed to move to a reservation. In his surrender speech, Chief Joseph said "I am tired of fighting. . . . It is cold and we have no blankets. The little children are freezing to death. . . . I am tired; my heart is sick and sad. From where the sun now stands, I will fight no more forever." The Nez Percé were sent to a reservation in Oklahoma. Chief Joseph was separated from his people and forced to move to a reservation in the state of Washington.

Helen Hunt Jackson wrote a book, *A Century of Dishonor*, that told Americans how unfair the government had been to Native Americans. Many members of Congress read Jackson's book. To improve the government's treatment of Native Americans, Congress passed the Dawes Act in 1887. For the first time, Native Americans were allowed to become American citizens. The Dawes Act encouraged Native Americans to become farmers. This law broke up land owned by different groups into small sections. Each family could receive 40 to 160 acres of their own land. But the land was not good for farming, and some Native Americans did not have the skills or the tools to be farmers. Many Native Americans sold their land, but then they had no way to earn a living. **Poverty** became a serious

▲ Chief Joseph was one of the leaders of the Nez Percé. From June to October 1877, they were pursued by the army through the Idaho, Wyoming, and Montana territories.

problem. The Dawes Act failed to help Native Americans.

The last battle between Native Americans and the United States Army happened in 1890 at Wounded Knee, South Dakota. The Sioux there were doing religious dances called Ghost Dances. Soldiers killed more than 200 Sioux men, women, and children. After the Wounded Knee Massacre, most Native Americans agreed to live on reservations.

By the 1890s the Great Plains had been settled by white people. Most Native Americans had been forced to move to reservations. Farms, railroads, and mining towns were being built across the West. Each year more Americans would make the Great Plains their home.

# Crazy Horse 1842–1877

Crazy Horse was one of the greatest warriors and chiefs of the Sioux nation. Crazy Horse was determined to protect Sioux land from settlers who were moving to the Great Plains. From 1866 to 1868 Crazy Horse fought alongside Chief Red Cloud to stop people from traveling west on the Bozeman Trail, which was in Sioux territory. Red Cloud and Crazy Horse attacked United States forts and settlements along the trail in Wyoming. Crazy Horse became famous for tricking and trapping his enemies. In 1868 the government signed a treaty with the Sioux. In that treaty the government gave up its forts along the Bozeman Trail. The Sioux were given the western part of South Dakota, including the Black Hills.

When gold was discovered in the Black Hills in 1874, the federal government broke the treaty. The government wanted to buy the Black Hills, but the Sioux refused to sell their land. So the United States Army sent General George Custer to fight for the land. In 1876 Crazy Horse and Chief Sitting Bull defeated General Custer at the Battle of Little Bighorn.

Crazy Horse and his warriors continued to fight, but in January 1877 they were defeated by General Nelson Miles. On May 6, 1877, Crazy Horse and hundreds of his followers surrendered to the army. A number of months later, Crazy Horse was killed when a soldier tried to force him into a jail cell. Crazy Horse's parents buried their son in a secret grave near Wounded Knee, South Dakota.

In 1948 Korczak Ziolkowski began carving a huge statue of Crazy Horse on one of the mountains in South Dakota's Black Hills. When it is completed, the statue will be more than 500 feet tall. Ziolkowski worked on that statue until he died in 1982. Others are now working to finish the statue. Although it is not yet finished, more than one million people visit the statue of Crazy Horse each year.

## In Your Own Words

In the journal section of your notebook, write a paragraph that tells why Crazy Horse was a great leader.

# REVIEW AND APPLY

## CHAPTER 2 MAIN IDEAS

- The Great Plains is a flat region between the Mississippi River and the Rocky Mountains. It receives little rain and has few forests.

- Congress passed the Homestead Act in 1862 to encourage people to settle on the Great Plains.

- Inventions such as the steel plow and the reaper helped farmers grow crops on the Great Plains.

- In 1869 the first transcontinental railroad was completed, allowing people to travel from New York to California in a week.

- The search for gold and other metals caused mining towns to develop throughout the West.

- As settlers moved onto the Great Plains, Native Americans were forced onto reservations. Some Native American groups fought for their land.

## VOCABULARY

**Matching** ■ Match the vocabulary word or phrase in Group B with the definition in Group A. Write the letter of the correct answer on the line. You will not use all the words in Group B.

### Group A

_____ 1. When the railroads were completed, a gold one of these was used to connect the railroads together.

_____ 2. This means having very little money.

_____ 3. This machine is used to harvest fields of wheat and corn.

_____ 4. This is the land where cattle grazed.

_____ 5. These were the places where Native Americans were forced to live.

_____ 6. This means "across the continent."

_____ 7. This invention made it easier to put up fences on the Great Plains.

### Group B

A. spike

B. technology

C. barbed wire

D. transcontinental

E. reservations

F. poverty

G. open range

H. reaper

## USING INFORMATION

**Writing an Opinion** ■ Many people today believe that the white settlers and the American government treated Native Americans unfairly. Do you agree or disagree? Give two or three reasons for your opinion.

## USING GRAPHIC ORGANIZERS

**Cause-and-Effect Chart** ■ Complete the graphic organizer by explaining how each event, or cause, affected life in the West.

| Cause (Event) | Effect on Life in the American West |
|---|---|
| Invention of the reaper | |
| First Transcontinental railroad | |
| Gold rushes | |
| Invention of barbed wire | |
| Settlers kill millions of buffalo | |
| Native Americans forced to live on reservations | |

## CRITICAL THINKING

**Fact or Opinion** ■ Write an **F** on the blank next to each statement that is a fact. Write **O** on the blank if the statement is an opinion. If the statement gives both a fact and an opinion, write **FO**. Then draw a line under the part of the sentence that is an opinion.

_____ 1. The Great Plains was called the Great American Desert, but it should have been called the Great American Farm.

_____ 2. The Homestead Act gave settlers 160 acres of free land on the Great Plains.

_____ 3. The transcontinental railroad cost too much money to build.

_____ 4. Miners in the West should not have given up so easily when they did not find gold at first.

_____ 5. By 1903 most of the buffalo in America had been killed.

_____ 6. Chief Joseph tried to save his people from being forced to live on a reservation.

# Region: The Great Plains

A region has places that may share similar climates, landforms, businesses, products, and culture. The Great Plains is a large region of flat plains and low hills stretching from western Texas to northern Canada and from the Mississippi River to the Rocky Mountains. The Great Plains has very hot summers and very cold winters. It has a dry climate with less than 20 inches of rain a year. Tornadoes, thunderstorms, and blizzards are common weather problems in this region.

**The Great Plains**

Read the paragraph above and study the map of the Great Plains. Then answer the questions below.

1. Name four states that are part of this region. _____,
   _____, _____, and _____.

2. Which four major rivers run through the Great Plains? _____,
   _____, _____, and _____

3. What are three features shared by places in this region? _____
   _____, _____, and _____

4. What is the climate like in the Great Plains? _____,
   _____

5. Why did the region known as the Great American Desert become known as
   America's breadbasket? _____,
   _____

# The Growth of Business and Industry

## Focus on Main Ideas

1. Why was the United States able to become an industrial nation?

2. How did new inventions help the growth of industry?

3. How did big business affect the growth of industry?

4. Why did Congress pass laws to control big business?

▲ Alexander Graham Bell's first telephone

After the Civil War, the United States became a nation with huge businesses and many different kinds of industries.

### The Industrial Revolution Changed America

The Industrial Revolution began in England in the 1700s. This revolution was a change from making products by hand at home to making products by machine in factories. After the Industrial Revolution started in England, it spread to other nations. The Industrial Revolution started in the United States when textile mills were built in New England. After the Civil War, industry grew rapidly throughout the United States. The United States became a great industrial nation between the years 1865 and 1900 for seven reasons.

First, the United States had people with **capital**, or money, to spend on developing industries and businesses.

Second, the United States had important **natural resources** such as iron, coal, and oil. These resources were needed to develop the steel, oil, and railroad industries. From these three industries, hundreds of other industries developed. For example, glass was needed for railroad car windows.

Third, the United States had the energy sources it needed to run railroads and factories. During the early days of the Industrial Revolution, steam and water power were the main types of energy used in factories. By the end of the 1800s, coal provided energy for many railroads and factories. Later, oil and electricity became important sources of energy.

Fourth, the United States was developing a large railroad system. The railroads moved natural resources, such as coal, oil, and iron, to where they were needed.

Fifth, new inventions helped the growth of industry. For example, the inventions of the telegraph and the telephone made it possible to communicate over long distances.

Sixth, the United States had a large population. There were plenty of people to work in factories, build railroads, and make new inventions.

Seventh, the American economy is based on **capitalism**. Under this system, also known as **free enterprise**, people can own businesses and industries and keep the profits that they earn. Each business owner tries to make as much money as possible. Capitalism encourages **competition** between businesses. Businesses try to make the best product to sell to customers.

The growth of industry led to new ways of selling products. Department stores, which sold many different kinds of products in one store, were common. Woolworth's and Macy's opened stores in many parts of the nation. Mail-order companies were started. They allowed people who lived far from stores to order products from catalogs and receive them by mail. Customers could order tools, clothes, and other items.

## Ways of Organizing Businesses

For hundreds of years, most businesses had been owned by one person or a family. Sometimes two or more people formed a **partnership** and owned a business together. This system had two problems. One problem was that if the business failed, the owners were personally responsible for paying all of the debts. The second problem was that this system could not raise enough capital, or money, to build very large businesses. For example, a partnership could not raise enough money to build a railroad.

▲ The growth of industry led to mail-order companies that sold products through the mail. Catalogs, such as this one from Sears, Roebuck and Company, advertised many different products.

Since the late 1800s, large businesses have been organized as **corporations**. A corporation is a company that can raise large amounts of money by selling **shares** of the company. People own a part of the corporation when they own shares. Shares are also called **stocks**. People who own shares are called shareholders or stockholders. If the corporation fails, shareholders cannot lose more money than they paid for their stock. If the company earns profits, the price of the stock will rise. Then shareholders can sell their stocks for a profit.

## New Inventions Helped the Growth of Industry

In 1856 Henry Bessemer, an English inventor, found a fast, cheap way to change iron into steel. Steel is a metal made from iron, which is found in rocks inside the earth. Iron is not a strong metal. It cracks and rusts easily. Steel is much stronger than iron.

The Bessemer process changed American industry. Bridges and machines in factories were made of steel. The invention of steel made it possible to build tall skyscrapers. Railroad companies began to make railroad tracks out of steel.

Besides steel, other inventions helped the growth of the railroad industry. After refrigerator railroad cars were invented, it became possible to ship meat and farm products across the nation. Granville T. Woods, an African American, invented a system that used electric power rather than steam engines to run trains.

In 1872 Elijah McCoy, another African American inventor, made the lubricating cup, which allowed oil to drip slowly onto the moving parts of a train so they would move smoothly. Before this invention every train had to stop frequently to be oiled. Others tried to copy McCoy's invention, but no one made one that worked as well. The owners of the railroads insisted on buying the "real McCoy" for their trains.

One of the most important American inventions was the electric light bulb. Thomas Edison made the first one in 1879. Soon factories, homes, offices, and trains were lit with electric bulbs. To use electric light bulbs, a large supply of electricity was needed. Power plants that produced electricity were invented. Electricity became the most important form of energy for homes and factories. Thomas Edison, one of America's greatest inventors, also made hundreds of other useful inventions.

The invention of the telegraph in 1837 made it possible to send messages across the nation in seconds. In 1866 Cyrus W. Field laid the first telegraph cable across the Atlantic Ocean. This underwater cable made it easy to send messages quickly between the United States and Europe.

The telegraph could send signals, but it could not send sounds made by the human voice. Alexander Graham Bell, a Scottish immigrant and a teacher of deaf children, invented the telephone in 1876. Ten years later thousands of telephones were being used across the nation.

## The Growth of Big Business

The corporations that ran the oil, steel, and railroad industries became huge and powerful by the end of the 1800s. These

▲ The Bessemer process, pictured above, made stronger steel. The improved steel brought about changes in many industries. It also changed the look of modern cities. Before the Bessemer process, city buildings were made with iron. New buildings called skyscrapers could be built using steel. The Home Insurance Building in Chicago was one of the first to use this new technology.

companies were called big businesses. A big business controls many other businesses. For example, one company controlled most of the steel industry in the United States.

To grow bigger, companies tried to gain a **monopoly**. As a monopoly a company controls an entire industry. These monopolies prevented competition from other companies. By controlling competition a monopoly could decide the price of a product everywhere. Several large corporations could become a single monopoly by forming a **trust**. A trust is a group of corporations that is run by a group of people called a board of directors. For example, the board of

directors of an oil trust could control most of the oil companies.

Three powerful leaders of big business were Cornelius Vanderbilt, Andrew Carnegie, and John D. Rockefeller. Vanderbilt controlled much of the railroad industry. He decided the rates that most people had to pay. By the time Vanderbilt died, he was worth about $100 million.

Andrew Carnegie became even richer than Vanderbilt. Carnegie owned most of America's steel mills. He also owned his own railroads and ships for shipping steel to different places. John D. Rockefeller became rich by controlling the oil industry. Oil was discovered in Pennsylvania in 1859. After oil was removed from the earth, it had to be cleaned in an oil **refinery** before it could be used. Rockefeller bought his first refinery after the Civil War. He started his own business called the Standard Oil Company.

Rockefeller's goal was to have complete control of the oil business. So he bought his own oil wells. Because he shipped so much oil, Rockefeller convinced railroad owners to charge him lower rates for shipping his oil than they charged other companies. Because he paid less for shipping, Rockefeller could sell his oil for less money than other companies.

Other companies lost money when they tried to sell their oil at the same low price. Then Rockefeller bought all the oil companies that were losing money. Before long he owned almost every oil refinery in America. Rockefeller became the richest man in the nation.

Some people called business leaders like Rockefeller and Carnegie "captains of industry" because they helped industry grow. People also praised these men because they gave away millions of dollars to help others. Rockefeller used his money to build many schools and churches. One of his schools became the University of Chicago.

Other people hated men like Carnegie and Rockefeller and called them "robber barons." People felt that these business leaders were evil because they forced many companies to go out of business. Robber barons also paid low salaries to most of their workers.

Not all business leaders were men. Madam C. J. Walker was a woman who built a business that made hair care products. Walker used part of her profits to create better schools for African Americans.

## Inventions that Changed America

| Inventor | Invention | Importance |
|---|---|---|
| Samuel F. B. Morse | telegraph 1837 | The telegraph could send messages quickly between places that were far apart. |
| Elias Howe | sewing machine 1846 | Clothing could be made much faster by machine. |
| Henry Bessemer | Bessemer Process 1856 | Steel could be made quickly and cheaply. |
| George Pullman | railroad sleeping cars 1858 | The sleeping car encouraged people to travel long distances by train. |
| Christopher Sholes | typewriter 1867 | The typewriter made it easier to prepare written material. |
| Elijah McCoy | lubricating cup 1872 | The lubricating cup used dripping oil to keep the parts of a train moving smoothly. |
| Joseph Glidden | barbed wire 1873 | Barbed wire made it possible to build fences around large areas. |
| Alexander Graham Bell | telephone 1876 | People could talk with each other over long distances. |
| Thomas Edison | phonograph 1877 | People could hear music and other sounds on records. |
| Thomas Edison | electric light bulb 1879 | Electric light bulbs are used to light homes, schools, offices, and streets. |
| Jan Matzeliger | shoemaking machine 1882 | Shoes are made in factories and sold in stores. |
| Wilbur and Orville Wright | airplane 1903 | The Wright brothers proved that it was possible to build a flying machine. |
| Henry Ford | moving assembly line 1913 | Cars and other items could be made quickly and cheaply. |

## The Government Tries to Control Big Business

Many Americans believed that the government should not try to control business. This idea is known as **laissez-faire**. However other Americans felt that big businesses had too much power. They wanted Congress to pass laws to control big business.

In 1887 Congress took the first step toward limiting the power of big business. Congress passed the Interstate Commerce Act. Congress said that railroads must charge fair rates on routes between states. Railroad companies had been charging huge companies like the Standard Oil Company lower rates than they charged small companies. To carry out the new law, Congress created the Interstate Commerce Commission, or the ICC.

The new agency found it difficult to force the railroads to charge fair rates. Sometimes the ICC took the railroad companies to court. Sixteen court cases against the railroad companies went to the Supreme Court by 1897. In 15 of those cases, the Court ruled in favor of the railroad companies.

The Sherman Antitrust Act was passed in 1890. The new law made monopolies and trusts illegal. The law's goal was to break up huge companies into smaller companies. Then competition between the smaller companies would force them to lower their prices. Unfortunately, the government found it very difficult to carry out the Sherman Antitrust Act. The law did not state clearly what businesses could or could not do.

▲ Madam C. J. Walker became a millionaire from her business that made hair care products. Her parents were sharecroppers, and she grew up working on a cotton plantation.

At first, the two laws that Congress passed in 1887 and 1890 did not succeed in limiting the power of big businesses. Now, however, these laws have been changed to allow Congress the power to make decisions about what businesses and industries can and cannot do.

During the years after the Civil War, the United States became an industrial nation. The oil, steel, and railroad industries became rich and powerful. While a small group of business leaders grew wealthy, millions of Americans led very difficult lives. In the next chapter, you will learn how immigrants and factory workers tried to solve their problems.

# Andrew Carnegie 1835–1919

When Andrew Carnegie was a young boy in Scotland, his family was so poor that they had to borrow money to move to America. This poor boy became one of the richest men in the world.

Carnegie's family moved to the United States when he was 12. He went to school for only a short time, but he continued to learn by reading as many library books as he could. Carnegie developed an appreciation for libraries.

Carnegie's first job was working in a cotton mill. He earned only $1.20 a week. By age 24, he had an excellent job and a very good salary with the Pennsylvania Railroad. Carnegie used part of his salary to buy shares in the oil, coal, and iron industries. In less than ten years, he was earning $50,000 a year from those shares.

In 1873 Carnegie used the money he had earned to build his first steel mill.

Before long Carnegie's mill was making more steel than any other American steel mill. Carnegie used his profits to buy other steel companies. He also bought railroads and ships to carry his steel. Carnegie's control of the steel industry made him a very rich man.

Many people felt that Carnegie was a cruel robber baron. Most of Carnegie's workers were poor immigrants from Europe. Although Carnegie was rich, he paid his workers very low salaries. He did not seem to care that the workers did very dangerous jobs but earned little money.

In 1901 Carnegie sold his steel company to J. P. Morgan, a rich banker, for about $500 million. Morgan then renamed the company the United States Steel Corporation. Today it is the largest steel company in the United States.

After Carnegie retired he gave away most of his money. He believed that money should be used to help others help themselves. He spent $60 million to build 3,000 libraries, and he gave millions of dollars to schools and colleges.

## In Your Own Words

Write a paragraph in the journal section of your notebook that explains how Carnegie was both a "captain of industry" and a "robber baron."

## CHAPTER 3 MAIN IDEAS

- The United States became a great industrial nation between the years 1865 and 1900.

- During the late 1800s, most large businesses became corporations which sold shares of the company to the public.

- Inventions helped the growth of industry in the United States.

- In an attempt to grow larger, some companies tried to gain a monopoly by trying to prevent competition from other companies.

- The government tried to control big business by passing the Interstate Commerce Act and the Sherman Antitrust Act.

## VOCABULARY

**Defining and Using Vocabulary Words** ■ Use the glossary to find the meaning of each word or phrase listed below. Write each word's definition in your social studies notebook. Then use each word in a sentence.

| | | |
|---|---|---|
| competition | free enterprise | monopoly |
| capital | partnership | trust |
| natural resources | corporations | laissez-faire |
| capitalism | stocks | |

## COMPREHENSION CHECK

**Choose the Answer** ■ Write the letter of the word or phrase that best answers each question.

_____ 1. Where did the Industrial Revolution begin?

    a. the United States
    b. England
    c. Russia

_____ 2. Who made the first electric light bulb?

    a. Thomas Edison
    b. Alexander Graham Bell
    c. Elijah McCoy

_____ 3. What is another name for free enterprise?

    a. capitalism
    b. competition
    c. partnership

_____ 4. What are people who own shares in a company called?

    a. borrowers
    b. inventors
    c. stockholders

_____ 5. What is capital?

    a. The building where
       Congress meets.

    b. Natural resources needed
       for a nation to industrialize.

    c. Money to spend on develop-
       ing business and industry.

_____ 6. Who invented a system that
used electric power rather than
steam engines to run trains?

    a. Henry Bessemer
    b. Granville Woods
    c. Cyrus Field

_____ 7. Who started the Standard Oil
Company?

    a. Cornelius Vanderbilt
    b. Andrew Carnegie
    c. John D. Rockefeller

_____ 8. Who owned most of
America's steel mills in the
late 1800s?

    a. Cornelius Vanderbilt
    b. Andrew Carnegie
    c. John D. Rockefeller

## USING INFORMATION

**Writing an Essay** ■ There were many reasons why the United States became a
great industrial nation. Identify and explain at least five of these reasons. Start
your essay with a topic sentence.

## CRITICAL THINKING

**Distinguishing Relevant Information** ■ Imagine you are telling a friend about the
growth of big business in the United States in the late 1800s. Read each sentence
below. Decide which sentences are relevant to what you will say. Put a check in
front of the relevant sentences. There are four relevant sentences.

_____ 1. The United States had important natural resources such as iron and coal.

_____ 2. Americans were moving onto the Great Plains.

_____ 3. Business owners wanted to be successful.

_____ 4. Many new inventions helped businesses.

_____ 5. John D. Rockefeller built schools and hospitals.

_____ 6. Cornelius Vanderbilt controlled much of the railroad industry.

_____ 7. Congress passed laws to try to limit big businesses.

★★★★★★★★★★★★★★★★★★★★★★★★★★★★★★★★★★★★★★★★★★★★★★★★★★★★★★★★★★★★★★★★

# Interpreting a Statistics Table

A table is a chart that contains **statistics**, or numbers, that provide information about a topic. The table below gives population statistics from 1850 to 1910. To read this table, first read the name of each heading. To find information about each heading, read the table from top to bottom. To find information about each year, read the table from left to right.

## Growth of City Population 1850–1910

| Year | United States Population | Percentage of Population in Cities | Percentage of Population in Rural Areas | Factory and Construction Workers in Cities | Farm Workers |
|------|------|------|------|------|------|
| 1850 | 23,191,876 | 15% | 85% | 2,140,000 | 4,982,000 |
| 1860 | 31,443,321 | 20% | 80% | 2,940,000 | 6,208,000 |
| 1870 | 39,818,449 | 26% | 74% | 4,560,000 | 6,850,000 |
| 1880 | 50,155,783 | 28% | 72% | 6,120,000 | 8,585,000 |
| 1890 | 62,947,714 | 35% | 65% | 8,860,000 | 9,938,000 |
| 1900 | 75,994,575 | 40% | 60% | 11,530,000 | 10,712,000 |
| 1910 | 91,972,266 | 46% | 54% | 15,601,000 | 11,340,000 |

**Study the table. Then answer the questions below.**

1. In what year did the largest percentage of people live in rural areas?

   _____.

2. How many people were farm workers in 1850? _____

3. Did the percentage of people in cities grow larger or smaller between 1850 and 1910?

   _____

4. How did the percentage of people in rural areas change between 1850 and 1910?

   _____

5. In what years were there more factory workers than farm workers?

   _____

## CHAPTER 4

### PEOPLE

- Emma Lazarus
- Samuel Gompers
- Mary "Mother" Jones
- George Pullman
- W.E.B. Du Bois

### PLACES

- Greece
- Austria-Hungary
- Japan
- Homestead, PA

### NEW VOCABULARY

- unskilled labor
- tenements
- ghettos
- quota system
- management
- riot
- collective bargaining
- arbitration
- injunction

# Immigration and Labor Movements Change America

## Focus on Main Ideas

1. Why did cities grow larger after the Civil War?

2. What problems did immigrants face in the United States?

3. What problems did workers face in the late 1800s?

4. How did unions try to help workers?

▲ 1870 union poster for eight-hour workday

In 1911 a terrible fire destroyed a clothing factory where immigrant women were working. While the fire burned throughout the factory, the women working inside the Triangle Shirtwaist Company factory could not escape. The owners had locked the factory doors to force the workers to stay at their jobs. In this tragedy, 146 Jewish and Italian immigrant workers died.

The fire at the Triangle Shirtwaist Company showed that worker safety was a problem. It proved that factory workers needed better working conditions. The fire also showed that immigrants to the United States faced many serious problems.

## The Division of Labor in Factories

To make factory products more quickly, a system called the division of labor had developed. Under this system, a factory worker did only one type of job all the time. For example, in a clothing factory, one worker would sew the sleeves onto a shirt. Another worker would sew on the buttons. Still another would sew on the pocket. One worker no longer made an entire product. Division of labor made it faster and cheaper to make many goods in factories. **Unskilled labor**, or workers with few skills, did most of the factory work. Their salaries were low because their jobs were easy to learn.

## American Cities Grow Larger

The growth of industry led to the growth of cities. By 1900 almost half of the nation's people lived in cities. New York City, Philadelphia, and Chicago became the nation's largest cities with more than one million people living in each city.

Cities developed better transportation that made travel easier. By the late 1800s, many cities had electric streetcars. Boston became the first American city with an underground subway system.

City populations grew as millions of immigrants moved to American cities after the Civil War. Many African Americans also moved to northern cities between 1890 and 1920. African Americans hoped to find better jobs in the North. But most factories would not hire them, so African Americans often took low-paying jobs, such as cleaning, cooking, and sewing.

As the population in cities grew larger, the cities' problems became more serious. There was not enough clean drinking water. Rats became a problem because city workers were not able to remove all the garbage that was produced. There were not enough police officers and firefighters.

▲ In the late 1800s, major cities around the country were growing rapidly. Immigrants filled cities like New York City, Boston, and Philadelphia. African Americans moved north to St. Louis and Chicago from farms in the South. Cities became more modern with taller buildings and public transportation.

▲ Most "new immigrants" to the United States came from southern and eastern Europe. Many of these immigrants were poor people who were looking for new opportunities.

Poor families lived in crowded **tenements**, or apartment houses, because there were not enough homes. Diseases spread quickly in these crowded, unhealthy conditions.

## New Immigration After the Civil War

Immigrants started coming to America in the 1600s. Those who had come before the 1880s were called "old immigrants." These immigrants had come from England, Scotland, Ireland, Germany, and other northern and western countries of Europe. Many of these immigrants knew how to read. Most were Protestants. Many spoke English.

Immigrants who came to America after the 1880s were called "new immigrants." Most of these new immigrants came from countries in southern and eastern Europe, such as Poland, Russia, Greece, Italy, and Austria-Hungary. About one third could not read or write. Most were Catholics, but ten percent were Jews. Most were very poor. Between 1880 and 1914, 22 million new immigrants moved to America.

Why did so many new immigrants come to America? First, many came to escape poverty. Second, they believed that America was a "golden door," or a land of opportunity. Third, people came to America for religious freedom and to escape persecution. For example, in Russia and Poland, Jews were often attacked and killed. Between 1881 and 1914, about 2 million Jews moved to America from Poland and Russia.

The first view of America for most immigrants was the Statue of Liberty. The statue, a gift to America from France, became a symbol of American freedom and opportunity.

Emma Lazarus, a Jewish American, wrote a famous poem about the Statue of Liberty. Lazarus's own family had come to America for religious freedom in the 1700s. Her poem stated that the statue welcomes all immigrants to America. These lines from the poem were placed at the base of the Statue of Liberty:

*"Give me your tired, your poor,*
*Your huddled masses yearning*
*to breathe free,*
*The wretched refuse of your teeming shore.*
*Send these, the homeless, tempest*
*tossed, to me,*
*I lift my lamp beside the golden door."*

## Immigrant Life in America

Many immigrants settled in large cities such as New York City, Chicago, and Boston. Most lived in crowded tenements and became factory workers. Because so many immigrants needed jobs, factory owners had a huge supply of cheap labor.

Immigrants usually lived in **ghettos**, or neighborhoods, with people from their own country. For example, in New York City, Italians lived in Little Italy while Jews lived nearby on the Lower East Side.

Many people did not welcome the new immigrants even though most Americans were descendants of immigrants. Because most Americans were Protestants, Catholic and Jewish immigrants met with prejudice. Also, many Americans were angry that immigrants would work for low wages. Factory owners did not want to pay the higher wages that workers had been earning because the factory owners could hire immigrants and pay them less money.

Some people wanted the government to stop allowing immigrants to come into the country. Congress began to pass laws to limit immigration. In 1882 the first law of this kind was the Chinese Exclusion Act. This law tried to stop Chinese people from coming to America. Starting in 1921 Congress passed laws that created a **quota system**. The quota system limited the number of immigrants who could move to the United States each year from different countries. The quota system favored immigrants from northern and western Europe.

At the same time, the Americanization movement was born. Americans volunteered to teach the English language and American history to immigrants so that they could become full citizens of the United States.

## Labor Unions

The number of workers in mines and factories increased as immigrants poured into the nation. These workers were needed as big businesses grew.

Most workers in mines and factories faced many serious problems. First, wages were very low. Few men earned more than $16 a week. Women and children earned much less. Second, people had to work 6 days a week for 14 hours a day. Third, there were no child labor laws to prevent children from working. By 1890 one fifth of all children worked 14 hours a day in mines, factories, and farms. Usually they earned less than $10 a week.

## People From Many Cultures Helped the United States

| Name | Nationality | Contribution |
|------|-------------|--------------|
| Michael Pupin | Serbian | Developed x-ray pictures |
| John Holland | Irish | Developed the submarine |
| Gideon Sundback | Swedish | Invented the zipper |
| Thomas Nast | German | Drew political cartoons |
| Albert Michelson | Polish | Developed instruments to measure the eye |
| Dr. Daniel William Hale | African American | Performed the first heart operation |
| Dr. Jokichi Takamine | Japanese | Found pure adrenaline in the human body |

Fourth, working conditions were dangerous and unhealthy. Workers who were hurt on the job received no money while they were unable to work. If they could not work, they often lost their jobs.

Many workers believed that they could win better salaries and working conditions by forming unions. To win better salaries and working conditions, union members could go on strike. During a strike, workers stopped working until union leaders reached an agreement with **management**. The chart on the next page shows some of the methods used by labor and management.

The first successful union was the Knights of Labor, which began in 1869. By 1886 more than 700,000 workers had joined the Knights of Labor. The Knights lost most of their members soon after a **riot** in Chicago's Haymarket Square in 1886. A meeting was held at Haymarket Square to protest the killing of strikers by police. As police tried to end the meeting, a bomb exploded in the crowd. Seven policemen were killed. A riot started. When the police tried to stop the riot, they killed other people in the crowd. The Knights of Labor did not start the riot, but they were blamed for it.

In 1886 Samuel Gompers started another labor union. This new union was the American Federation of Labor, or the AFL. The AFL was made up of several

▲ In the late 1800s, there were few laws in the nation to control child labor. Children could work as many hours as adults. Working conditions for children were often harsh, and injuries were common. In this photograph, children work without shoes or other protective clothing in a textile mill.

# Methods Used By Labor and Management

| Labor Methods | How it Works | Management Methods | How it Works |
|---|---|---|---|
| strike | Workers stop working. | strikebreakers or "scabs" | Management hires new non-union workers. |
| collective bargaining | Leaders from both sides find ways to solve problems. | blacklist | Management sends a list of union members to other businesses to prevent them from being hired. |
| closed shop | Management can hire only union members. | injunction | Management gets a court order to prevent or end a strike. |
| boycott | The public agrees not to buy products until the union ends the boycott. | yellow-dog contract | To get a job, workers must sign a contract that they will not join a union. |
| picket line | Union members stop non-union workers from entering a shop or factory. | lockout | Management closes the factory so workers must give in or lose their jobs. |

skilled craftworkers' unions such as the shoemakers' union and the printers' union. Since only skilled workers could join these unions, few women, immigrants, and African Americans could become members of the AFL. Still the AFL became the nation's most important union. By 1904 more than one million people had become members of this union. However, most skilled workers were not union members in the early 1900s.

The goals of the AFL were to get better salaries for workers, to win better working conditions, and to have an eight-hour workday. To reach these goals, the AFL used strikes and **collective bargaining** as its weapons. Collective bargaining happens when factory owners and union leaders meet to discuss ways to solve problems. Sometimes the union and the management agree to use **arbitration** as a way to settle a serious problem. In arbitration both the union leaders and the management present their arguments to another person. That person tries to make a decision that is fair for both sides.

Mary Harris Jones, often called "Mother" Jones, helped unions grow. "Mother" Jones was an Irish immigrant. In America she worked for laws to end child labor. "Mother" Jones believed mining work was so dangerous that workers needed unions to protect their rights. So she traveled around the country and helped miners join unions. "Mother" Jones continued working for unions until she was more than ninety years old.

## Striking for Better Conditions

As more people joined unions, workers often went on strike. In 1892 the Homestead Strike began in Homestead, Pennsylvania. Workers at the Carnegie steel plant went on strike because the company had cut their wages. Andrew Carnegie was away on vacation, and management would not discuss the lower wages with the striking workers. Instead the management called in armed guards. A small war was fought between the guards and the union members. Although the strike lasted for months, the union failed to win better salaries. Union members finally returned to work for the lower wages.

Another famous strike, the Pullman Strike, also failed to help union members. George Pullman owned the company that made sleeper cars for railroads. Pullman's workers went on strike in 1894 when their salaries were cut. The American Railway Union, or the ARU, supported the Pullman workers. The ARU refused to

▲ Many people were injured during the Homestead Strike in 1892. Armed union men are shown here leading away company guards that had surrendered.

handle Pullman cars on any railroads. This action stopped railroad traffic throughout the West. It also interfered with the delivery of the United States mail. A federal court issued an **injunction** to end the strike. Finally the government sent troops to force the workers to go back to work. The ARU lost its power and soon fell apart. Most of the striking workers were allowed to return to work at lower salaries. The actions of the federal government during the strike showed that it favored big business over the needs of poor workers.

As more people joined unions, the government began to pass laws to improve working conditions. In the 1900s better laws and stronger unions would help millions of workers achieve better working conditions.

# W.E.B. Du Bois 1868–1963

W.E.B. Du Bois spent his life trying to help African Americans win equal rights. He was born in Massachusetts after the Civil War. Du Bois went to Fisk University in Nashville where he graduated second in his class. Then he became the first African American to earn a Ph.D. at Harvard. Du Bois became a teacher at Atlanta University in Georgia. While living in the South, he realized how unfairly African Americans were treated. He was upset that they were often lynched, or killed, by angry mobs. Du Bois was also angry that most African Americans in the North worked at cooking, cleaning, and sewing jobs. It was difficult for them to join labor unions. Du Bois wrote a book called *The Souls of Black Folk* that explained these problems.

Du Bois strongly disagreed with the ideas of another African American leader, Booker T. Washington. Washington said that African Americans should not demand equal rights. Instead they should improve their lives by working hard and earning good salaries. W.E.B. Du Bois thought African Americans should try to win equal rights immediately.

In 1905 Du Bois started the Niagara Movement. This movement encouraged educated African Americans to demand full voting rights and civil rights for their people.

In 1909 Du Bois joined with African Americans and white people to start the National Association for the Advancement of Colored People, or the NAACP. The NAACP worked to end segregation. Du Bois became the editor of *The Crisis*, the NAACP's magazine. In the magazine Du Bois wrote that African Americans should feel proud of their race and their culture. During elections the NAACP supported candidates who said they would work for equal rights.

Today the NAACP continues the fight for equal rights. Du Bois is remembered as a leader who worked to end prejudice in the United States.

## In Your Own Words

Write a paragraph in the journal section of your notebook that explains the goals and the work of W.E.B. Du Bois.

## CHAPTER 4 MAIN IDEAS

■ American factories in the early 1900s had many problems including unsafe working conditions and unfair treatment of employees.

■ By 1900 almost one half of the country's population lived in cities. Chicago, New York City, and Philadelphia each had more than one million people.

■ As cities grew larger, problems such as overcrowding and the spread of disease became more serious.

■ Most immigrants lived in crowded tenements. Many Americans did not welcome the new immigrants.

■ The first successful labor union in the United States was the Knights of Labor. The American Federation of Labor was later started by Samuel Gompers.

■ Unions used methods such as strikes and collective bargaining to win better salaries and working conditions.

## VOCABULARY

**Finish the Sentence** ■ Choose one of the words or phrases from the box to complete each sentence. You will not use all the words in the box.

1. In the early 1900s, _____ did most of the work in factories.

2. Many immigrants who came to the United States lived in crowded buildings called _____.

3. In 1921, Congress passed laws that created a _____ that limited the number of immigrants from different countries.

4. One way that management agreed to settle labor problems was by using _____.

5. Sometimes federal courts would issue an _____ to end a strike.

> unskilled labor
> collective bargaining
> arbitration
> tenements
> quota system
> injunction

## USING INFORMATION

**Writing an Opinion** ■ In the late 1800s, unions were started to help workers. Write a paragraph in your social studies notebook that tells your own opinion about whether you agree or disagree with the methods used by unions to achieve their goals.

## USING GRAPHIC ORGANIZERS

**Concept Web** ■ Complete the graphic organizer with information about immigration or the labor movement.

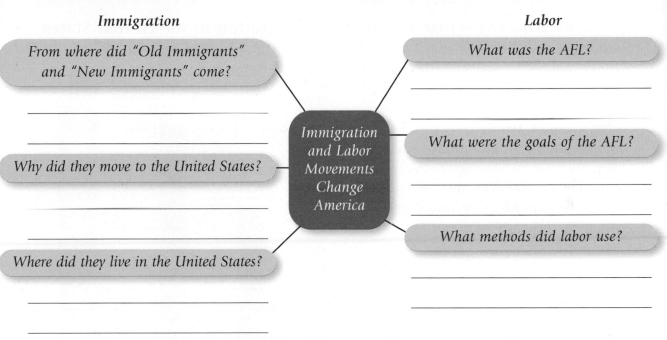

*Immigration*

From where did "Old Immigrants" and "New Immigrants" come?

_____

_____

Why did they move to the United States?

_____

_____

Where did they live in the United States?

_____

_____

*Immigration and Labor Movements Change America*

*Labor*

What was the AFL?

_____

_____

What were the goals of the AFL?

_____

_____

What methods did labor use?

_____

_____

## CRITICAL THINKING

**Drawing Conclusions** ■ Read the paragraph below and the sentences that follow it. Put a check in front of the conclusions that can be drawn from the paragraph. You should find three conclusions.

In the late 1800s, many immigrants came to the United States looking for a better life. Immigrants usually lived in ghettos with other immigrants from the same country. Most immigrants worked in factories. Working conditions in the factories were very bad. The workers were paid low wages and had to work many hours. Some Americans were angry that immigrants would work for lower wages. In 1921 Congress passed laws limiting the number of immigrants that could come into the United States from different countries.

_____ **1.** Life was not always easy for immigrants living in the United States.

_____ **2.** Factories were only found in the Northeastern part of the United States.

_____ **3.** Fewer immigrants came to the United States after 1921.

_____ **4.** Immigrants enjoyed living near people from their own countries.

_____ **5.** Immigrant children could not work in factories.

# Reading a Bar Graph

The bar graph on this page shows the number of immigrants who came to the United States from five countries between 1860 and 1900. Study the key for the bar graph. Each country is represented by a different color. Using the key, you can compare how immigration to America from one country changed between 1860 and 1900. Or you can compare immigration to America from different countries during the same year.

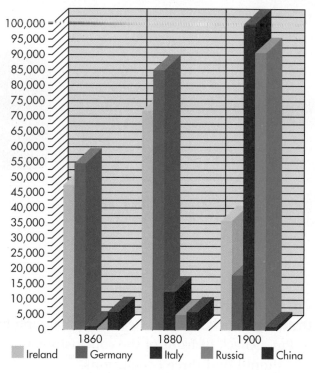

**Immigration to the United States 1860-1900**

Study the bar graph. Then answer the questions below.

1.  Which nation sent the most immigrants in 1860? _____.

2.  About how many Chinese immigrants were there in 1860? _____.

3.  Which two nations had the most immigrants come to the United States in 1880?
    _____ and _____.

4.  About how many Italian immigrants were there in 1880? _____.

5.  Which nation sent the most immigrants to the United States in 1900?
    _____.

6.  How did immigration of Germans change between 1860 and 1900?
    _____.

# Reform and the Progressive Movement

## Focus on Main Ideas

1. How did farmers try to solve their debt problems before 1900?

2. How did the Pendleton Act change the civil service?

3. How did Jane Addams help immigrants and workers?

4. What did the American people learn from the muckrakers?

▲ Jacob Riis photograph of Little Katie, 1892

By 1903 baseball had become the most popular sport in the country. Fans were thrilled when Boston's team defeated Pittsburgh's team in the first World Series. While the growth of industry gave middle-class Americans time to enjoy sports, millions of poor workers were struggling to survive. By the end of the 1800s, many reforms, or changes, were needed.

### Hard Times for Farmers

Between 1870 and 1900, American farmers grew more food than ever before. However, farmers earned less money because crop prices had dropped. Many farmers were also in debt because they had borrowed money to buy expensive machines like seeders and reapers. They felt that their enemies were the railroad companies that charged farmers very high rates for shipping their crops.

In the 1870s farmers tried to help themselves by joining the **National Grange**. Grange members worked to get laws passed to control railroad rates. Several states passed such laws, which were called Granger laws.

The railroad companies went to court to end these laws. The Supreme Court ruled in favor of the railroads in the 1886 case called *Wabash* v. *Illinois*. The Supreme Court said that only Congress could control railroad rates if the railroad company had routes between states. The next year Congress passed the Interstate Commerce Act to control business between states.

### The Populist Party

The Granger laws did not help farmers as much as they had hoped. Farmers looked for another answer. Many farmers believed that they could not earn enough money because all paper money had to be backed by gold. This was called the **gold standard**. Since gold was scarce, the amount of paper money the government could print was limited. Most business leaders wanted to keep the gold standard. Farmers wanted a new law that would allow paper money to be backed by both gold and silver. Since the nation had more silver than gold, the government could print more paper money. Increasing the amount of paper money would cause **inflation**. Farmers wanted inflation to make farm products more expensive so they would earn more money and be able to pay their debts.

In 1892 the farmers formed the Populist party. The main goal of the Populist party was to end the gold standard, but the new party also

▲ Farmers tried to help themselves by getting new laws passed. This meeting of the Grange in Illinois in 1873 was just one of many meetings where farmers could voice their opinions. By the 1890s, meetings of the Grange led to a new political party, the Populist party.

supported other important changes. The Populists wanted an income tax that would require the rich to pay more taxes than the poor. They wanted an eight-hour workday. And they wanted to change the law so that the people of each state voted for United States senators, instead of allowing state legislatures to elect them.

The **depression** of 1893 brought hard times to millions of people. Many Americans blamed the gold standard for causing this depression. At the Democratic convention in 1896, Congressman William Jennings Bryan spoke out against the gold standard. He ended his "Cross of Gold" speech with these words: "We will answer their demand for a gold standard by saying to them: You shall not press down upon the brow of labor this crown of thorns, you shall not crucify mankind upon a cross of gold."

William Jennings Bryan became the presidential candidate for both the Democratic and Populist parties. The Republican candidate, William McKinley, supported the gold standard. Bryan lost the election, and the Populist party soon came to an end.

## Reforms in Government

Since the days of Andrew Jackson, people who supported a new President had been rewarded with jobs in the federal government, or **civil service** jobs. The Civil Service Act of 1883, also called the Pendleton Act, reformed the civil service. Under the new law people had to pass tests in order to get civil service jobs. Under this law, people would not lose their jobs when a President left office.

▲ Thomas Nast drew this political cartoon of Boss Tweed as a vulture feeding on the people of New York. Nast's cartoons were seen by many people who would later turn against Tweed.

City governments also needed reform because many were controlled by "bosses." These leaders were not elected to the government. Instead they became powerful by controlling a city's main political party. By controlling the political party, the bosses controlled the elected leaders. Elected leaders needed the support of the bosses and their political party to stay in power.

William Tweed, a New York City boss, had great power in the 1860s and 1870s. He was called Boss Tweed, and he controlled the city's Democratic party. He used his power to steal about $100 million from the government. Thomas Nast drew political cartoons in newspapers that showed Boss Tweed stealing government money. Because of Nast's cartoons, Tweed lost his power and was sent to jail.

## The Reform Movement

The growth of American industry brought serious problems to factory workers, immigrants, and the nation's big cities. During the late 1800s, many Americans began to work for change, or reform. One important reformer was Jane Addams. In 1889 Addams started a **settlement house** called Hull House. Hull House was in an immigrant neighborhood in Chicago. Included in its many services were English classes for immigrants, a summer camp for children, and a nursery to care for the children of working mothers. By 1900 about 2,000 people received services from Hull House each day.

▲ Marches were held to bring attention to the women's suffrage movement. The Nineteenth Amendment gave women the right to vote in local, state, and national elections.

Addams did far more than take charge of Hull House. Her work led to the first child labor law in Illinois. She helped win an eight-hour workday for women. She fought for other laws to protect workers. In 1931 Addams became the first American woman to receive the Nobel Peace Prize.

Many people admired Addams for her work at Hull House. About 400 other settlement houses were started across the country. Lillian Wald, a nurse, started the Henry Street Settlement House in New York City. To help sick people who were too poor to visit doctors, Wald started a "visiting nurse" program. This program sent nurses to treat sick people in their homes. Jane Edna Hunter, also a nurse, started the Working Girls' Home Association in Cleveland. She helped African American women find jobs in Cleveland.

While women worked for reform, they also worked for **suffrage**, or the right to vote. They fought for an amendment to the Constitution that would allow women's suffrage. Susan B. Anthony became a leader in the suffrage movement. In 1920 women finally won the right to vote when the Nineteenth Amendment became part of the Constitution.

## The Progressive Movement

Between 1890 and 1914, a new reform movement known as the Progressive Movement made possible some of the important changes that the Populist party had wanted. Writers called **muckrakers** were an important part of this movement. These writers were called muckrakers

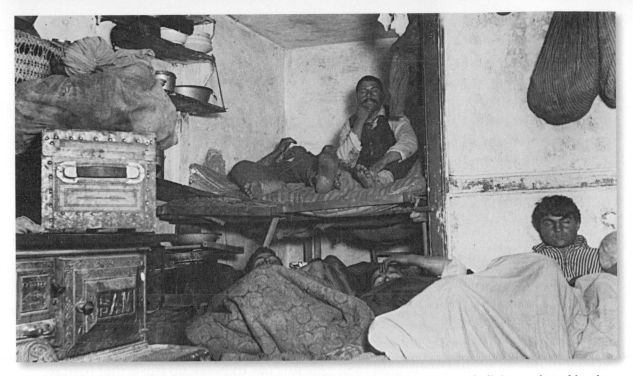

▲ Jacob Riis was a muckraker who wrote about what life was like for poor people living and working in cities. In 1889 Riis took this photograph of an apartment in New York City. Each person paid five cents for a place to sleep in the room.

because they raked up the muck, or dirt, in American life. Americans across the nation read their works and learned about many serious problems in business and in society.

Theodore Roosevelt became President in 1901 after President McKinley was assassinated. Roosevelt believed that big business helped the growth of the nation, but he also thought the federal government should have more control over business.

President Roosevelt became known as a **trustbuster**. He used the Sherman Antitrust Act to attack trusts that were harming the country. Huge companies were broken up into smaller companies.

In 1904 Roosevelt was elected to a second term as President. He promised

Americans a "Square Deal," a program that would be fair to all. Roosevelt worked to pass more laws that would control trusts. These laws gave more power to the Interstate Commerce Commission. Many more trusts were broken up.

Roosevelt and others learned about problems in the meat-packing industry by reading Upton Sinclair's novel *The Jungle*. Sinclair wrote the book to explain how people had to work under dangerous conditions. But it was his description of how the food was made that got people's attention. Canned meats and sausages often contained meat from sick animals and rats because of poor conditions in the meat-packing plants. In 1906 two laws were passed to protect people from unsafe food. The Pure Food and Drug Act required companies to make only safe foods and medicines. The Meat Inspection Act allowed federal workers to check all meat shipped out of a state.

Roosevelt started **conservation** programs to protect the nation's natural resources. Too many forests were being destroyed. Mining and manufacturing were using up other natural resources. The conservation programs were the first to protect America's forests, animals, and natural resources.

Roosevelt did not run for President a third time. In 1908 William Howard Taft was elected President. Taft continued to break up trusts. However, Roosevelt was not pleased with Taft's work. Roosevelt decided to run for President again in the election of 1912. The Republican party chose Taft as its candidate. So Roosevelt's supporters started a new **third party**, the Progressive party. The Progressive Party was also called the Bull Moose party. Roosevelt and Taft were defeated by Woodrow Wilson, a Democrat.

## Wilson Works for Change

Under Wilson two new amendments were added to the Constitution in 1913. The Sixteenth Amendment allowed Congress to pass income tax laws. The Seventeenth Amendment allowed citizens, instead of lawmakers, to vote for United States senators.

President Wilson worked with Congress to pass the Clayton Antitrust Act in 1914. The new law said that companies could not limit competition. Wilson used this law to break up trusts that tried to stop competition. To carry out the laws against trusts, the Federal Trade Commission was started.

Wilson also supported the passing of the nation's first child labor law. Another law gave railroad workers an eight-hour workday. Still another law made it easier for farmers to borrow money.

The growth of big business and the arrival of immigrants brought progress and problems to the growing nation. During the time of the Progressive Movement, Americans began to solve the problems that were created by big business and industry.

# Famous Muckrakers

| Muckraker | Title of Well-known Work | Why Was the Work Important? |
|---|---|---|
| Jacob Riis | *How the Other Half Lives* 1890 | Riis used photographs to show the terrible conditions in tenements. |
| Ida Tarbell | *A History of the Standard Oil Company* 1903 | Tarbell wrote about John D. Rockefeller and the oil industry. |
| Lincoln Steffens | *The Shame of the Cities* 1904 | Steffens told about the illegal methods used by city leaders. |
| Upton Sinclair | *The Jungle* 1906 | Sinclair described unhealthy methods and terrible working conditions in the meat-packing industry. |
| Ray Stannard Baker | *Following the Color Line* 1908 | Baker wrote about segregation of African Americans. |

# Susan B. Anthony 1820–1906

Susan B. Anthony helped women win equal rights. Anthony was born in Massachusetts to a Quaker family. Her parents taught her that men and women of all races should have equal rights. As a child, Anthony saw that women had few opportunities. Often their choices were limited to being wives, factory workers, or teachers.

As a young woman, Susan B. Anthony became a teacher in Rochester, New York. There she earned only one dollar a week. When she learned that the male teachers were earning better salaries, she became very angry. She wanted to change what was unfair for women.

After 1854 Anthony's goal was to help women win the right to vote. She believed that once women could vote, they would use their voting power to win other rights. Anthony and Elizabeth Cady Stanton became close friends and worked together for women's rights.

Anthony never gave up her goal of women's suffrage. In 1872 she voted in an election for President. Because it was against the law for a woman to vote, Anthony was arrested. A jury trial found Anthony guilty. Her punishment was a $100 fine. Anthony believed that her punishment was unfair, so she never paid the fine. After the trial, Anthony spent the next twenty years traveling across the nation giving speeches about women's rights.

She spoke to senators and other members of Congress about the need for an amendment to the Constitution. Because of her work, people began to understand why women should be allowed to vote. Susan B. Anthony's efforts helped women win the right to vote in four western states by 1900. Anthony died in 1906 before she reached her goal. Fourteen years later the Nineteenth Amendment to the Constitution was ratified. This amendment gave women the right to vote. The amendment quickly became known as the Susan B. Anthony Amendment.

## In Your Own Words

Write a paragraph in the journal section of your notebook that explains how Susan B. Anthony's work has helped American women.

# The Jungle by Upton Sinclair

**Upton Sinclair wrote *The Jungle* to show the terrible working conditions in meat-packing plants. The setting was the Durham meat packing plant in "Packingtown," a part of Chicago. Sinclair showed the unfair hardships that Jurgis, a Lithuanian immigrant, had to deal with in order to earn a living.**

Jurgis fell into his trap. . . . At first he hardly noticed it, it was such a slight accident . . . he turned his ankle . . . and in the morning his ankle was swollen out nearly double its size, and he could not get his foot into his shoe. Still, even then, he did nothing more than swear a little, and wrapped his foot in old rags. . . . It chanced to be a rush day at Durham's . . . by noontime the pain was so great that it made him faint, and . . . he . . . had to tell the boss. They sent for the company doctor, and he examined the foot and told Jurgis to go home to bed, adding that he had probably laid himself up for months. . . . The injury was not one that Durham and Company could be held responsible for. . . . Jurgis got home somehow, scarcely able to see for the pain, and with an awful terror in his soul. . . . He knew that the family might starve to death. . . .

The latter part of April Jurgis went to see the doctor, and was . . . told that he might go back to work. . . . However . . . he was told by the foreman that it had not been possible to keep his job for him. Jurgis knew that this meant simply that the foreman had found some one else to do the work. . . . He went out and took his place with the mob of the unemployed.

He must get work, he told himself, fighting the battle with despair every hour of the day. . . .

But there was no work for him. He went to every one he knew. . . . There was not a job anywhere. . . .

## Write Your Answers

**Write the answers to these questions in your social studies notebook.**

1. How did Jurgis's accident affect his work at Durham?

2. What did the foreman tell Jurgis?

3. **Think and Respond** What would happen to Jurgis and all the people who lost their jobs?

# Being an American Citizen

Throughout his years as a politician, Theodore Roosevelt fought to make life better for all Americans. In 1883 he made this speech about American citizenship. In the speech, he urged Americans to be active in politics and to vote. He also said Americans should treat people of every background and religious faith fairly.

No man can be a good citizen who is not a good husband and a good father, who is not honest in his dealings with other men and women, faithful to his friends and fearless in the presence of his foes [enemies]. . . .

Every man must devote a reasonable share of his time to doing his duty in the Political life of the community. . . . If freedom is worth having, if the right of self-government is a valuable right, then the one and the other must be retained [kept] exactly as our forefathers acquired [gained] them, by labor. . . .

There was one time that a number of men who think as we do here tonight (one of the number being myself) got hold of one of the assembly districts of New York, and ran it in really an ideal way. . . . We did it by hard work and good organization. . . ; especially did we do it by all turning in as straight-out Americans without any regard to distinctions of race origin. Among the many men who did a great deal in organizing our victories was the son of a Presbyterian clergyman, the nephew of a Hebrew rabbi, and two well-known Catholic gentlemen. We also had a Columbia College professor. . . , a noted retail butcher, . . . and a stone-mason. . . .

Again, questions of race origin, like questions of creed [religious beliefs], must not be considered: we wish to do good work, and we are all Americans, pure and simple. . . .

## Write Your Answers

**Answer these questions in the assignment section of your notebook.**

1. What does Roosevelt believe makes a good citizen?

2. Why does Roosevelt believe every person should give some time to the "Political life of the community"?

3. **Think and Respond** What do you think Roosevelt would have thought of Jurgis?

# REVIEW AND APPLY

## CHAPTER 5 MAIN IDEAS

- One of the reasons the Populist party was formed was to help farmers.

- During the late 1800s, many Americans began to work to reform child labor laws, living conditions in cities, women's rights, and city governments.

- Jane Addams started Hull House to help immigrants in Chicago.

- In 1920 women gained the right to vote when the Nineteenth Amendment was passed.

- The Progressive Movement made changes in controlling big business and trusts, improving working conditions, and conserving natural resources.

## VOCABULARY

**Choose the Meaning** ■ Write the letter of the word or phrase that best completes each sentence.

_____ 1. The **National Grange** was formed to help _____ .

    a. immigrants
    b. farmers
    c. politicians

_____ 2. The **gold standard** was used to back _____ .

    a. paper money
    b. coins
    c. stocks

_____ 3. **Suffrage** is _____ .

    a. the right to an eight-hour workday
    b. the right to vote
    c. the right to buy gold

_____ 4. **Muckrakers** were _____ .

    a. writers
    b. politicians
    c. farmers

_____ 5. **Conservation** is the protection of _____ .

    a. big business
    b. city governments
    c. natural resources

_____ 6. President Roosevelt was called a **trustbuster** because he _____ .

    a. could not be trusted
    b. attacked harmful trusts
    c. did not want to give women the right to vote

## USING INFORMATION

**Writing an Essay** ■ During the late 1800s and early 1900s, many Americans started to work to change American society. Write a paragraph in your social studies notebook that describes one of these reform movements and the effects it had on the United States.

## COMPREHENSION CHECK

**Reviewing Important Facts** ■ Match each sentence in Group A with the word or phrase from Group B that the sentence explains. You will not use all the words in Group B.

### Group A

_____ 1. The Supreme Court ruled in favor of the railroads in this court case.

_____ 2. William Jennings Bryan gave this speech to end the gold standard.

_____ 3. This person started the Henry Street Settlement House in New York City.

_____ 4. This law reformed the civil service in 1883.

_____ 5. He promised Americans a Square Deal.

_____ 6. This cartoonist showed that Boss Tweed was stealing from the government.

### Group B

A. Lillian Wald

B. *Wabash* v. *Illinois*

C. The Pendleton Act

D. Thomas Nast

E. Jane Addams

F. Cross of Gold

G. Theodore Roosevelt

## CRITICAL THINKING

**Cause and Effect** ■ Choose a cause or an effect from Group B to complete each sentence in Group A. Write the letter of the correct answer on the blank. Group B has one more answer than you need.

### Group A

_____ 1. The Supreme Court ruled in favor of the railroads in *Wabash* v. *Illinois,* so _____ .

_____ 2. _____ , so the amount of paper money the government could print was limited.

_____ 3. Jane Addams fought for laws to protect workers, so she _____ .

_____ 4. _____ , so the Pendleton Act was passed to reform the civil service.

_____ 5. Upton Sinclair wrote *The Jungle,* so _____ .

### Group B

A. Gold was scarce

B. the Federal Reserve Act was passed in 1913

C. Americans learned about the problems in the meat-packing industry

D. won the Nobel Peace Prize

E. Congress passed the Interstate Commerce Act

F. People were given jobs in the federal government even if they could not do the job

55

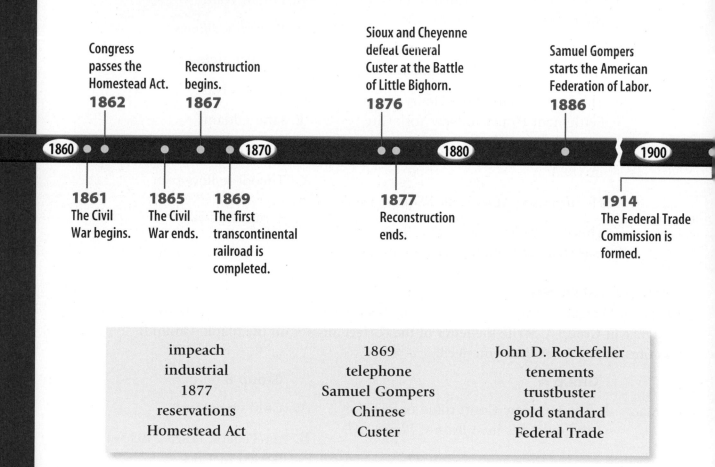

Study the time line on this page. You may want to read parts of Unit 1 again. Then use the words and dates in the box to finish the paragraphs. The box has one possible answer that you will not use.

In 1867 Congress passed the Reconstruction Act, so the South could rejoin the Union. Congress did not like President Andrew Johnson. In 1868 the House of Representatives voted to **1**_____ President Johnson. The Senate did not have enough votes to find Johnson guilty, so he finished his term as President. In **2**_____ federal troops were removed from the South and Reconstruction ended. After the Civil War, many factories were built, and the United States became an

3_____ nation. Many Americans also moved west because the

4_____ gave settlers 160 acres of free land on the Great Plains. The first

transcontinental railroad was completed in 5_____ . As people settled the

Great Plains, Native Americans were forced onto 6_____ . A combined force

of Sioux and Cheyenne defeated General 7_____ at the Battle of

Little Bighorn.

The growth of industry was helped by the invention of the 8_____ and

the electric light bulb. By the end of the 1800s, 9_____ and Andrew

Carnegie were leaders of big business. As millions of immigrants moved to American

cities, they lived in crowded 10_____ . Because many factory workers worked

under terrible conditions and earned low salaries, 11_____ started the

American Federation of Labor.

Farmers blamed hard times on the money system called the 12_____ .

Theodore Roosevelt became known as a 13_____ . President Woodrow

Wilson helped control big business with the Clayton Antitrust Act and the

14_____ Commission.

## Looking Ahead to Unit 6

At the end of the 1800s, the United States won control of Alaska, Hawaii, Puerto Rico, and other territories. The United States began to act as a police officer for Latin America. With American help, England and France won World War I. The years after the war brought some good times to the nation.

As you read Unit 6, think about the ways the United States won control of new land. Find out why World War I began in 1914. Discover how the United States entered World War I and how the nation changed in the years after the war. Read on and learn how the United States became an important world power.

# The United States

The United
States annexes
Hawaii.
**1898**

**1850**

**1853**
Commodore
Matthew Perry
visits Japan.

**1867**
The United States buys
Alaska from Russia
for $7.2 million.

**1898**
The United States
defeats Spain in the
Spanish-American War.

# as a World Power

In 1898 Theodore Roosevelt led a group of Americans against Spanish soldiers in the Battle of San Juan Hill in Cuba. The Rough Riders, as they were called, won the battle, and their success helped the United States win the Spanish-American War. This victory moved the United States closer to becoming a world power.

As you read Unit 2, you will learn how the United States became a world leader. Find out how the United States tried to control Latin America. Learn the reasons the United States entered World War I. Discover the many ways the nation changed during the 1920s.

## Think About It

- Hawaii is a group of islands in the Pacific Ocean. How did Hawaii become part of the United States?

- For more than 100 years, the United States stayed out of Europe's affairs. Then in 1917 American soldiers went to France to fight in World War I. Why did Americans decide to fight in Europe?

- Before World War I, most American women wore long skirts and did not work outside their homes. Why did life change for women between 1917 and 1929?

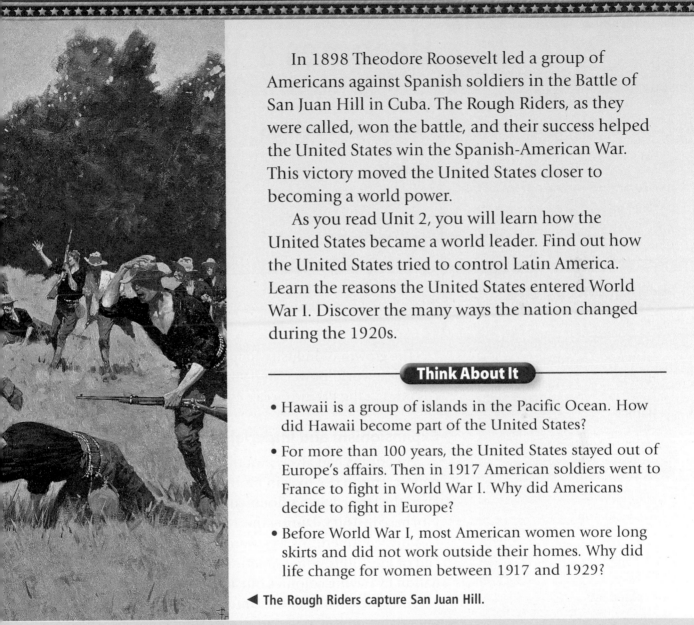

◀ The Rough Riders capture San Juan Hill.

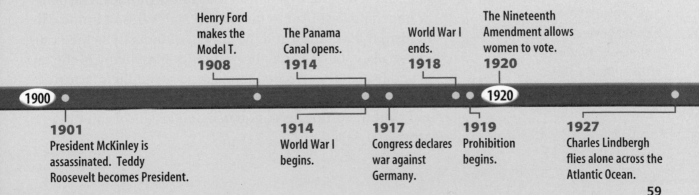

Henry Ford makes the Model T.
**1908**

The Panama Canal opens.
**1914**

World War I ends.
**1918**

The Nineteenth Amendment allows women to vote.
**1920**

**1900**

**1920**

**1901**
President McKinley is assassinated. Teddy Roosevelt becomes President.

**1914**
World War I begins.

**1917**
Congress declares war against Germany.

**1919**
Prohibition begins.

**1927**
Charles Lindbergh flies alone across the Atlantic Ocean.

# The United States Becomes a World Power

## Focus on Main Ideas

1. Why did the United States want to rule colonies?

2. How did the United States win control of Alaska and Hawaii?

3. How did the Spanish-American War help the United States?

4. How did the United States deal with Japan and China?

▲ Campaign button from election of 1900

The growth of industry helped the United States to become a **world power**. By 1900 the United States ruled colonies in the Pacific Ocean as well as in the Caribbean Sea.

### Expansionism and Imperialism

Americans had always wanted to increase the size of their nation. This desire to gain more land is called **expansionism**. First, the United States doubled in size with the Louisiana Purchase in 1803. During the 1800s the idea of Manifest Destiny led Americans westward, to the Pacific Ocean. By the end of the 1800s, some Americans wanted to expand the nation by having colonies outside the United States.

After the Civil War, the United States became an imperialist nation, or a nation that rules colonies. The belief in imperialism spread to the United States from Europe. The Industrial Revolution and the growth of industry helped cause imperialism. European nations did not have many of the raw materials that they needed to make goods in their factories. Colonies would provide raw materials such as oil, rubber, and cotton. Europeans conquered and ruled colonies in Africa and Asia.

Americans also wanted colonies as a source of raw materials for their factories. By ruling colonies the United States hoped to become an important, powerful nation. To conquer and control colonies, the United States had to build up its army and navy.

Some people in the United States believed that imperialism was wrong. They remembered that Americans had been unhappy when they were the colonists of Great Britain. People who were against imperialism thought it was wrong for Americans to take away the freedom and independence of people in other countries.

## Trade with Japan

Japan is an island nation in the Pacific Ocean in eastern Asia. During the 1630s Japan ended relations with other nations. It became an **isolationist** nation.

In 1853 the American government sent Commodore Matthew C. Perry to Japan with a group of warships. The United States wanted Japan to end its isolationist policy. Perry had two goals—to develop trade between the two nations and to improve Japan's treatment of American sailors. When American sailors had been shipwrecked off the coast of Japan, the Japanese had treated them badly.

In 1854 Japan's government signed a friendship treaty with the United States. The treaty allowed the United States to trade in two Japanese ports. The Japanese promised to treat American sailors fairly. The 1854 treaty helped Japan become a modern nation. The Japanese began their own Industrial Revolution. They built new factories and a strong army and navy.

▲ Matthew Perry opened Japan to trade. For more than 200 years, the Japanese had refused to trade with other nations. The 1854 treaty with Japan opened trade in two port cities.

Soon Japan became one of the most powerful nations in Asia.

## The Purchase of Alaska

William Henry Seward, the secretary of state under President Andrew Johnson, believed in expansionism. Seward wanted the United States to own Alaska, which was then owned by Russia. Most people thought that Alaska was nothing more than a huge northern icebox. In 1867 Russia agreed to sell Alaska to the United States for $7.2 million. People laughed at Seward and called the purchase of Alaska "Seward's Folly." Soon Americans learned that Alaska was rich in natural resources such as oil, forests, and metals. After the gold rush in Alaska, everyone agreed that Alaska was a real bargain. In 1959 Alaska became the forty-ninth state.

In the same year that Seward bought Alaska, the United States **annexed** two small islands in the Pacific Ocean.

61

▲ This check for $7,200,000 was used to buy Alaska from Russia. The United States and Russia had talked about a deal since the 1850s, but they did not agree until 1867.

Altogether the Midway Islands had a very small population, but they were an excellent place for steamships to **refuel** before sailing on to Asia and Australia.

### Annexation of Hawaii

Hawaii is a group of islands in the Pacific Ocean about 2,000 miles from California. During the 1800s American missionaries moved to Hawaii to teach Hawaiians to be Protestants. **Descendants** of these missionaries became planters who raised sugar on plantations. Most of the sugar was sold to the United States, and Americans in Hawaii grew wealthy.

By the late 1800s, Hawaii had become an important place to refuel American ships. In 1887 Hawaii's king allowed the United States navy to use Pearl Harbor as an American **naval** base.

By 1891 the Americans in Hawaii wanted the islands to be part of the United States. But Hawaii's new queen, Queen Liliuokalani, wanted Hawaii to remain an independent nation. In 1893 Americans revolted against the queen. The revolution ended quickly, before anyone was killed. As a result, Queen Liliuokalani had to give up her throne. For a few years, Hawaii was an independent republic. In August 1898 the United States annexed Hawaii. In 1959 Hawaii became the nation's fiftieth state.

### The Spanish-American War

Spain had once been a powerful nation that ruled a large empire. By the 1890s Spain had lost most of its colonies. But Spain continued to rule the islands of Cuba and Puerto Rico in the Caribbean Sea and the Philippines and Guam in the Pacific Ocean. In 1898 the United States fought and won a short war against Spain. As a result of that war, Spain lost these four colonies.

The United States went to war against Spain for several reasons. First, the United States wanted to help Cuba, an island near Florida, win its independence. The Cubans had revolted against Spain, but they lost their fight for freedom. José Martí was an important leader in the Cuban struggle. After ending the Cuban revolt, the Spanish treated the Cubans more cruelly than before.

Americans also wanted to protect their trade with Cuba. Americans owned property and businesses in Cuba that were worth about $50 million.

The *New York Journal* and the *New York World* wrote exciting but often untrue stories about Cuba's revolution. They wrote these types of stories to sell more newspapers. The stories were examples of **yellow journalism**. They encouraged the United States to go to war against Spain.

In February 1898 an American battleship called the *Maine* exploded in a Cuban harbor, killing most of the sailors onboard. The *Maine* had been sent to Cuba to protect American citizens and their property. The explosion was caused by a problem in the engines of the ship. But at the time no one knew why the *Maine* had exploded. Newspaper stories blamed Spain for the explosion. "Remember the *Maine!*" Americans cried, as they encouraged Congress to declare war against Spain.

President William McKinley tried to avoid war with Spain. But because more and more Americans and members of Congress wanted war, McKinley finally asked Congress to declare war against Spain. In April 1898, the Spanish-American War began.

## Winning the Spanish-American War

The first battle of the Spanish-American War was fought in the Philippines, which was a Spanish colony. Theodore Roosevelt, the assistant secretary of the navy, ordered Commodore George Dewey to attack. Dewey and the American navy destroyed the Spanish fleet, quickly giving Americans control of the Philippines.

▲ This artist's version of the explosion on the *Maine* was painted in 1898. Because of the articles and drawings in newspapers, many people believed that the Spanish were to blame. Today we know that it was not the Spanish. The explosion was caused by a problem in the engines of the ship.

More fighting in the war took place in Cuba. Theodore Roosevelt resigned his job as assistant secretary of the navy to join the fight in Cuba. Roosevelt led a group of men known as the "Rough Riders" to capture San Juan Hill. On July 17, 1898, the Spanish surrendered the city of Santiago de Cuba, in yet another battle.

Next, Americans fought to free the nearby island of Puerto Rico. The fight for Puerto Rico ended quickly with an American victory. In August 1898 the Spanish surrendered. Americans had won

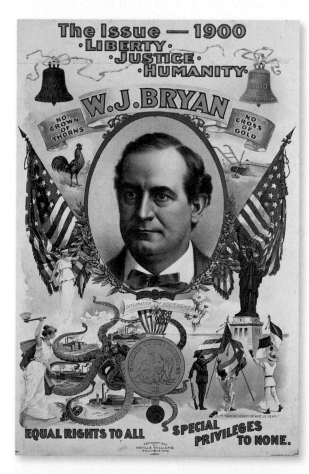

▲ This poster is from the election of 1900. The drawing at lower right shows that control of Cuba, Puerto Rico, and the Philippines was still being debated two years after the war.

the Spanish-American War in less than four months. Secretary of State John Hay said the Spanish-American War was "a splendid little war." About 5,000 Americans died from diseases during this war. Only a few hundred died in battle.

The United States and Spain signed the Treaty of Paris. The Treaty of Paris ended the war and forced Spain to give Cuba, Puerto Rico, Guam, and the Philippines to the United States. Control of these islands and the people living there led to a debate, or argument, in the United States. Should these places be treated as territories? Could they become states? Could the people there become citizens of the United States with the same rights under the Constitution? Eventually the government treated each of these islands differently.

Congress passed the Platt Amendment, which gave Cuba its independence. However, that law also gave the United States the right to interfere in Cuba. Eventually the island of Puerto Rico became a **commonwealth** of the United States. Guam became a territory.

The Philippines were promised that they would get independence when they were ready. But the people of the Philippines had expected to be independent after the Spanish-American War. When the United States would not give them independence, they revolted against American rule. It took the United States several years to end the revolt.

As time passed, the people of the Philippines were given more power to rule themselves. It was not until 1946 that the United States allowed the Philippines to become independent.

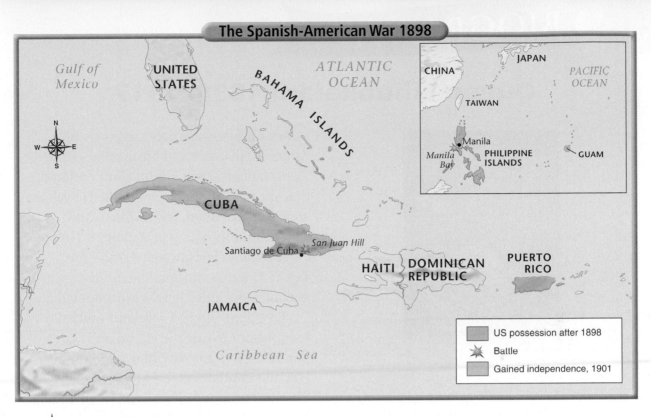

## The Spanish-American War 1898

---

✴ MAP STUDY

The Spanish-American War started because the United States wanted to help Cuba. But the war was fought in the Philippines, in Cuba, and in Puerto Rico. Which country gained its independence in 1901?

(Geography Theme: place)

## China and the Open Door Policy

The United States wanted to trade with China. But it was difficult for Americans to trade with China because China had been divided into **spheres of influence**. A sphere of influence was an area in China that was controlled by a European nation or by Japan. The United States did not have a sphere of influence in China, so it could not trade with China.

The Chinese were unhappy that foreign nations had taken control of their country. In 1900 a large group of Chinese, known as Boxers, decided to force the foreigners to leave China. Their fight was called the Boxer Rebellion. Soldiers from Europe and the United States fought back and defeated the Boxers.

After the Boxer Rebellion, Secretary of State John Hay said that China should have an **Open Door Policy**. He meant that all nations should be allowed to use any of China's ports. There would be no more spheres of influence. With this policy China would remain an independent nation. Although the United States wanted an Open Door Policy to improve its own trade with China, the new policy was also good for China.

By 1900 the United States had become a world power. It ruled colonies in the Pacific Ocean and the Caribbean Sea.

# Queen Liliuokalani 1838–1917

Queen Liliuokalani was the last royal leader of Hawaii. Although she loved her country and wanted it to stay independent, she could not prevent Hawaii from becoming a territory of the United States.

When she was a child, Hawaii's last queen was called Lydia Kamekeha. She was the daughter of a Hawaiian chief. Lydia's brother became king of Hawaii. Since he did not have children, he chose Lydia to be the next royal ruler. When her brother died in 1891, Lydia became queen. After that she was known as Queen Liliuokalani.

Queen Liliuokalani's goal was to protect Hawaii's independence so it would not become an American territory. She was not pleased that American business leaders had great power in Hawaii's government. Queen Liliuokalani tried to increase her own royal power so she could limit the power of American planters and business leaders.

In January 1893 Liliuokalani declared that she held all the power in the Hawaiian government. Americans revolted, and American troops prepared to fight. The Queen knew the Hawaiians could not defeat American troops. She did not want anyone to be killed, so she surrendered.

President Grover Cleveland wanted Liliuokalani to rule the Hawaiian Islands. But the Americans who had taken over Hawaii would not give up control of the islands. They made Hawaii an independent republic. Sanford B. Dole, one of the American business leaders, was president of Hawaii until 1898. At that time President McKinley decided to annex Hawaii. The islands became part of the United States.

Queen Liliuokalani had tried unsuccessfully to protect Hawaii's independence. She was loved and respected by her people until her death. Today millions of people visit the royal palace where Hawaii's last queen once lived.

## In Your Own Words

Write a paragraph in the journal section of your social studies notebook that tells why Queen Liliuokalani was forced to give up her throne.

# REVIEW AND APPLY

## CHAPTER 6 MAIN IDEAS

■ The United States and the countries of Europe wanted to rule colonies. This was known as imperialism.

■ In 1854 the United States and Japan signed a friendship treaty that opened trade between the two nations.

■ In 1867 the United States bought Alaska from Russia for $7.2 million.

■ The United States annexed Hawaii in 1898.

■ As a result of the Spanish-American War, Spain gave the United States control of Cuba, Puerto Rico, Guam, and the Philippines.

■ The Open Door Policy ended the spheres of influence in China.

## VOCABULARY

**Finish the Sentence** ■ Write the correct word or phrase that best completes each sentence. You will not use all the words in the box.

1. During the 1630s, Japan ended its relations with other nations, becoming an _____ nation.

2. Secretary of State John Hay wanted China to have an _____, which would allow all nations to use China's ports.

3. The desire to gain more land is called _____.

4. It was difficult to trade with China because the country had been divided into _____.

5. The growth of industry helped the United States become a _____.

6. In 1898 the United States _____ Hawaii, making it part of the country.

> world power
> expansionism
> isolationist
> annexed
> spheres of influence
> refuel
> Open Door Policy

## USING INFORMATION

**Writing an Opinion** ■ Write a paragraph in your social studies notebook that tells your opinion about whether the United States was right or wrong to keep control of Guam, Puerto Rico, and the Philippines.

## COMPREHENSION CHECK

**Who Said It?** ■ Read each statement in Group A. Then look at the names in Group B for the person who might have said it. Write the letter of the correct answer on the blank. There is one name you will not use.

### Group A

_____ 1. "I was sent to Japan to develop trade between the United States and Japan."

_____ 2. "I wanted the United States to buy Alaska from Russia."

_____ 3. "I wanted Hawaii to remain an independent country."

_____ 4. "I led Cuba's fight for independence from Spain."

_____ 5. "I led the Rough Riders up San Juan Hill."

_____ 6. "I wanted China to have an Open Door Policy."

### Group B

A. William Henry Seward

B. William McKinley

C. José Martí

D. Theodore Roosevelt

E. John Hay

F. Matthew C. Perry

G. Queen Liliuokalani

## CRITICAL THINKING

**Categories** ■ Read the words in each group. Write a title for each group on the line above each group. There is one title you will not use.

| Reasons for the Spanish-American War | Reasons for Imperialism |
| --- | --- |
| American Expansionism | Americans Trade with Japan    Hawaii |

1. _____

islands in the Pacific Ocean
Americans owned sugar plantations
   there
ruled by Queen Liliuokalani

2. _____

bought Alaska in 1867
annexed Hawaii in 1898
gained control of Guam, Puerto Rico,
   and the Philippines

3. _____

wanted to rule more land
wanted colonies for raw materials
wanted larger market for finished
   products

4. _____

wanted to protect American
   businesses in Cuba
wanted to help Cuba gain its
   independence from Spain
Americans were angry about the
   sinking of the *Maine*

# Using Lines of Latitude and Longitude

Lines of latitude and longitude are imaginary lines that form a grid on maps. Lines of latitude run east and west around the earth. Lines of longitude run north and south. Lines of latitude and longitude are identified with a direction and a number that stands for the degrees, or parts of a circle. The latitude of the Equator is 0 degrees, or 0°. To locate a place on a map, find the nearest lines of latitude and longitude.

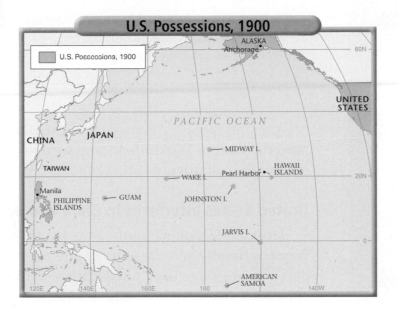

U.S. Possessions, 1900

**A.** Write the latitude for each island.

1. Wake Island _____

2. Jarvis Island _____

3. Midway Islands _____

**B.** Write the longitude for each island.

1. Wake Island _____

2. Jarvis Island _____

3. Midway Islands _____

**C.** Match each place with the correct latitude and longitude.

_____ 1. Manila, Philippines

_____ 2. Anchorage, Alaska

_____ 3. Guam

_____ 4. Pearl Harbor, Hawaii

a. 21°N/158°W

b. 13°N/145°E

c. 15°N/121°E

d. 61°N/150°W

# The United States and Latin America

### Focus on Main Ideas

1. Why did the United States become involved in the problems of Chile and Venezuela?

2. How did the United States gain control of the Panama Canal?

3. In what different ways did Presidents Theodore Roosevelt, William Howard Taft, and Woodrow Wilson treat Latin America?

▲ Dr. Carlos Finlay

After the Spanish-American War, the United States was a powerful nation. The United States used its power to try to control the countries of Latin America.

## United States Interferes in Chile and Venezuela

Most of the nations south of the United States in the **Western Hemisphere** are part of Latin America. Trade developed between the United States and its southern neighbors. American industries bought raw materials from Latin America. They sold their factory products in Latin American countries. Americans who owned land and businesses there wanted **stable governments** in Latin America so that their land and businesses would be protected.

In 1891 the United States interfered in a civil war in Chile. The United States supported the forces that wanted to keep Chile's president in power. However, the forces that opposed Chile's president won the civil war. After the war, Chileans were angry with the United States.

A mob of Chileans attacked a group of American sailors who were visiting Chile. Two sailors were killed, and 16 others were hurt. The United States threatened to go to war unless Chile apologized and paid money to the families of the dead sailors. Chile's government apologized and paid $75,000 to the families. Fortunately, war between the nations was avoided.

In 1895 the United States interfered in Venezuela. The problem began when Great Britain and Venezuela claimed the same piece of land near the colony of British Guiana. According to the Monroe Doctrine, Great Britain could not take control of more land in Latin America. The United States even threatened to go to war against Great Britain if the British would not agree to accept the decision of a committee that did not favor either Great Britain or Venezuela. The committee decided that most of the land belonged to Great Britain. The United States accepted this decision. But the United States had shown that it was willing to use its power to keep Europe out of Latin America. Today British Guiana is the independent nation of Guyana.

## Puerto Rico and Cuba After the Spanish-American War

After the Spanish-American War, the island of Puerto Rico belonged to the United States. The United States chose the governor and some members of the government. But the Puerto Rican people were allowed to elect other leaders.

**Latin America**

Legend:
- North America
- Central America
- South America

★ MAP STUDY

Latin America includes countries in the Western Hemisphere that are south of the United States and where Spanish, Portuguese, and French are the main languages. Which Latin American country is the farthest to the east?

(Geography Theme: location)

▲ This woman wants Puerto Rico to remain a commonwealth of the United States. Her sign calls the commonwealth "the best of both worlds."

Since 1917 all Puerto Ricans have been American citizens. In 1952 Puerto Rico became a commonwealth. This means the island belongs to the United States, but the people rule themselves. People who live in Puerto Rico are American citizens, but they do not pay federal taxes and cannot vote in United States presidential elections. Not all Puerto Ricans want their island to be a commonwealth. Some want it to become a state of the United States. Others want Puerto Rico to be an independent nation.

After the Spanish-American War, the United States had military control of Cuba. The United States greatly improved Cuban health conditions while it ruled Cuba. Many Cubans had died every year from a disease called yellow fever. Carlos Finlay, a Cuban doctor, believed a certain type of mosquito spread the disease. The American Army killed the deadly mosquitoes, and yellow fever was no longer a problem.

In 1901 the United States agreed to allow Cuba to rule itself. But first Cuba had to accept a new constitution that included the Platt Amendment. The Platt Amendment gave the United States the right to interfere in Cuba. It also allowed the United States to have naval bases in Cuba. Cuba's Guantánamo Bay became an American naval base.

The American Army left Cuba in 1902, and the Cubans began to rule themselves. However, the American Army returned to Cuba four times when there were problems.

## Winning Control of the Panama Canal

In order to reach Asia, ships in the Atlantic Ocean had to sail around South America. After the United States won control of Guam and the Philippines, it needed a faster way to send warships from the Atlantic Ocean to the Pacific Ocean.

The shortest route to the Pacific Ocean would be a canal through the narrowest part of Central America. The narrowest part was in the **Isthmus** of Panama, a narrow strip of land connecting North America and South America.

The United States was not the first country to think of building a canal through Panama. A French company had already tried and failed. The project became too expensive for the French, and too many workers had died of disease. The French company wanted the United States to build the canal because the United States would have to buy the right to build it from their company. The United States decided to build the Panama Canal.

Colombia had ruled Panama since it had become independent from Spain in the early 1800s. The United States offered to pay Colombia for the right to build the canal through Panama. The United States promised to pay rent to Colombia each year. But Colombia wanted more money than the United States was willing to pay. So Colombia refused to allow the United States to build the Canal.

People in Panama did not want to lose the trade that the Canal would bring. In 1903 the people of Panama revolted against Colombia. President Roosevelt sent an American warship to help Panama win its freedom. With American help, Panama won its independence in only three days.

The United States quickly signed a treaty with Panama. The treaty said that the United States would build the Canal and control a ten-mile-wide zone around the Canal. The United States paid $10 million to Panama. The United States would also pay $250,000 a year to rent the Canal zone. In 1977 the United States and Panama signed another treaty. The new treaty gave Panama control of the Canal on December 31, 1999.

The region where the Panama Canal was built had many mosquitoes that carried yellow fever and **malaria**. These diseases

▲ It took more than ten years to build the Panama Canal. This photograph shows the construction of one of the Canal locks. The ship in the inset photograph is the *Cristobal*, which in 1914 was the first ship to sail through the Panama Canal.

▲ Roosevelt said that his policy was to "walk softly and carry a big stick." In this political cartoon, he is shown walking with a big stick and the United States Navy in the Caribbean.

had killed many of the French company's workers. An American doctor, Colonel William C. Gorgas, worked hard to stop these diseases. It took about two years to cut down the tall grass and to drain the swamps where the mosquitoes laid their eggs. With the mosquitoes gone, people building the Canal no longer died from yellow fever and malaria.

The Panama Canal was a great achievement in engineering. The Canal opened in 1914. Ships from all nations were allowed to use it. The Panama Canal gave the United States the shortcut it needed from the Atlantic to the Pacific.

## Roosevelt and Big Stick Diplomacy

As President, Teddy Roosevelt changed the meaning of the Monroe Doctrine. To James Monroe, the Doctrine meant that

Europe must not start new colonies in Latin America. To Roosevelt, the Monroe Doctrine meant that the United States could interfere in Latin America with military force.

Roosevelt said that the United States would act as a police officer in Latin America by using military force to settle problems. This was known as **big stick diplomacy**. He also stated that European countries would not be allowed to interfere in Latin America. Together these policies were called the Roosevelt **corollary** to the Monroe Doctrine.

Roosevelt used military force in several Latin American nations that had borrowed money from Europe. They did not have enough money to repay what they had borrowed. Instead of allowing Europeans to send ships and troops to force the countries to pay, the United States forced those nations to pay their debts. At different times Roosevelt sent troops to Venezuela, Cuba, and the Dominican Republic. Those nations were forced to pay their debts. But the use of American troops caused many Latin Americans to hate the United States.

## Latin American Policies of Presidents Taft and Wilson

William Howard Taft became President after Roosevelt. Taft's policy toward Latin America became known as **dollar diplomacy**. This policy encouraged the growth of large American businesses in Latin America. Through these businesses the United States gained power in Latin America. The United States sent troops to Latin America to protect these businesses. Nicaragua, a country in Central

America, was one of the nations into which Taft sent troops. American troops remained in Nicaragua for more than 20 years. Nicaraguans were angry at the United States for interfering.

President Woodrow Wilson also sent troops to Haiti, Cuba, and the Dominican Republic. Wilson wanted Latin American countries to have democratic governments that supported the United States.

After the Mexican Revolution began in 1910, Mexican leaders fought over who would rule the country. President Wilson interfered by supporting Pancho Villa, a Mexican leader. But later President Wilson changed his mind and supported Villa's enemy. This decision made Villa so angry that he entered the United States and killed some Americans in 1916. President Wilson then sent General John J. Pershing with thousands of American soldiers into Mexico to find Pancho Villa. Villa was never captured. Mexicans were furious that American soldiers had invaded their country.

## Improving Relations

Big stick diplomacy and dollar diplomacy in Latin America created great anger toward the United States. Presidents Herbert Hoover and Franklin D. Roosevelt worked to improve relations with Latin America. They started a **Good Neighbor Policy** toward Latin America in the 1930s. Both Presidents promised not to use military force there. However, other Presidents since then have found it necessary to send troops to Latin America. The Good Neighbor Policy opened the way for friendship and trade between the United States and its southern neighbors. That friendship has continued to grow between the United States and many parts of Latin America.

▲ Pancho Villa was one of several leaders who tried to control Mexico's government after the Mexican Revolution. Many Mexicans supported him when he was being chased by American troops.

# Theodore Roosevelt 1859–1919

As a child Theodore Roosevelt, nicknamed Teddy, was small, weak, and often very sick. At the age of 12, he began to exercise and lift weights. Through hard work, Theodore Roosevelt became a strong, powerful man.

When Roosevelt was 22, he married a beautiful woman named Alice. Alice died soon after giving birth to a daughter, whom he named after his wife. Roosevelt's mother also died on the same day. After the deaths of his wife and his mother, Roosevelt moved west to the Dakota Territory. He owned a cattle ranch and worked as a cowboy. Roosevelt developed a deep love for the American West.

A few years later, Roosevelt married again. Roosevelt and his new wife, Edith, had five children.

Roosevelt was a member of the Republican party, and he helped William McKinley become President in 1896. McKinley appointed Roosevelt to be the assistant secretary of the navy.

When the Spanish-American War began, Roosevelt became famous for leading the Rough Riders. After the war Roosevelt was elected governor of New York.

McKinley chose Roosevelt to run as his Vice President in 1900. McKinley was reelected, and Roosevelt became the new Vice President. Six months after his inauguration, McKinley was killed. Roosevelt then became President.

Teddy Roosevelt was the first President to show support for labor unions. He worked with Congress to pass laws protecting the nation's food, meat, and medicines. Roosevelt passed conservation laws to protect America's land, forests, resources, and wild animals. Roosevelt was given the Nobel Peace Prize because he helped end a war between Russia and Japan. Roosevelt felt that his greatest achievement was the Panama Canal.

Cowboy, soldier, governor, Vice President, and President were all jobs that Theodore Roosevelt did well.

## In Your Own Words

Write a paragraph that tells about three of Roosevelt's achievements.

## CHAPTER 7 MAIN IDEAS

- The United States used its power to try to maintain stable governments in Latin America.

- Puerto Ricans became American citizens in 1917. In 1952 Puerto Rico became a commonwealth of the United States.

- The United States helped the country of Panama gain its independence from Colombia because Americans wanted to build a canal across the Isthmus of Panama that would connect the Atlantic and Pacific oceans.

- The United States built the Panama Canal and controlled a ten-mile-wide zone around the Canal. The Canal opened in 1914.

- President Roosevelt started his policy of "big stick diplomacy" in Latin America. He stated that the United States would use military power to settle problems in the region. Roosevelt also said that European countries would not be allowed to interfere in Latin America.

- Taft's policy toward Latin America, called dollar diplomacy, encouraged the growth of large American businesses there. Wilson wanted to have democratic governments in Latin America that supported the United States, so he sent troops into Haiti, Cuba, and the Dominican Republic.

- Presidents Herbert Hoover and Franklin D. Roosevelt started a Good Neighbor Policy toward Latin America, which promised that no military force would be used there.

## VOCABULARY

**Writing with Vocabulary Words** ■ Use five or more words below to write a paragraph that describes how different American Presidents treated Latin America.

| | | |
|---|---|---|
| Western Hemisphere | stable governments | corollary |
| big stick diplomacy | Good Neighbor Policy | isthmus |
| dollar diplomacy | | |

## USING INFORMATION

**Journal Writing** ■ Imagine being on the American warship that helped Panama win its independence from Colombia. How would you feel about helping Panama become an independent nation? Write a paragraph in your journal that describes your feelings. Support your opinions with facts.

## USING GRAPHIC ORGANIZERS

**Concept Web** ■ Complete the concept web with information about United States involvement in the politics of each Latin American country listed.

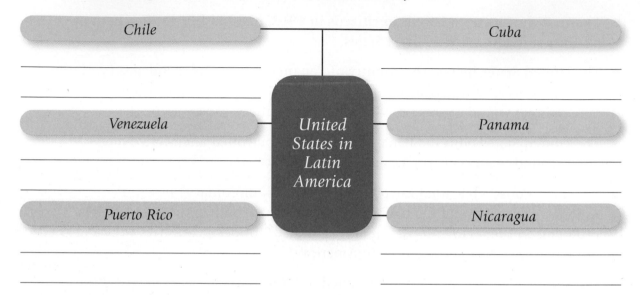

## CRITICAL THINKING

**Cause and Effect** ■ Choose a cause or an effect from Group B to complete each sentence in Group A. Write your answers on the blank lines. Group B has one more answer than you need.

### Group A

_____ 1. Two American sailors were killed in Chile, so _____ .

_____ 2. The United States needed a shorter route between the Atlantic Ocean and the Pacific Ocean, so _____ .

_____ 3. Malaria and yellow fever killed many French workers, so _____ .

_____ 4. _____ , so Roosevelt used big stick diplomacy to force them to pay.

_____ 5. People in Panama began to revolt against Colombia, so _____ .

### Group B

**A.** Colonel William Gorgas worked to destroy mosquitoes that carried diseases

**B.** it wanted to build a canal through Panama

**C.** Roosevelt sent an American warship to help Panama

**D.** the United States threatened to go to war with Chile

**E.** In the year 2000, Panama gained control

**F.** Some Latin American countries could not pay their debts

# Human/Environmental Interaction: The Panama Canal 1904–1914

Human/Environmental Interaction tells how people can change an area and how an area can change people. By digging the Panama Canal, Americans changed a 50-mile strip of land into a 50-mile water route that joined the Atlantic and Pacific oceans. Before digging the Canal, Americans first built a railroad across the Isthmus. The railroad was used to move workers and supplies to the Canal. Trains carried away tons of dirt.

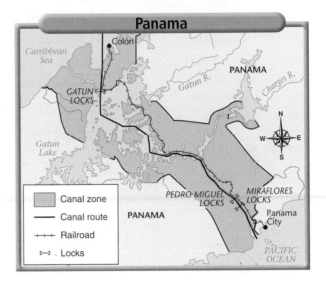

One big problem in building the Canal was that the land was 85 feet above sea level. To solve this problem, engineers built three pairs of sea elevators called locks. These locks raised and lowered the level of the water to allow ships to pass through. It takes about eight hours for a ship to pass through all three pairs of locks of the Canal. Panama's mountains and jungles were another problem, so workers used dynamite to cut through them.

**Study the map of Panama on this page. Use the map and the paragraphs to answer the questions.**

1. What large lake is part of the Panama Canal? _____

2. Why did Americans need a railroad in Panama? _____

_____

3. What were two problems that had to be solved in order to build the Panama Canal?

_____

4. How did Americans solve these two problems? _____

_____

5. What are the names of the Canal's three pairs of locks? _____,

_____ , and _____

# The United States in World War I

### Focus on Main Ideas

1. What were the causes of World War I?

2. How was World War I different from other wars?

3. Why did the United States enter the war?

4. What were the results of the Treaty of Versailles?

▲ Tank used during World War I

Imagine being told not to eat wheat on Wednesdays. From 1917 to 1918, millions of Americans obeyed government rules and did not eat meat and wheat on certain days. The government needed wheat and meat to send to soldiers in Europe who were fighting in World War I.

## Causes of World War I

World War I, or the Great War, began in 1914. The causes of World War I developed over a period of many years. First, the growth of **nationalism** led to World War I. Nationalism is pride in one's own people or country. Nationalism made people of different **ethnic groups** want to fight to have their own nations. For example, Poles and Finns wanted their independence from Russia, and the Irish wanted to be free from Great Britain.

Second, imperialism helped lead to war. Great Britain and France had colonies. Austria-Hungary and Germany were willing to fight to win control of colonies, too.

**Militarism** was a third cause of the war. European nations were building large armies and navies. They had huge supplies of weapons that were more dangerous than weapons that had been used in earlier wars. Another cause was the growth of **alliances**. Nations had signed secret treaties that said they would fight for each other during a war. Great Britain, France, Russia, and some other nations had formed an alliance. During World War I, they were called the Allied Powers, or the Allies. Germany, Austria-Hungary, Turkey, and some other nations also formed an alliance. During the war these nations were called the Central Powers.

By 1914 Europe was like a bomb that was ready to explode. The spark that started the war happened on June 28, 1914. On that day Archduke Francis Ferdinand of Austria-Hungary and his wife were shot and killed. The **assassin** was a Serbian who was angry that Austria-Hungary was ruling his country. Archduke Ferdinand was supposed to become the next emperor of Austria-Hungary.

Austria-Hungary blamed Serbia for Ferdinand's death. So Austria-Hungary declared war on Serbia. Since Russia, Great Britain, and France had alliances with Serbia, they went to war against Austria-Hungary. Some nations were neutral and did not favor either side. At the start of the war, Italy was neutral. But in 1915 Italy joined the Allies. Germany went to war to protect its ally, Austria-Hungary. World War I had begun.

### World War I Alliances

**MAP STUDY**

Most of the fighting during World War I took place in Europe. Many of the nations of Europe fought for either the Allies or the Central Powers. Some nations remained neutral. Which countries were part of the Central Powers?

(Geography Theme: region)

### The Early Years of the War

The war in Europe was fought on two fronts. The eastern front was in Russia and in parts of Germany and Austria-Hungary. The western front was in Belgium and northeastern France. Although Belgium wanted to be neutral, Germany invaded that country in order to attack France.

Germany planned to defeat France quickly and then use its army to defeat Russia. To defeat France the Germans had to capture Paris, the French capital. In September 1914 the battle for Paris began. It was called the First Battle of the Marne. The Allied Powers defeated Germany in this battle, but the Great War would continue for four more years.

World War I was fought differently from all earlier wars. At the start of the Great War, the Allies and the Central Powers were about equal in military power. For more than four years, the two sides fought without victory. Soldiers in World War I used **trench warfare**. Trenches were long ditches dug in the earth. Soldiers on both sides hid in hundreds of miles of trenches, which were often separated with barbed wire. They fired machine guns and **poison gas** at the enemy from the trenches.

For the first time, airplanes were used to find the enemy. Airplanes were also used to shoot down other airplanes in battles called **dogfights**. New weapons such as tanks, poison gas, and **submarines** were also used.

▲ For months at a time, soldiers lived in trenches. They hid in the trenches and fired their weapons from the trenches. The trenches were cold, damp, and often filled with rats. Exploding cannon shells destroyed much of the land around the trenches.

The war was also fought in the Middle East and in North Africa. Turkey, one of the Central Powers, controlled much of the Middle East. Great Britain and France fought against Turkey for control of the Middle East.

World War I was also fought at sea. The British blockaded Germany's ports so that Germany could not receive supplies. Germany used submarines to sink ships that were sailing to Britain and France. Americans were furious when German submarines sank their **merchant ships**.

## The Russian Revolution and the Russian Surrender to Germany

On the eastern front, the Germans began to defeat the Russians. The Russians did not have enough food, fuel, or weapons for the war. By 1917 almost two million Russians had been killed. The Russian ruler, Czar Nicholas II, refused to surrender.

In March 1917 the angry Russian people started a revolution. The Russians forced Nicholas to resign. The leaders of this revolution started a new government. Russia continued to fight in World War I.

In November 1917 Russia had a second revolution, called the Russian Revolution. In this revolution, **Communists** won control of the government. The ideas of communism had been started back in 1848 by a German named Karl Marx. In a Communist nation, the government owns all businesses. In 1917 the Russians used Marx's ideas to start the first Communist government. In Russia a man named V.I. Lenin became dictator. In 1918 Lenin signed a peace treaty with Germany. As part of that treaty, the Russians

▲ Lenin was the leader of the Russian Revolution. His powerful speeches and writings convinced Russians to revolt and create the world's first Communist country.

surrendered and gave large amounts of land to Germany. The treaty helped Germany. Thousands of German soldiers left the eastern front to fight in France.

## America Goes to War

The foreign policy of the United States had always been to stay out of Europe's affairs. When World War I began, President Wilson announced that the United States would remain neutral. But as time passed, the majority of Americans favored the Allies. Americans favored Great Britain and France because they were democracies. However, many Americans supported the Central Powers. Millions of German Americans wanted Germany to win the war. Many Irish Americans were against the Allies because the British refused to allow Ireland to be a free nation.

The United States moved closer to war against Germany in 1915. The *Lusitania*, a British passenger ship, sank after being hit by two **torpedoes** fired from a German submarine. The Germans believed that the *Lusitania* was secretly carrying weapons to Great Britain. Of about 1,200 passengers who died, 128 were Americans. The sinking of the *Lusitania* turned millions of Americans against Germany.

Americans were still hoping to stay out of World War I. In 1916 Woodrow Wilson was reelected. Wilson's campaign slogan had been, "He kept us out of war."

In 1917 the British captured a message that helped push the United States into the war. In the message, called the Zimmermann Note, Germany asked Mexico to go to war against the United States. If Germany won World War I, Mexico could take back the land it had lost to the United States in 1848. Mexico never agreed to this plan. American anger towards Germany grew stronger when the Zimmermann Note was published in American newspapers.

Americans were also angry because Germany had said that its submarines would sink all neutral ships sailing to Great Britain. Germany's goal was to stop the United States and other nations from sending food, weapons, and other supplies to the British.

After German submarines sank several American ships, President Wilson asked Congress to declare war on Germany. In his speech to Congress, Wilson said, "The world must be made safe for democracy." On April 6, 1917, Congress declared war against Germany.

## Life in America During the War

Preparing to fight a war was a difficult job for Americans. The nation had to collect money to pay for the war, raise a huge army, grow enough food to feed the Allies, and keep up the spirits of the American people.

Congress raised taxes to collect money for the war. The federal government also sold billions of dollars worth of Liberty Bonds. By buying bonds, Americans were lending money to the government for the war effort.

To raise an army, Congress passed the Selective Service Act. By 1918 all men ages 18 to 45 were required to register for the draft. About four million served as soldiers during the war.

To raise enough food to feed the American soldiers and the Allies in France, the federal government paid farmers to grow more food. Americans were asked not to eat meat and wheat on certain days of the week. Americans everywhere grew food in small gardens in their backyards.

To build support for the war, the Committee on Public Information created and spread **propaganda**. Propaganda encouraged men to become soldiers and told Americans to buy Liberty Bonds. The government also tried to stop people from speaking and writing against the war. Congress passed laws that limited freedom of speech and freedom of the press. People wrote songs to encourage support of the war. One popular war song, "Over There," had these lines:

> Over there, over there,
> Send the word over there
> That the Yanks are coming
> And we won't come back till it's over,
> Over there.

Because millions of men were in the American armed forces, women worked making tanks, machine guns, and ships. These were jobs that had always been done by men. Women did not serve as soldiers. However, they did dangerous work in Europe as army nurses and ambulance drivers.

Many African American and Mexican American families left the South to work in northern factories. They could get better jobs and better salaries in the North. African American women also became factory workers. However, they often received lower salaries than white women.

**FOOD WILL WIN THE WAR**
You came here seeking Freedom
You must now help to preserve it
**WHEAT is needed for the allies**
Waste nothing

▲ Wheat, sugar, and meat were the foods most needed by the Allies. So Americans were asked not to waste these products.

Many Americans began to hate Germany and German culture during the war. Many towns would not allow the German language to be taught in schools.

## Americans Help the Allies

General John J. Pershing, the general who had once tried to capture Pancho Villa, led the American Army in Europe. The American forces were called the American Expeditionary Force, or the AEF.

The first American soldiers reached France in June 1917. They arrived at a time when they were really needed. German soldiers were leaving Russia to fight in France. But the AEF made the Allies stronger than the Germans. The turning point of the war was the Second Battle of the Marne in 1918. Americans helped defeat the Germans near the Marne River, not far from Paris. After this battle the Allies won more battles and recaptured land that they had lost earlier in the war. The fighting moved away from Paris. The Allies had saved the capital of France.

Americans of different backgrounds—Polish, Greek, German, Irish, and Italian—fought together against Germany. Thousands of Jewish Americans fought in Europe, and about 6,000 Native Americans helped defeat the Germans.

Many African American soldiers won French medals for their courage in battle. Thousands of African Americans fought for the Allies, but they were not allowed to live with or fight in the same units as white soldiers. However, soldiers everywhere owed their lives to an African American inventor, Garrett Morgan. Morgan invented the gas mask.

His invention saved thousands of soldiers from the effects of poison gas.

By November 1918 the Germans knew that the Allies would win. They agreed to stop fighting. At 11:00 A.M. on November 11, 1918, fighting in Europe finally stopped.

## The Treaty of Versailles

Before the end of the war, President Wilson had begun to think about creating a fair peace treaty. In January 1918 Wilson presented his ideas for peace to Congress. In a speech called the "Fourteen Points," Wilson said, "What we demand . . . is that the world be made fit and safe to live in. . . ." In his speech Wilson listed fourteen ways to keep peace between nations. Many of the points addressed the causes of World War I. For example, nations would not form secret alliances. All nations would have freedom of the seas and free trade. Nations would have smaller armies with fewer weapons. Also, people of different ethnic groups would be allowed to form their own nations. Finally, a League of Nations would be started to solve problems between nations. Wilson believed the League would prevent future wars.

In 1919 the Allied leaders met in Paris to write a peace treaty. The treaty was called the Treaty of Versailles. The treaty placed all blame for the war on Germany and forced Germany to pay billions of dollars to the Allies. Germany also lost a large amount of land to the Allies. Woodrow Wilson felt that the Treaty of Versailles was unfair. Wilson did not want to punish Germany and the Central Powers. But the other Allies wanted the Central Powers to pay for the war. Wilson accepted the Treaty of Versailles only because it included his plan for a League of Nations.

Although Wilson signed the treaty, the United States Senate had to ratify, or approve, it. The treaty needed the votes of two thirds of the senators. Senator Henry Cabot Lodge led the fight to defeat the treaty because many Americans did not want to join the League of Nations. They feared that the League would involve Americans in future European wars. The Senate refused to ratify the treaty. As a result the United States did not join the League of Nations.

## Results of World War I

World War I caused terrible damage and loss of life. The Allies lost more than five million soldiers. The Central Powers lost more than three million. Americans lost 126,000 soldiers. Millions of soldiers were wounded. Large areas of France were destroyed during the war. The war had cost both sides billions of dollars.

The Treaty of Versailles created a new map of Europe and the Middle East. Austria-Hungary's Empire and Turkey's Ottoman Empire were broken up. New nations were created from those empires. The treaty gave ethnic groups such as Poles, Finns, and Czechs their own countries and the right to rule themselves.

Americans had fought to make the world safe for democracy. But the world was less safe for democracy after the war. The Treaty of Versailles had planted seeds of anger in Germany that would grow and lead to World War II.

# Woodrow Wilson 1856–1924

President Woodrow Wilson led the American people through the difficult years of World War I.

Wilson came from a family of ministers. Not only was his father a minister, but both of his grandfathers were ministers. His wife was also the daughter of a minister.

As a child Wilson did not learn to read until he was nine years old. Although he later became an excellent speaker, teacher, and writer, he was never a fast reader. As a young man, Wilson became a college teacher. Later he became famous as the president of Princeton University.

In 1910 Wilson was elected governor of New Jersey. Two years later he was elected President of the United States.

Wilson was a progressive President. Together with Congress he worked to end child labor and to lower tariffs on goods from other nations. He also worked to control the growth of big business.

Wilson led the nation during World War I. Throughout the war Wilson's goal was "to make the world safe for democracy." Wilson's peace plan became the "Fourteen Points." Wilson wanted a fair peace plan. Most of all, Wilson wanted a League of Nations. He believed the League would prevent future wars.

Wilson decided to tour the country to win support for the League from the American people. In 1918 he began traveling west. He made speech after speech in many different cities. The trip exhausted Wilson. He became ill, and he suffered a terrible stroke. He would never be strong and well again.

In 1920 the Senate defeated the treaty. Wilson believed that the League would not succeed in keeping peace without the United States. Wilson feared that the unfair Treaty of Versailles would lead to another world war. All of Wilson's fears would turn out to be true. In 1920 he received the Nobel Peace Prize. Wilson is remembered as a President who led Americans through peace and war.

## In Your Own Words

Write a paragraph in your journal that describes Wilson's achievements.

# The Sinking of the *Lusitania*

On Friday, May 7, 1915, a German submarine torpedoed a British passenger ship, the *Lusitania*. The ship, owned by the Cunard Company, sank near Ireland. This news article was in *The New York Times* the next day. Americans were shocked that Germany had attacked a ship that had so many passengers. On that day no one knew all the details about the disaster. Later people learned that 1,198 people had died, and 128 of those people were Americans.

**LONDON, Saturday, May 8.**

—The Cunard liner *Lusitania*, which sailed out of New York last Saturday with 1,918 souls aboard, lies at the bottom of the ocean off the Irish coast.

She was sunk by a German submarine, which sent two torpedoes, crashing into her side, while the passengers, seemingly confident that the great, swift vessel could elude [avoid] the German underwater craft, were having luncheon.

Probably at least 1,000 persons, including many Americans, have lost their lives.

**Sank in Fifteen Minutes.**

The stricken vessel went down in less than half an hour, according to all reports. The most definite statement puts fifteen minutes as the time that passed between the fatal blow and the disappearance of the *Lusitania* beneath the waves.

There were 1,253 passengers from New York on board the steamship, including 200 who were transferred to her from the steamer *Cameronia*. The crew numbered 665.

## Write Your Answers

Write the answers to these questions in your social studies notebook.

1. How did the German submarine sink the *Lusitania*?

2. What were passengers doing when the ship was attacked?

3. **Think and Respond**  Why was the sinking of the *Lusitania* a tragedy?

# Response to the Sinking of the *Lusitania*

After the *Lusitania* was sunk, President Wilson's government sent a statement to Germany. The German government wrote back that the sinking was necessary. The letter was written by Germany's foreign minister, Gottlieb von Jagow.

**BERLIN, May 28, 1915**

The Imperial Government has subjected the statements of the Government of the United States to a careful examination and has the . . . wish . . . to clear up any misunderstandings. . . .

With regard to the loss of life when the British passenger steamer *Lusitania* was sunk, the German Government has already expressed its deep regret [sorrow]. . . .

The Imperial Government must [say] . . . that certain important facts . . . connected with the sinking of the *Lusitania* may have escaped the attention of the Government of the United States. . . .

The . . . United States [thinks] . . . that the *Lusitania* is to be considered as an ordinary unarmed merchant vessel. The Imperial Government begs . . . to point out that . . . English merchant vessels have been provided with guns, ammunition and other weapons, and . . . a crew specially practiced in manning guns. According to reports at hand here, the *Lusitania* . . . undoubtedly had guns on board. . . .

The German Government believes that it acts in just self-defense when it seeks to protect the lives of its soldiers by destroying ammunition destined for the enemy. . . . The English steamship company must have been aware of the dangers to which passengers on board the *Lusitania* were exposed. . . .

In taking them on board . . . the company . . . tried to use the lives of American citizens as protection for the ammunition carried. . . . The company thereby . . . caused the death of so many passengers. . . .

## Write Your Answers

Write the answers to these questions in your social studies notebook.

1. Why did Germany sink the *Lusitania*?

2. Why does Gottlieb von Jagow blame the steamship company for the passengers' deaths?

3. **Think and Respond** What might a passenger on the *Lusitania* have said in response to Germany's reason for sinking the ship?

## CHAPTER 8 MAIN IDEAS

- The four main causes of World War I were nationalism, imperialism, militarism, and the growth of alliances. World War I started when Archduke Francis Ferdinand of Austria-Hungary was assassinated by a Serbian on June 28, 1914.

- World War I was fought differently from earlier wars. Trench warfare lasted for years. New technology, such as airplanes, tanks, and poison gas, was used.

- In 1917 the Russian Revolution created a communist government in Russia.

- The United States entered World War I in 1917 on the side of the Allies.

- On November 11, 1918, World War I came to an end. The Treaty of Versailles included some of Wilson's "Fourteen Points."

## VOCABULARY

**Choose the Meaning** ■ Write the letter of the word or phrase that best completes each sentence.

1. **Militarism** leads to the creation of large _____ .

   a. cities
   b. armies
   c. farms

2. **Nationalism** makes people want their own _____ .

   a. factories
   b. houses
   c. countries

3. Nations in an **alliance** _____ .

   a. protect each other
   b. fight against one another
   c. share the same political leaders

4. **Trench warfare** is fought in _____ .

   a. ditches
   b. ships
   c. planes

5. **Propaganda** tries to influence _____ .

   a. the goods that factories produce
   b. the way people think
   c. the alliances countries make with each other

6. **Communists** believe that all businesses should be _____ .

   a. owned by the military
   b. owned by private citizens
   c. owned by the government

## USING INFORMATION

**Writing an Essay** ■ The United States had to prepare quickly for World War I. Write a paragraph in the assignment section of your notebook in which you list and explain two ways that the United States prepared for war. Start your paragraph with a topic sentence.

## USING GRAPHIC ORGANIZERS

**Cause and Effect** ■ Complete the graphic organizer to show the causes and effects of World War I. Part of the chart has already been done for you.

> **Four Causes of World War I:**
> 1. Nationalism
> 2. _____
> 3. _____
> 4. _____

↓

> **Event in June 1914 that led to the start of World War I:**
>
> _____

↓

> **Four Results of World War I:**
> 1. Great loss of life
> 2. _____
> 3. _____
> 4. _____

## CRITICAL THINKING

**Sequencing Information** ■ Write the numbers 1, 2, 3, 4, and 5 next to these sentences to show the correct order.

_____ The Allies won the First Battle of the Marne.

_____ Austria-Hungary declared war on Serbia after Archduke Francis Ferdinand was assassinated by a Serb.

_____ The Treaty of Versailles was signed.

_____ On November 11, 1918, Germany agreed to stop fighting.

_____ A German submarine sank the *Lusitania*, a British passenger ship.

# Comparing Historical Maps

You can learn some of the results of World War I by comparing a map of Europe before World War I with a map of Europe after the Treaty of Versailles was signed. After World War I, the Austria-Hungary Empire and the Ottoman Empire were broken up into new nations. The map of Europe was changed so that some of the large ethnic groups could have their own nations.

**Europe After World War I**

Compare the map on page 81 with the map on this page. Then answer the questions.

1. What nations were on Russia's western border before World War I?

   _____

2. What nations were on Russia's western border after World War I?

   _____

3. What nations were formed from Austria-Hungary in 1920?

   _____

4. Name four nations with borders that did not change because of World War I.

   _____

# America in the 1920s

### Focus on Main Ideas

1. How did the Republican Presidents help big business?

2. What were some of the problems in the United States in the 1920s?

3. How did American lives change in the 1920s?

4. Who were some important people involved in the Harlem Renaissance?

▲ A radio from the 1920s

In the 1920s, a woman would have shocked people if she came to a party wearing a skirt that was just long enough to cover her knees. Women had always worn long skirts that covered their ankles. Women dared to wear shorter skirts because America changed during the 1920s.

## New Amendments to the Constitution

In 1919 the Eighteenth Amendment to the Constitution made it a crime to manufacture, sell, drink, or ship alcoholic beverages anywhere in the United States. The period when alcoholic beverages were illegal was called **Prohibition**. Supporters of Prohibition believed that alcohol caused crime and social problems.

Prohibition was supposed to reduce crime, but it actually caused more crime. Millions of people found illegal ways to manufacture, sell, and use alcohol. By the 1930s most people agreed that Prohibition laws were impossible to carry out. In 1933 the Twenty-first Amendment to the Constitution ended Prohibition.

During World War I, women had worked in factories and on farms across the nation. Women insisted that if they could serve their country in so many ways, they should have the right to vote. Alice Paul and Carrie Chapman Catt became the new leaders in the fight for women's suffrage. In 1920 the Nineteenth Amendment, which allowed women's suffrage, was ratified. Many women voted for the first time in the 1920 presidential election.

## Republican Presidents

Republicans controlled the White House from 1921 until 1933. President Warren G. Harding wanted the United States to return to the way it had been before the Progressive Movement and World War I. During Harding's presidency, the United States returned to being isolationist. Americans wanted to stay out of Europe's affairs so that they would not have to fight in future wars.

Many **scandals** occurred during Harding's years as President. The people he appointed to federal jobs stole money from the government. The Teapot Dome Scandal was the worst scandal while Harding was President. The navy owned oil fields in Teapot Dome, Wyoming, and Elk Hills, California. Albert Fall, the secretary of the interior, agreed to rent these oil fields to two oil companies. In return the oil companies gave Fall about $400,000. It was against the law for Fall to rent the oil fields or to take money from the oil companies. Fall was later sent to jail for one year, and he paid a fine of $100,000.

Harding died while traveling in the West, and Vice President Calvin Coolidge

▼ During the years of Prohibition, it was illegal to manufacture, sell, drink, or ship alcoholic beverages. Federal police tried to stop the illegal use of alcoholic beverages. When they found illegal alcohol, they destroyed it and arrested the people who made it.

became the next President. Under Presidents Calvin Coolidge and Herbert Hoover, the government continued to favor big business. Coolidge said, "The business of America is business."

Coolidge was a popular President. He was elected to serve again in 1924 and chose not to run in 1928. In 1928 Herbert Hoover defeated Alfred Smith. Hoover won because businesses had been successful under Republican Presidents. Hoover promised that Americans would continue to enjoy **prosperity**. Hoover also won because Al Smith was a Catholic. Prejudice against Catholics stopped millions of people from voting for Smith.

## Threats to American Democracy

In the years after World War I, many Americans were afraid that the democracy they had fought for in the war would be lost. So Americans tried to protect their way of life, but some of their attempts became serious threats to democracy.

The fear of communism in 1919 caused a time of panic called the **Red Scare**. Red was a symbol of communism. Americans feared Communists might win control of the United States. Americans were also afraid of **anarchists**, people who did not want any government. The government unfairly arrested thousands of people who might be anarchists or Communists. By 1920 Americans realized that Communists were not going to take control of the country. But the government's actions during the Red Scare had been a threat to democracy.

Another threat to democracy was **nativism**, or the fear of foreigners. In 1921 a quota system allowed only a certain

▲ Warren G. Harding (left) was upset by the many scandals that occurred while he was President. In 1923 Calvin Coolidge (right) became President when Harding died.

number of immigrants to come to the United States from each nation. By 1929 only 150,000 European immigrants were allowed to come to America each year. Other laws stopped immigration to the United States from China and Japan. Asians living in America were not allowed to become citizens. However, immigrants were allowed into the United States from Mexico and other Latin American nations.

**Racism** threatened democracy because the Constitution was supposed to protect the freedom of all Americans. During the 1920s the Ku Klux Klan spread deep hatred for African Americans, Jews, Catholics, and immigrants. The Klan had about 2 million members. When some members of the Klan murdered African Americans, other members left the

Klan. By 1930 the Klan had fewer than 10,000 members. However, racism continued to grow throughout the nation.

Marcus Garvey tried to fight racism. He told African Americans to be proud of their African culture. He encouraged them to leave the United States and move back to Africa. Most African Americans did not want to move, but Garvey helped them feel pride in their culture.

## The Sacco and Vanzetti Trial

The fear of foreigners and anarchists led to the Sacco and Vanzetti trial. Nicola Sacco and Bartolomeo Vanzetti were Italian immigrants who were anarchists.

▲ Marcus Garvey was an immigrant from Jamaica who told African Americans to be proud of their African culture.

In 1920 the two men were arrested for murder and robbery. Both men said that they were not guilty.

There was little evidence to prove that Sacco and Vanzetti were guilty. But the judge was prejudiced against them because they were anarchists and Italian immigrants. The two men were found guilty. Another man later confessed to the murders, but Sacco and Vanzetti were not given a new trial. Instead the two men were **executed** in 1927. To this day no one knows if Sacco and Vanzetti were guilty. We do know that fear of foreigners and anarchists prevented Sacco and Vanzetti from receiving a fair trial.

## Prosperity in the 1920s

During the 1920s prosperity increased among Americans. New jobs were created, and many products were inexpensive.

Henry Ford owned a car factory named the Ford Motor Company. In 1908 Ford made a car called the Model T. Ford's goal was to make his Model T so inexpensive that most Americans could buy one. He invented a moving **assembly line** to produce cars faster and cheaper than ever before. By 1926 there were 23 million Model T cars in America. Each car cost less than $500.

The Model T brought prosperity to America. Making tires, gasoline, and glass windows for cars became new industries. The steel industry grew because cars were made of steel. Motels, restaurants, and gas stations were built to serve Americans as they traveled farther from home. All of these industries created many new jobs.

The millions of cars on the roads also created dangerous traffic problems.

Garrett Morgan, the inventor of the gas mask, also invented the traffic light, which made American roads safer.

Other new industries made American life easier. Airplane travel became popular. Appliance industries grew larger as more homes had electricity. Americans bought refrigerators, washing machines, and other appliances.

Radio was another industry that grew during the 1920s. Popular radio programs brought music, plays, ball games, and news reports into American homes. Businesses used radio commercials to sell their products to millions of people.

## The Roaring Twenties

The 1920s were called the Roaring Twenties. It was a time when American culture changed in many ways. New fashions, music, literature, and entertainment appeared in the 1920s.

Fashions changed when women said goodbye to long skirts. Instead they wore short skirts, pants, and shorts. They also wore short haircuts and used makeup.

The 1920s were also called the Jazz Age. Jazz was a new type of music that became popular in the 1920s.

Young people wrote literature about life after World War I. Ernest Hemingway later won a Nobel Prize for his novels. F. Scott Fitzgerald wrote *The Great Gatsby*. Hemingway and Fitzgerald questioned the meaning of American life and values.

Movies were a popular kind of entertainment during the 1920s. At first only silent movies were made. Rudolph Valentino and Mary Pickford were two stars of the age of silent movies. By the

1915 FORD MODEL 'T'

▲ The Ford Motor Company was a success because millions of Model T cars were built on a moving assembly line. The company also had the highest paid workers in the industry— $5 per day.

end of the 1920s, Americans were watching "talkies," or movies with sound. Hollywood, California, became the center of the film industry. In 1928 the artist Walt Disney created a cartoon character named Mickey Mouse.

The Roaring Twenties brought some opportunities for African Americans and Hispanic Americans. A. Philip Randolph started the first labor union for African American railroad workers. In 1928 Oscar De Priest of Chicago became the first African American to be elected to Congress in the north. That same year Octaviano Larrazolo from New Mexico became a United States senator. He had been the first Mexican American governor of New Mexico.

▲ Pictured above are some of the people who were famous during the 1920s. From left to right, they are Charles Lindbergh, first person to fly alone across the Atlantic Ocean; Babe Ruth, baseball player with the New York Yankees; Mary Pickford, movie star; Gertrude Stein, writer; and Louis Armstrong, trumpet player and bandleader.

## The Harlem Renaissance

The largest **urban** African American community was in a New York City neighborhood called Harlem. During the 1920s African Americans created new music, art, and literature. This growth of African American culture was called the Harlem Renaissance.

One writer, Langston Hughes, became famous for his poems and novels about his experiences as an African American. Another well-known poet of the Harlem Renaissance was Countee Cullen.

The music of the Harlem Renaissance became famous. Bessie Smith was a popular singer of the African American music called the "blues." Louis Armstrong became the most famous trumpet player in America. Duke Ellington created his own style of music that was loved by people across the nation.

## The Age of Heroes

Americans found many people to admire in the 1920s. They loved the famous baseball player Babe Ruth. Ruth was a good pitcher and a great hitter. During his career with the New York Yankees, he hit 714 home runs.

Charles Lindbergh and Amelia Earhart also became popular heroes. In 1927 Lindbergh became the first person to fly alone across the Atlantic Ocean. He landed safely near Paris after flying for about 33½ hours without sleep. In 1928 Amelia Earhart became the first woman to fly across the Atlantic Ocean.

The 1920s were a time of change and prosperity. Millions of people thought that the good times would last forever. In the 1930s the prosperity ended, and the United States faced very difficult years.

# Paul Robeson 1898–1976

Paul Robeson was one of the greatest actors and singers of the Harlem Renaissance.

Robeson grew up in New Jersey. Robeson's father, who had been enslaved, ran away to freedom when he was 15. He later became a minister. Paul Robeson finished high school at the top of his class. Then he attended Rutgers College in New Jersey where he became a star football player. After four years of college, Robeson graduated at the top of his college class.

After college Robeson attended Columbia University Law School. At that time it was hard for an African American to find work as a lawyer. Robeson found a job with a firm of white lawyers. He was unhappy there and decided to resign.

Robeson began performing as a singer and an actor in Harlem in the early 1920s.

In 1927 Robeson moved to London, England, where he became famous for playing the title role in Shakespeare's play *Othello*. Robeson traveled and performed in many parts of Europe, including the Soviet Union. He thought that the Soviet people were less prejudiced towards African Americans. While in Europe, Robeson spoke out about the need for African colonies to become independent nations. He returned to the United States during the years of World War II.

In the United States, Robeson spoke against racism and prejudice. He praised the Soviet Union for its lack of prejudice toward Africans and African Americans. Before long Paul Robeson was being called a Communist. From 1951 to 1958, he was not allowed to travel outside the United States. In 1958 he was allowed to return to London, where he began singing and acting again.

Robeson was a lawyer, an athlete, a singer, and an actor. He could have used his talents to live an easy, comfortable life. Instead he spent his life helping people of the world win equality.

## In Your Own Words

Write a paragraph in the journal section of your social studies notebook explaining how Paul Robeson used his talents to help himself and other people in many parts of the world.

## CHAPTER 9 MAIN IDEAS

- The Eighteenth Amendment made it illegal to use, buy, or sell alcoholic beverages. The Nineteenth Amendment gave women the right to vote.

- Many scandals, including the Teapot Dome Scandal, occurred during Harding's years as President.

- Republican Presidents Calvin Coolidge and Herbert Hoover favored big business.

- After World War I, fear of communism grew, racism increased, and immigration to the United States was limited.

- Henry Ford's Model T led to new industries and increased prosperity in America.

- The 1920s, called the Roaring Twenties and the Jazz Age, was a period of many cultural changes.

- During the Harlem Renaissance, many African Americans created new art, music, and literature.

## VOCABULARY

**Matching** ■ Match the vocabulary word or phrase in Group B with the definition from Group A. You will not use all the words in Group B.

| Group A | Group B |
|---|---|
| _____ 1. During this time it was illegal to use alcoholic beverages. | A. racism |
| _____ 2. This is a period when people earn more money and live well. | B. nativism |
| | C. prosperity |
| _____ 3. Fear of communism led to this time of panic. | D. Prohibition |
| _____ 4. This fear of foreigners leads to favoring people who were born in the United States and limiting immigration. | E. executed |
| | F. Red Scare |
| _____ 5. This means prejudice towards people because of their race. | |

## USING INFORMATION

**Journal Writing** ■ In your journal, list and explain what you feel were the most important changes that took place during the 1920s.

## COMPREHENSION CHECK

**Finish the Paragraph** ■ Use the words, names, and terms in the box to finish the paragraph. Next to each number, write the correct word you choose. There is an extra word, name, or term in the box that you will not use.

| | | |
|---|---|---|
| Charles Lindbergh | | Harlem Renaissance |
| Republican | immigrants | Model T |
| Roaring Twenties | anarchists | Red Scare |

During the 1920s Americans feared that Communists would take control of the United States. This became known as the **1**_____ . Also as a result of the fear of foreigners, Congress passed laws that lowered the number of **2**_____ that could enter the United States. During the 1920s the United States had three **3**_____ Presidents. The first type of automobile that was bought by millions of Americans was called the **4**_____ . The 1920s were called the **5**_____ because people enjoyed jazz, new fashions, new literature, and movies. The **6**_____ produced new African American music, art, and literature. **7**_____ became an American hero after he became the first person to fly alone across the Atlantic Ocean.

## CRITICAL THINKING

**Fact or Opinion** ■ Write **F** on the blank next to each statement that is a fact. Write **O** on the blank if that statement is an opinion. If the statement gives both a fact and an opinion, write **FO** on the blank. Then draw a line under the part of the sentence that is an opinion.

_____ **1.** The Eighteenth Amendment made it illegal for Americans to drink alcoholic beverages.

_____ **2.** Women should have been given the right to vote long before 1920.

_____ **3.** Calvin Coolidge and Herbert Hoover supported big business.

_____ **4.** Both Sacco and Vanzetti said that they were not guilty.

_____ **5.** During the Roaring Twenties, fashions changed for women, but women wore nicer clothes at the beginning of the 1900s.

Study the time line on this page. You may want to read parts of Unit 2 again. Then use the words and dates in the box to finish the paragraphs. The box has one possible answer you will not use.

The United States starts the Open Door Policy with China.
**1900**

Russia becomes a Communist nation.
**1917**

World War I begins.
**1914**

World War I ends.
**1918**

The Nineteenth Amendment is ratified.
**1920**

Herbert Hoover is elected President.
**1928**

**1900**

**1898**
The United States defeats Spain in the Spanish-American War.

**1903**
Work begins on the Panama Canal.

**1915**
A German submarine sinks the *Lusitania*.

**1917**
The United States enters the war against Germany.

**1919**
Prohibition begins.

**1927**
Sacco and Vanzetti are executed.

| | | |
|---|---|---|
| 1898 | malaria | Allies |
| 1920s | McKinley | Serbia |
| Alaska | Hawaii | 1917 |
| Latin America | Panama Canal | Prohibition |
| Open Door Policy | *Lusitania* | Communist |

The United States expanded in 1867 when it bought **1**_____ from Russia. In **2**_____ the United States became an imperialist nation after it defeated Spain in the Spanish-American War. In that same year, the United States annexed **3**_____ . The United States wanted to have trade with China, so in 1900 it announced the **4**_____ . Teddy Roosevelt became President after

President 5_____ was assassinated in 1901. Teddy Roosevelt used military force to control events in 6_____ . Roosevelt encouraged Americans to build the 7_____ . Before the Canal could be built, the region had to be made safe from yellow fever and 8_____ .

World War I began after a Serbian killed Archduke Francis Ferdinand of Austria-Hungary. American anger toward Germany grew after more than 100 Americans were killed when a German submarine sank the 9_____ in 1915. During World War I, Russia became a 10_____ nation. After Germany sank several American ships, President Wilson asked Congress to declare war in 11_____ . With American help the 12_____ defeated Germany and the other Central Powers. The Eighteenth Amendment made alcoholic beverages illegal during the time known as 13_____ . During the 14_____ , new fashions, new music, new literature, and movies became popular.

## Looking Ahead to Unit 3

The good years of the 1920s came to an end in 1929. In that year the Great Depression began. Millions of people were out of work during the Great Depression. During these difficult years, dictators came to power in Germany, Italy, and Japan. The actions of these dictators led to World War II. From 1941 to 1945, millions of American soldiers fought around the world. After the war Americans tried to prevent a third world war from starting.

As you read Unit 3, think about the ways life changed during the Great Depression. Discover how the United States helped the Allies win World War II. Read on and learn about the difficult challenges Americans faced during the Depression and World War II.

Adolf Hitler
becomes dictator
of Germany.
**1933**

Congress passes the
Social Security Act.
**1935**

**1925**      **1930**      **1935**

**1929**
The stock market crashes and
the Great Depression begins.

**1932**
Franklin D. Roosevelt
is elected President.

**1933**
The New Deal
begins.

# and World War II

After weeks of deadly fighting on the island of Iwo Jima, six brave marines raised a large American flag on top of Mount Suribachi. About 6,800 Americans died as they fought for victory against the Japanese on Iwo Jima. After capturing the island, Americans continued their fight against Japan during World War II.

As you read Unit 3, you will learn about the difficult years of the Great Depression and World War II. Find out why millions of Americans became very poor during the Great Depression. Discover the ways Americans helped the Allies defeat Germany, Italy, and Japan.

## Think About It

- In the early 1930s, farmers grew plenty of food for the nation. Why did many people need breadlines and soup kitchens to survive?

- During World War II, Germany conquered France in 1940. Why did the Allies wait until 1944 to help France become free from Germany?

- Iwo Jima had few people, few natural resources, and poor soil. Why did Americans fight so hard for this island in 1945?

◄ Statue of Marines raising American flag on Iwo Jima

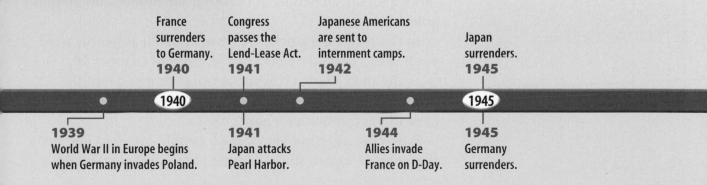

| France surrenders to Germany. **1940** | Congress passes the Lend-Lease Act. **1941** | Japanese Americans are sent to internment camps. **1942** | Japan surrenders. **1945** |

**1940**  **1945**

**1939**
World War II in Europe begins when Germany invades Poland.

**1941**
Japan attacks Pearl Harbor.

**1944**
Allies invade France on D-Day.

**1945**
Germany surrenders.

# The Great Depression

## Focus on Main Ideas

1. What caused the stock market to cras in 1929?

2. What were the causes of the Great Depression?

3. How did the Great Depression hurt the United States?

4. How did the federal government try to end the Great Depression?

UNEMPLOYED
BUY
APPLES
5¢ EACH

▲ A sign that was common during the 1930s

Many hungry Americans waited in breadlines to receive free bread. Millions of people were so poor that they needed help to survive. During the 1930s Americans lived through the difficult years of the Great Depression.

## The Crash of '29

The Great Depression began when the **stock market** crashed in 1929. During the 1920s many Americans had **invested** money in the stock market by buying stocks, or shares, of corporations. You learned about stocks and corporations in Unit 5.

Many people took great risks when they bought stocks during the 1920s. Some people used all their savings to buy stocks. Other people bought stocks with money that they had borrowed from banks. From 1925 to 1929, the price of most stocks went up. So people borrowed more money and bought more stocks.

In October 1929 stock prices began to fall as people tried to sell stocks that no one wanted to buy. On October 29, 1929, the stock market crashed as prices dropped rapidly. People called that day "Black Tuesday." It was the worst day the stock market had ever had.

When the stock market crashed, people who had invested all of their savings in stocks became poor overnight. People who had borrowed money from banks to buy stocks were unable to repay their loans. Banks had also invested in stocks. Many banks lost millions of dollars and were forced to close. People who had their savings accounts in those banks lost all their money.

Years of hard economic times followed the stock market crash. This time period is called the Great Depression. This was not America's first depression. But the Great Depression was the longest and most difficult one in American history. This depression lasted more than ten years.

## Causes of the Great Depression

The stock market crash started the Great Depression but did not cause it.

There were many causes of the Great Depression.

First, the nation's wealth was not shared by everyone during the 1920s. About half of all Americans were poor. Half of the nation's wealth was owned by only 200 businesses.

Second, farmers suffered during the 1920s. During World War I, farmers raised huge amounts of food for the Allies. After the war farmers grew more crops than people could buy. They were forced to sell their crops at very low prices. Many farmers lost so much money that they were forced to sell their farms. Third, overproduction caused people to lose their jobs. Factories were producing more than people could buy. When

▲ When the stock market crashed on October 29, 1929, many people lost all of their money. This photograph shows a crowd of people on the street in front of the stock market building on Black Tuesday. In one day the value of the stock market dropped $14 billion.

people did not buy the products, the factories closed. About 75,000 people lost their jobs when a Ford Motor Company plant closed.

Fourth, Congress had placed high tariffs on European goods. Then European nations placed high tariffs on American goods. American businesses suffered because Europeans bought fewer American goods.

Fifth, the banking system had many problems. Laws did not require banks to protect money in savings accounts.

Sixth, the government did not pass laws to correct problems in the economy. The three Republican Presidents in the 1920s believed in laissez-faire government. They refused to interfere with business.

## Hard Times During the Great Depression

Herbert Hoover was President when the Great Depression began. He was sure that this depression would soon end by itself. Unfortunately the depression grew worse each year. In 1932 Hoover asked Congress to start an agency that would lend money to banks and businesses. Hoover believed that if banks and businesses had more money, they would provide jobs for workers. Hoover's plan failed to help the nation.

By 1933, 13 million people, or 25 percent of Americans, were unemployed. Many people who had jobs were working for lower salaries. People became homeless. They built shacks out of old boxes and whatever junk they could find. Every city had large areas filled with shacks. People named these areas **Hoovervilles** because they blamed President Hoover for the depression. By 1933, one million people lived in Hoovervilles.

As the depression continued, people throughout the country suffered. Schools closed because towns could not afford to pay their teachers. Hungry people searched for scraps of food in garbage cans. People who lost their jobs had no money to buy food. A loaf of bread cost only five cents, but many people did not even have a nickel for bread. So they waited in breadlines for a loaf of free bread. And they went to soup kitchens to get a free bowl of soup.

Prejudice grew during the depression. Often the first workers to be fired were African Americans or Mexican Americans. It became harder for immigrants to find jobs. Many women were fired so that men could have their jobs.

As the depression continued, farm prices dropped lower because people could not afford to buy the crops. Most farmers could no longer earn a living. Starting in 1931 a seven-year drought destroyed many farms on the Great Plains. After the drought caused soil to dry up and blow away, there were huge dust storms. This area of the nation became known as the Dust Bowl. Thousands of farmers sold their farms and moved west to California. There they became **migrant farm workers** as they moved from place to place looking for work on farms.

John Steinbeck, a famous American writer, wrote a novel about migrant farm workers. In that novel, *The Grapes of*

▲ Dorothea Lange took this photograph of a family during the depression. Lange was a famous photographer who captured in her pictures the sad suffering of people during the 1930s.

*Wrath*, Steinbeck told how migrants struggled as they moved to California during the depression.

> And the migrants streamed in on the highways and their hunger was in their eyes, and their need was in their eyes. They had no argument, no system, nothing but their numbers and their needs. When there was work for a man, ten men fought for it— fought with a low wage.
>
> If that fella'll work for thirty cents, I'll work for twenty-five.

## The Bonus Army

In the summer of 1932, about 20,000 World War I **veterans** went to Washington, D.C., to demand bonus money that the government had promised them. They were supposed to receive the bonuses in 1945, but the hungry veterans did not want to wait. President Herbert Hoover and Congress refused to pay the bonuses, so the veterans camped out in Washington, D.C., in protest. They became known as the Bonus Army.

President Hoover sent General Douglas MacArthur with federal troops to attack the Bonus Army. The troops forced them to leave Washington. Most Americans were angry at Hoover for attacking the veterans.

## Roosevelt and the New Deal

By 1932 most Americans wanted a new President. Franklin D. Roosevelt, the Democratic candidate, easily defeated Herbert Hoover in the election of 1932.

Roosevelt promised to end the depression. He brought new hope during his campaign when he promised a "New Deal" for the American people. At his inauguration on March 4, 1933, he told the frightened nation, "The only thing we have to fear is fear itself."

Two days after becoming President, Roosevelt closed all of the banks in the nation. The government examined how each bank was handling money. After a few days, safe banks were allowed to reopen. Roosevelt encouraged people to keep their savings in banks again.

Roosevelt spent his first 100 days working with Congress to pass many new programs. His plan to end the Great Depression was called the New Deal.

The New Deal had three main goals. They were relief, **recovery**, and reform.

▲ The WPA was one of the New Deal agencies that put people to work. WPA workers often built or repaired public places.

Americans needed relief from poverty and hunger. The nation needed to recover from the depression. And reform, or change, was needed to prevent future depressions.

The New Deal created many agencies to carry out the goals of relief, recovery, and reform. Some agencies gave states money to help the poor. Other agencies helped farmers. Some agencies helped provide jobs for the many people who were unemployed. Once people were earning money, they could buy food, clothing, and other goods. This would help businesses grow stronger.

New Deal agencies created millions of new jobs. The government hired workers to plant trees, build bridges, and clean streets. One New Deal agency, the Tennessee Valley Authority, or TVA, hired thousands of workers to build dams to control floods. The TVA also built power plants that used waterpower to make electricity. See the chart on the next page for names and descriptions of other New Deal agencies.

The New Deal also helped correct problems that had caused the Great Depression. The Federal Deposit Insurance Corporation, or FDIC, provided **insurance** for money in savings accounts. People would no longer lose their savings if a bank failed. Another New Deal agency, the Securities and Exchange Commission, or SEC, made it safer for people to invest in the stock market.

From 1935 to 1936, Roosevelt worked with Congress to pass more laws. Congress passed the Social Security Act, which required all workers to pay a special tax. In return, workers would receive **pensions** when they retired at age 65. The new law also provided money for poor families with children.

## Roosevelt's Plan to Pack the Supreme Court

After the Supreme Court found some New Deal agencies unconstitutional, Roosevelt wanted more control over the Supreme Court. So in 1937 he asked Congress to pass a law that would allow him to appoint a new justice to the Supreme Court for every judge who was older than age 70. If the law passed, Roosevelt could appoint six more justices.

Congress defeated Roosevelt's plan to "pack the Supreme Court" with his own judges. It was defeated because the Constitution requires the Supreme Court to be independent from both Congress and the President. However, many justices retired while Roosevelt was President. By 1944 he had appointed seven of the nine justices on the Supreme Court.

## Roosevelt Selects His Cabinet

Roosevelt was very popular. He was the first President to be elected more than twice. Eleanor Roosevelt, the President's wife, was also popular. She traveled around the country to help women, workers, and African Americans have equal rights. When a women's group

### Important New Deal Agencies

| New Deal Agency | | What Did the Agency Do? |
|---|---|---|
| CCC | Civilian Conservation Corps | It provided conservation jobs for unemployed young men. They planted trees and built dams and roads. |
| FERA | Federal Emergency Relief Administration | It worked with states to provide relief money to the unemployed or to people hurt by the drought. |
| FDIC | Federal Deposit Insurance Corporation | It protected the safety of banks. It insured savings deposits so people would not lose money if banks failed. |
| TVA | Tennessee Valley Authority | It built dams on the Tennessee River to control floods, provide cheap electricity, and improve life in the region. |
| PWA | Public Works Administration | It created public works jobs. People built bridges, roads, dams, schools, hospitals, and courthouses. |
| SEC | Securities and Exchange Commission | It controls the stock market so it will not crash again. It tries to protect people from investing in unsafe stocks. |
| SSB | Social Security Board | It provides workers with pensions and unemployment insurance. It gives aid to poor families with children and to some people with disabilities. |
| WPA | Works Progress Administration | It employed more than eight million needy people. They built roads, parks, and buildings. The WPA also created jobs for artists, actors, and musicians. |

refused to allow Marian Anderson, a famous African American singer, to sing inside its building, Eleanor Roosevelt invited Anderson to sing in front of the Lincoln Memorial. Anderson sang "America" before almost 75,000 people.

President Roosevelt appointed many kinds of Americans to important government jobs. Frances Perkins became the first woman Cabinet member. Roosevelt appointed Felix Frankfurter, a Jewish American, to be a Supreme Court justice. Matthew T. Abruzzo was the first Italian American to be a federal judge.

Roosevelt often met with a group of African American leaders who were called the Black Cabinet. One member of the Black Cabinet was Mary McLeod Bethune. She had started a school for African American girls. Bethune led the Office of

▲ Eleanor Roosevelt was a very active President's wife. She traveled for the President, and she supported many social causes.

▲ Marian Anderson sang at the Lincoln Memorial after a women's group refused to let her sing because she was an African American.

**Minority** Affairs for President Roosevelt from 1935 to 1944.

Roosevelt made the Democratic party very popular. Most factory workers became Democrats. Most African Americans had been Republicans, but they became Democrats during the New Deal.

## Results of the New Deal

The New Deal made the federal government larger and more powerful than ever before. The President became a more powerful leader.

Some people believed that the New Deal hurt the nation. People had to pay more taxes in order to pay for expensive programs. The national debt grew larger because the government borrowed billions of dollars to pay for the New Deal. Many believed the New Deal did not end the depression.

However, the New Deal helped America by providing relief to the poor and hungry. Many of the nation's roads, bridges, dams, and airports were built by New Deal agencies. Some New Deal agencies, such as the Social Security Board and the FDIC, continue to help millions of people.

The New Deal may have protected American democracy. Other nations in the world were also faced with depressions during this time. Some nations turned to dictators to solve their problems, while the United States did not.

The Great Depression finally ended soon after World War II began in Europe in 1939. Americans began to worry more about the terrible events around the world instead of their problems at home.

# Franklin D. Roosevelt 1882–1945

Franklin D. Roosevelt was the only President elected four times. He was President for 12 years. Roosevelt was born in New York into a wealthy family. Roosevelt was called FDR by his friends. In 1905 FDR married Eleanor Roosevelt, his distant cousin. Teddy Roosevelt, Eleanor's uncle and President of the United States, came to the wedding and gave away the bride. Franklin and Eleanor would later have six children.

Franklin Roosevelt's life changed after he was struck by **polio** in 1921. He spent years trying to learn to walk again, but he could never walk again without leg braces and a cane. Roosevelt went to Warm Springs, Georgia, to swim in a warm pool of mineral water. Roosevelt bought the springs and used his own money to provide low-cost treatment for polio patients.

In 1932 Roosevelt, a Democrat, ran for President of the United States. He had been a state senator and a governor of New York. As President, Roosevelt developed the New Deal program to end the Great Depression.

FDR used the radio to speak to the American people. In talks that he called "fireside chats," he told the nation that the depression would end.

During the 1930s Roosevelt worked at building friendship and trade with Latin America. His policy was called the Good Neighbor Policy.

During World War II, Roosevelt had the nation produce weapons and supplies for the war. The United States sent supplies to its ally, Great Britain.

Soon after Japan attacked the American naval base at Pearl Harbor, the United States went to war against Japan, Germany, and Italy. FDR led the nation through the difficult years of World War II.

FDR died suddenly on April 12, 1945, only months before the United States and the Allies won the war. Roosevelt is remembered as the President who led the nation through 12 hard years of depression and war.

## In Your Own Words

Write a paragraph in your journal that tells how FDR helped the United States during his years as President.

## CHAPTER 10 MAIN IDEAS

- The stock market crash on October 29, 1929, started the Great Depression.

- There were six main causes of the Great Depression: the nation's wealth was not shared by everyone, farmers suffered during the 1920s, overproduction caused people to lose their jobs, Congress placed high tariffs on European goods, banks failed, and the government did not pass laws to correct problems in the economy.

- During the Great Depression, millions of Americans were unemployed. Many people went hungry and homeless.

- Franklin D. Roosevelt promised Americans a "New Deal" that would end the Great Depression. President Roosevelt was reelected three times.

- The New Deal had three main goals: relief, recovery, and reform. Many government agencies were created as part of the New Deal to end the Great Depression and to prevent future depressions.

- Roosevelt tried to "pack the Supreme Court" to protect New Deal agencies.

- The Cabinet selected by President Roosevelt included the first woman Cabinet member.

- The Great Depression ended soon after World War II began.

## VOCABULARY

**Defining and Using Vocabulary** ■ Use the glossary to find the meaning of each word or phrase listed below. Write the definition of each word in your social studies notebook. Then use each word in a sentence.

| stock market | Hoovervilles | veterans |
|:---:|:---:|:---:|
| recovery | pensions | polio |
| invested | insurance | minority |

## USING INFORMATION

**Writing an Essay** ■ The New Deal had three main goals. Write an essay that lists and explains each goal. Then provide one example of how government agencies tried to reach each New Deal goal. Start your essay with a topic sentence.

## USING GRAPHIC ORGANIZERS

**Compare and Contrast Chart** ■ Complete the graphic organizer below to compare and contrast the Great Depression and the New Deal.

| | **Great Depression** | **New Deal** |
|---|---|---|
| Year started | | |
| Reason it started | | |
| President who was in office | | |
| Effect on jobs in the united States | | |
| Savings accounts | | |
| Effect on federal government | | |

## CRITICAL THINKING

**Distinguishing Relevant Information** ■ Imagine that you are telling your friend how difficult life was during the Great Depression. Read each sentence below. Decide which sentences are relevant to what you will say. Put a check next to the relevant sentences. There are four relevant sentences.

_____ 1. When the stock market crashed, many people became poor overnight.

_____ 2. Starting in 1931, a seven-year drought destroyed many farms on the Great Plains.

_____ 3. The country's population grew larger during the Great Depression.

_____ 4. Millions of Americans depended on breadlines and soup kitchens for free food.

_____ 5. Many new movies were made during the Great Depression.

_____ 6. President Roosevelt created New Deal programs to help the poor and the hungry.

# Region: The Dust Bowl

**Region** tells us the way places in an area are alike. During the 1930s part of the Great Plains became a region called the Dust Bowl.

When farmers planted wheat, they destroyed the prairie grass that held the soil on the Great Plains. Then came seven years of drought in the 1930s. The crops died, and the soil became dry and loose.

Wind storms hit the Great Plains and blew dust off of the dry fields. Thick dust buried farms, animals, cars, and houses. Dust storms also damaged other areas of the Great Plains. To prevent another dust bowl, thousands of trees have been planted to hold down the soil and block the wind on the Great Plains.

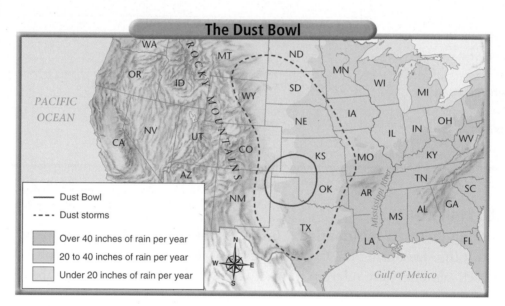

**The Dust Bowl**

— Dust Bowl

- - - Dust storms

Over 40 inches of rain per year

20 to 40 inches of rain per year

Under 20 inches of rain per year

**Read the paragraphs and study the map of the Dust Bowl. Answer the questions below.**

1. What five states were part of the Dust Bowl? _____

   _____

2. What made the Dust Bowl a region? _____

   _____

3. What caused the Dust Bowl? _____

   _____

4. What have people in this region done to prevent future dust bowls? _____

   _____

# Comparing Line Graphs

Line graphs are used to show changes over a period of time. By comparing two line graphs that have different information for the same period, we can draw conclusions. The graph on the left shows how the percentage of people without jobs changed from 1929 to 1940. The graph on the right shows how the amount of money the federal government spent on programs changed from 1929 to 1940.

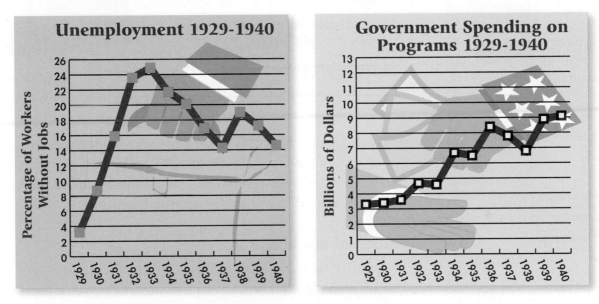

Study the two graphs. Write the answers to the questions.

1. Which year had the most people unemployed? _____

2. Which year had the most government spending? _____

3. What was the amount of government spending in the year with the highest unemployment? _____

4. How did the lack of government spending in 1938 affect unemployment?

   _____

5. How might government spending have changed unemployment between 1933 and 1937?

   _____

   _____

# CHAPTER 11

# The Beginning of World War II

### Focus on Main Ideas

1. What were the causes of World War II?

2. What did Hitler do after he became dictator of Germany?

3. What happened in Europe during the early years of World War II?

4. Why did the United States enter World War II?

▲ Winston Churchill

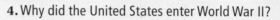

World War II began in Europe in 1939. By the time the war ended in 1945, about 17 million soldiers from many nations had been killed. More Americans died fighting in World War II than in any other war in the twentieth century.

## Causes of World War II

World War II had many causes. First, the Treaty of Versailles that ended World War I created new problems. The people of Germany were angry because the treaty punished Germany for its role in World War I. Germany had to pay billions of dollars to France and Great Britain. Also, Germany lost much of its land and was not allowed to rebuild its military. The League of Nations had been created in the treaty to keep peace between nations. However, the League had no power to stop one nation from attacking another.

Second, dictators came to power in Italy, Germany, Japan, and the Soviet Union. People turned to dictators to solve serious economic problems during the Great Depression. Millions of poor people in Europe did not have jobs. These unhappy people wanted leaders who could make their countries strong again. So dictators won control of the governments of Germany, Italy, and the Soviet Union. These dictators had total power, or **totalitarian** governments.

Third, nationalism and imperialism grew in Germany, Italy, and Japan. Imperialism made those nations want to conquer other countries.

A fourth cause was militarism. Germany, Italy, and Japan built powerful armies, navies, and air forces. Germany built a huge military even though it was not allowed to do so according to the Treaty of Versailles.

## Dictators Come to Power

Benito Mussolini became the dictator of Italy in 1922. Mussolini promised to bring order, prosperity, and jobs to the people of Italy. Mussolini became the leader of the **Fascist** party. Fascists wanted to build a powerful army, and they wanted to have a totalitarian government.

Joseph Stalin became the dictator of the Soviet Union in 1929. Unlike Mussolini, Stalin was a Communist. But Stalin also ruled with total power. People who spoke out against him were killed or sent to prison.

Germany also turned to a Fascist dictator, Adolf Hitler, to solve its problems in the 1930s. Hitler was the leader of the **Nazi** party. After becoming dictator in 1933, Hitler immediately began building a huge military. The Nazi party became Germany's only political party.

Nationalism was important to the Nazis. In powerful speeches Hitler told the Germans that they were a "master race." He said that other people, such as Eastern Europeans, gypsies, blacks, and Jews, were inferior. Hitler promised that Germany would become a powerful empire that would rule the world. He

▲ The rise of dictators led to World War II. Pictured left to right are Benito Mussolini of Italy and Adolf Hitler of Germany. Both were Fascist dictators of their countries. Joseph Stalin was the Communist dictator of the Soviet Union. Hideki Tojo became the military dictator of Japan in 1941.

▲ Adolf Hitler often gave strong speeches to large crowds. Many of his speeches, which inspired German nationalism, were about pride in Germany and the German people.

promised jobs and food for Germans.

Hitler blamed some of Germany's problems on the Treaty of Versailles and the country's Communists. But he blamed most problems on Jews. He said that the Jews had caused the defeat of Germany in World War I and the Great Depression. As Hitler repeated lies about the Jews, more and more people believed them. Hatred of Jews, or **anti-Semitism**, spread throughout Germany.

Hitler **persecuted** Germany's Jews. Stores owned by Jews were destroyed. Jews lost their jobs. Thousands of Jews were arrested and sent to **concentration camps**, where they became prisoners and were often killed. Many Jews tried to escape from Germany. Most countries in Europe did not want them. Strict immigration quotas allowed only a small number of Jews to come to America. The government refused to change the quota laws.

In Japan, military leaders made all important government decisions, although the nation also had an emperor. In 1941 General Hideki Tojo became Japan's military dictator.

## Steps Toward World War II

In 1936 Germany and Italy formed an alliance and agreed to fight in wars for each other. They became known as the **Axis nations**. In 1940 Japan also joined the Axis alliance.

During the 1930s Germany, Italy, and Japan used **aggression**, or military force, to attack and conquer other countries. In 1931 Japan conquered Manchuria, a mineral-rich area in northern China. Japan later invaded eastern China and other parts of Asia in order to get raw materials. In 1935 Italy conquered Ethiopia, a country in Africa.

Hitler began building a German empire. Hitler said that all German-speaking people must form one nation. So in 1938 Hitler's army marched into Austria and made Austria part of Germany. Next Hitler said that a German part of Czechoslovakia should be ruled by Germany.

Great Britain and France had an alliance with Czechoslovakia. So in 1938 Hitler met with the leaders of Britain and France in Munich, Germany. Hitler promised that he would not want more territory after he had taken the German region of Czechoslovakia. The British and the French gave in to Hitler, using a policy known as **appeasement**. Britain's leader, Neville Chamberlain, said that by giving in to Hitler's demands he had kept "peace in our time." But six months later, Hitler took control of the rest of Czechoslovakia.

In 1939 Hitler signed a **nonaggression pact** with Joseph Stalin. In the pact, Germany and the Soviet Union agreed not to attack each other during a war.

## The Beginning of World War II

On September 1, 1939, Germany invaded Poland. Germany used a new method called **blitzkrieg**, or lightning war, to attack and conquer. Blitzkrieg meant making quick, surprise attacks using tanks and airplanes in many places at the same time. Two days later Poland's allies, Great Britain and France, declared war on Germany. World War II had begun.

As in World War I, Britain and France were called the Allies. The Allied armies were not strong enough to save Poland. Later in September the Soviet Union attacked eastern Poland, and by the end of the month Poland surrendered. Germany controlled western Poland and the Soviet Union controlled the eastern part.

Hitler quickly conquered more nations in Western Europe. By 1940 Denmark, Norway, Belgium, Luxembourg, and the Netherlands were ruled by Germany. Then the battle for France began. Germany captured Paris by the end of June, and France surrendered.

The Allied soldiers in France had to escape before Hitler's army surrounded

▲ Nazis persecuted Germany's Jews. During the night of November 9, 1938, Nazis destroyed Jewish businesses across Germany in what has been called The Night of Broken Glass.

them. They escaped from the French port of Dunkirk and crossed the English Channel in small and large British boats and ships. More than 300,000 French, British, and Belgian soldiers escaped to Great Britain. There they prepared to continue the war against Hitler. Winston Churchill, the new prime minister of Great Britain, inspired the British people after the escape from Dunkirk. ". . . We shall fight on the fields and in the streets. We shall fight in the hills. We shall never surrender. . . ."

From July 1940 until May 1941, Germany tried to conquer Great Britain with bombs from airplanes. These attacks were called the Battle of Britain. Night

▲ During the Battle of Britain, thousands of buildings were destroyed in cities throughout Great Britain.

after night German planes bombed British air force bases, cities, and towns. The bombs destroyed buildings and caused fires. Thousands of **civilians** were killed. In the city of London, people slept in subway stations in order to be safe. But the British people would not surrender.

## Hitler Invades the Soviet Union

Hitler dreamed of conquering the huge Soviet Union. In June 1941 he broke his agreement with Stalin. He invaded the Soviet Union with 3 million soldiers. Hitler wanted to control the Russian wheat and oil fields.

Hitler did not know how difficult it would be for his soldiers to survive Russia's bitterly cold winters. Their trucks and tanks froze, and thousands of German soldiers froze to death in the cold. The Germans failed to capture the Russian capital of Moscow. Heavy fighting in the Soviet Union continued until 1944.

## The United States Helps the Allies

As Hitler grew more powerful and more dangerous, most Americans continued to favor a policy of **isolationism**. In 1935 Congress started passing laws to keep the United States neutral. Although most Americans did not want to fight, they did want the Allies to win. President Franklin D. Roosevelt looked for ways to help the Allies. The Neutrality Act of 1939 allowed nations that were fighting aggression to buy weapons from the United States. This was a "cash and carry" policy because nations had to pay for the weapons with cash and use their own ships to carry them back to their countries.

In 1940, Winston Churchill asked the United States for fifty old **destroyers**, which are small warships that carry weapons. President Roosevelt agreed. In return for the warships, the British allowed the United States to use several British naval and air bases.

In November 1940 Roosevelt became the first President to be reelected to a third term. During the campaign, Roosevelt said that the United States would not fight in World War II. But in January 1941, Roosevelt made his famous "Four Freedoms" speech before Congress. In that speech, Roosevelt said that all people in the world should have freedom

## World War II in Europe, 1939–1942

**Legend:**
- Axis countries
- Allied countries
- Neutral countries
- Axis-occupied areas
- ✴ Major battle

✴ **MAP STUDY**

From September 1939 through the end of 1941, Germany was able to conquer many countries in Europe. Hitler broke his pact with Stalin and invaded the Soviet Union. What region of Europe was occupied by the Axis countries?

(Geography Theme: region)

of speech and religion. And all people should have freedom from want, or hunger, and freedom from fear.

In March 1941 Congress passed the Lend-Lease Act. This law said that the United States would lend Britain all the weapons and supplies it needed to fight Hitler. Britain would return or replace the supplies after the war. By providing Britain with weapons, Roosevelt said the United States would "become the great arsenal of democracy." After Hitler invaded the Soviet Union, the United States used the Lend-Lease Act to give the Soviets weapons and supplies.

Roosevelt also took steps to prepare America for war. Laws were passed to raise taxes. Tax money was used to build a larger American military. In 1940 Congress passed a law that required all men between the ages of 18 and 35 to register for military service.

## Japan Attacks Pearl Harbor

Japan had gone to war against China and had won control of eastern China. Then in 1941 it began attacking France's colony in Indochina in Southeast Asia. Japan wanted this region's supplies of rubber, tin, and rice.

The United States was worried about Japanese aggression. To stop Japanese attacks in Asia, the United States stopped

**123**

selling scrap iron and oil to Japan. Later the United States stopped all trade with Japan. Japan was furious because it needed these supplies for its industries and its military forces.

In November 1941 Japanese and American leaders met to solve the problems between the two nations. At the same time, Japan secretly made plans to attack American bases in the Pacific if an agreement was not reached. When the two nations did not reach an agreement, Japan decided to carry out its secret attack plans.

Early in the morning on Sunday, December 7, 1941, Japan surprised the United States with an attack. Pearl Harbor,

an American naval base in Hawaii, was bombed by 350 Japanese planes. About 2,400 Americans were killed in the attack on Pearl Harbor.

News of the surprise attack on Pearl Harbor spread quickly. Americans were upset and angry. The next day, December 8, President Roosevelt asked Congress to declare war on Japan. Roosevelt said that the attack on Pearl Harbor was "a date which will live in infamy." Congress declared war that day. Three days later Germany and Italy, the other Axis Powers, declared war on the United States. America's isolationism was over.

▲ On the morning of December 7, 1941, Japanese planes attacked the American naval base at Pearl Harbor, Hawaii. Almost 200 American planes were destroyed, and 18 warships were sunk or badly damaged. Only the top of the *USS Arizona*, a large battleship, remained above the water when the ship sank.

# Jesse Owens 1913–1980

Jesse Owens won four gold medals at the 1936 Olympic Games. This great athlete was born in Alabama to a poor family with nine children. His grandfather had been enslaved. Owens's father was a sharecropper who struggled to earn enough money for his family. In 1921 Owens's family moved to Ohio.

When Owens was in the fifth grade, the coach at his school asked him to join the track team. After six years of training, Owens became a high school track star.

After high school Owens studied at Ohio State University. Owens attended classes, trained for the track team, and worked at three part-time jobs.

At a track meet in 1935, Owens broke four track records for running and jumping.

He was chosen to represent the United States in the 1936 Olympic Games. The Olympics were to be held in Berlin, Germany. In 1936 Adolf Hitler was the dictator of Germany.

Hitler was sure that German athletes would win most of the gold medals at the Olympics. Hitler believed that the Germans were better than other people because the Germans were a "master race." Hitler also believed that black athletes were inferior people. Owens embarrassed and angered Hitler by winning four gold medals at the Olympic Games.

Hitler left the stadium so that he would not have to give Owens his awards at the medal ceremony. But Owens had proved that no group of people is superior or inferior. He proved that black athletes could be the best in the world.

After the Olympics Owens finished college. He spoke and wrote about ways to help African Americans and whites get along.

Owens is remembered as a great athlete. He showed that Hitler's ideas about race were wrong.

### In Your Own Words

Jesse Owens embarrassed Hitler when he won four gold medals at the Olympic Games in 1936. Write a paragraph in your journal that tells why Hitler was embarrassed and what Owens proved to the world.

## CHAPTER 11 MAIN IDEAS

- There were several causes of World War II, including problems created by the Treaty of Versailles, the rise of dictators, economic problems in Europe, and nationalism, imperialism, and militarism.

- Adolf Hitler became the leader of Germany's Nazi party. Germany formed an alliance with Japan and Italy called the Axis Powers.

- The British and the French tried to contain Hitler and the Germans through a policy called appeasement, but World War II started when Hitler invaded Poland on September 1, 1939.

- The Germans captured many nations in Europe, but they did not defeat Great Britain and the Soviet Union.

- The United States stayed out of World War II until December 7, 1941, when the Japanese attacked the American naval base at Pearl Harbor in Hawaii.

## VOCABULARY

**Find the Meaning** ■ Write the word or phrase that best completes each sentence.

1. A _____ system of government has full control over its people and allows little individual freedom.
   **appeasement**      **democratic**      **totalitarian**

2. The _____ party in Germany stressed total power by the government and a strong love for Germany.
   **Communist**      **Nazi**      **Germanic People's**

3. A _____ was a quick, powerful attack by the German army and air force.
   **blockade**      **blitzkrieg**      **boycott**

4. The policy of not becoming involved in the affairs of other nations is called _____ .
   **militarism**      **isolationism**      **appeasement**

5. Great Britain and France used a policy of _____ to try to avoid a war with Germany.
   **appeasement**      **anti-Semitism**      **blitzkrieg**

6. _____ is attacking other nations with military force.
   **Aggression**      **Isolationism**      **Appeasement**

## COMPREHENSION CHECK

**Write a Paragraph** ■ Use seven or more words or phrases below to write a paragraph that tells how Germany fought to control Europe from 1939 to 1941.

appeasement
Poland
Dunkirk
invaded

Adolf Hitler
Great Britain
Allies
Battle of Britain

Joseph Stalin
Winston Churchill
Lend-Lease Act

## CRITICAL THINKING

**Drawing Conclusions** ■ Read the paragraph below and the sentences that follow it. Put a check in front of the conclusions that can be drawn from the paragraph. You should find three conclusions.

In order to have a supply of raw materials, Japan began to conquer other lands in Asia. It conquered Manchuria, eastern China, and French Indochina. In an effort to put an end to Japanese aggression, the United States stopped trading with Japan. This angered the Japanese. They decided to weaken American power in the Pacific by attacking the American naval base at Pearl Harbor, Hawaii. Early on the morning of December 7, 1941, Japanese bombers staged a surprise attack on Pearl Harbor. As a result of this act, the United States entered World War II by declaring war against Japan and Germany.

_____ 1. Japan, Germany, and Italy had formed an alliance called the Axis Powers.

_____ 2. Japan had a powerful military.

_____ 3. Japan did not have enough of its own raw materials.

_____ 4. The attack on Pearl Harbor was planned by the Japanese emperor.

_____ 5. The United States was not prepared for the Japanese attack on Pearl Harbor.

## USING INFORMATION

**Writing an Opinion** ■ World War II began in 1939, but the United States did not enter the war until 1941. Americans were split over the issue of involvement in the war. Do you think that the United States should have become involved in World War II sooner? Write a paragraph in your social studies notebook that explains your opinion. Start your paragraph with a topic sentence.

# The Fight to Win World War II

### Focus on Main Ideas

1. How did American life change on the home front during World War II?

2. How did the Allies win the war in Europe against the Axis Powers?

3. What happened during the Holocaust?

4. How did the Allies win the war in the Pacific against Japan?

▲ Rosie the Riveter

In December 1941 the United States entered World War II. The Americans and the Allies would not defeat the Axis nations until 1945.

## Life on the Home Front

American life changed after the United States entered the war. Millions of men served in the armed forces. For the first time, women were allowed to join the armed forces. They did many types of military jobs, but they did not fight directly against the enemy. Because many men were away fighting the war, women worked in factories, building tanks, planes, and battleships. Rosie the Riveter became the symbol of the millions of women who entered the work force during World War II.

World War II helped to end the Great Depression. The war created millions of jobs in **defense industries**. Americans had to produce enormous amounts of weapons and war equipment for the American and Allied armed forces. By 1945 Americans had produced 15 million guns and 300,000 warplanes.

Because the United States was supplying the Allies with food and equipment, many goods became scarce. The government **rationed** scarce items, such as soap, shoes, gasoline, meat, sugar, and butter, by using coupon books. Once people used up their coupons, they could not buy any more rationed items. **Recycling** of tin, rubber, and other goods was also important.

Prejudice toward Japanese Americans increased after the attack on Pearl Harbor. In 1942 President Roosevelt ordered that all Japanese Americans living on the West Coast, about 112,000 people, move to **internment camps**. About two thirds of these people were American citizens. Each camp contained **barracks** to house families. A high barbed-wire fence and armed guards surrounded each camp.

About 33,000 Japanese Americans fought for the United States. One Japanese American, Daniel Inouye, lost an arm in battle. Inouye later became a senator. In 2000 the National Japanese American Memorial was dedicated in Washington, D.C., to honor all who were interned and those who fought in World War II.

## Fighting in Africa and in Europe

After the United States entered the war, Churchill, Roosevelt, and Stalin disagreed on a **strategy**, or plan. They finally decided to free North Africa from Italy and Germany. Next they would attack the southern part of Europe. Then they would invade and free France. And finally, they would invade Germany.

General Dwight D. Eisenhower became the leader of all the Allied troops. He led the battles in North Africa. In May 1943 the Axis army in North Africa surrendered.

▲ LINKING PAST AND PRESENT Recycling was important for the war effort. Americans collected goods, which were later reused to make war supplies. Rubber and tin were used to make airplanes. Steel was used to make ships and tanks. Why do people recycle newspapers, bottles, cans, and other items today?

From Africa, the Allied armies invaded Italy. The Italian people were tired of war. They forced Mussolini to resign and later killed him. In September 1943 the Italian government surrendered. German soldiers in Italy did not surrender until May 1945.

While the Allies fought in Africa and in Italy, British and American planes bombed Germany. Many factories and railroads in Germany were destroyed. The Soviets continued to fight the Nazis in the Soviet Union. The turning point of the war in the Soviet Union was at the city of Stalingrad in February 1943. The Germans repeatedly failed to capture Stalingrad. After that the Soviets slowly pushed the German Army out of the Soviet Union.

## Victory in Europe

The Allies made plans to cross the English Channel and invade France. D-Day, the day of the invasion, was June 6, 1944. Early that morning about 200,000 Allied soldiers and about 4,600 ships landed in Normandy, a region in northern France. It was the largest invasion by sea in world history. Within a month about one million troops arrived in France.

After D-Day Hitler had to send soldiers to fight on three fronts—in the Soviet Union, in Italy, and in France. The Allies freed Paris on August 25, 1944. The Soviets drove the German Army out of Poland, Romania, and Hungary. At the

World War II in Europe and in North Africa, 1942–1945

## MAP STUDY

After the invasion of Normandy in 1944, the Germans had to fight on three fronts. Hitler's weakened armies could not withstand the Allied advances. From which direction was Berlin captured?

(Geography Theme: movement)

▶ **This survivor of the Holocaust shows the number that had been tattooed onto his arm at a concentration camp like the one above.**

the last meeting between these leaders. Roosevelt died on April 12, 1945. Harry S Truman became President.

The Soviets captured the city of Berlin in April 1945. On April 30, 1945, Hitler committed suicide. On May 8, 1945, Germany surrendered. Europe had peace at last.

## The Holocaust

After the Allies defeated the Axis Powers, prisoners in concentration camps were **liberated**, or set free. People around the world learned that the Nazis had killed six million Jews and several million other people. This mass murder of Jews and other people is called the **Holocaust**.

The Holocaust happened in every country that Hitler captured. Jews were crowded into railroad cars and sent to concentration camps, such as Buchenwald, Dachau, Auschwitz, and Treblinka, in Germany and in Poland. Barbed wire and armed guards made escape from the camps almost impossible.

In the concentration camps, all Jews were forced to have identification numbers tattooed onto their arms. They were given only small amounts of food each day, so they slowly starved. People who were strong and healthy when they arrived had to work for the Nazis. Young children, old people, and all people who were sick or weak were killed. Millions were killed in **gas chambers**, rooms filled with poison gas. Then their bodies were burned in huge ovens. Thick black smoke from these ovens filled the sky day after day.

end of 1944, the Soviet Union controlled most of Eastern Europe.

In December 1944 the Germans started the Battle of the Bulge, the last major battle against the Allies. The battle took place in Belgium and in Luxembourg. In January 1945 the Allies won the Battle of the Bulge.

In February 1945 Churchill, Roosevelt, and Stalin met at Yalta in the Soviet Union. They agreed that Great Britain, France, the United States, and the Soviet Union would each control an area in Germany after the war. They also planned a peacekeeping organization called the United Nations. The meeting at Yalta was

Some people knew what was happening to the Jews, but they did nothing to help. Others risked their lives to help Jews hide or escape. People are still trying to figure out what could have been done to save millions of innocent people from being killed.

## Americans at War in Asia

While the Allies were fighting in Europe, they were also at war with Japan. Admiral Chester W. Nimitz became commander of the navy in the Pacific. Nimitz worked closely with General Douglas MacArthur, the commander of the army in the Pacific. Allied soldiers from many countries fought alongside American soldiers.

After attacking Pearl Harbor, Japan conquered the Philippines. In 1942 Roosevelt ordered General MacArthur to leave the Islands. MacArthur promised the people of the Philippines, "I shall return."

As you can see on the map on the opposite page, the Japanese controlled eastern China, the Philippines, Guam, part of Southeast Asia, and islands near Australia. The Allies knew that it would be difficult to defeat the Japanese.

In June 1942 the Battle of Midway became a turning point in the war in the Pacific. The Japanese attacked the Midway Islands, which are near Hawaii. The Allies sank four of Japan's **aircraft carriers** while winning the battle. The American victory at Midway gave the Allies control of the central Pacific.

After the Battle of Midway, the Allies began a strategy called "island hopping." They planned to capture important islands that would bring them close enough to invade Japan. In August 1942, United States Marines landed on the island of Guadalcanal in the Solomon Islands. After six months of deadly jungle fighting, the Japanese left Guadalcanal.

After capturing Guam and other Pacific islands, General MacArthur returned to the Philippines. He landed there in October 1944. While MacArthur fought on land, Admiral Nimitz used the navy to destroy Japan's fleet of ships in the sea around the Philippines. By February 1945 Americans had won control of the Philippine capital.

In February 1945 Americans won control of Iwo Jima. One of the most famous photographs of World War II was taken on Iwo Jima. It shows six brave marines raising an American flag in victory. In June 1945 they captured Okinawa. The Allies planned to use Iwo Jima and Okinawa as bases to invade Japan and force it to surrender.

## The Atomic Bomb and Japan's Defeat

By 1945 the Japanese had lost most of their Asian empire. Most of their navy was destroyed. American planes bombed Japanese cities day and night. However, Japan refused to surrender.

American military leaders told President Truman that one million Americans would probably be killed if the Allies had to invade and conquer Japan. To save the lives of these soldiers, Truman decided to use a powerful new bomb to defeat Japan. The **atomic bomb** was about 2,000 times more powerful than an ordinary bomb. Truman warned Japan to surrender or its cities would be destroyed.

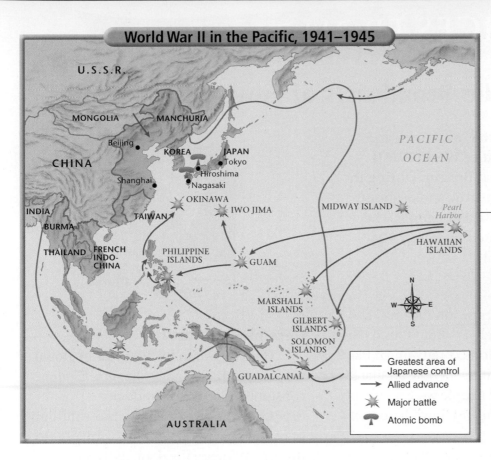

## World War II in the Pacific, 1941–1945

✴ MAP STUDY

After the Battle of Midway, the Allied strategy of island hopping led to Allied advances throughout the Pacific. The goal was to get closer to Japan so that it could be invaded. From what direction did the Allies advance toward Japan?

(Geography Theme: movement)

Map legend:
— Greatest area of Japanese control
→ Allied advance
✴ Major battle
☁ Atomic bomb

Japan still refused to surrender. On August 6, 1945, an American plane dropped an atomic bomb on the Japanese city of Hiroshima. In seconds much of the city was destroyed. About 75,000 people were killed and thousands more were injured. But Japan still refused to surrender. On August 9, Americans dropped a second atomic bomb, this time on the city of Nagasaki. The bomb killed about 40,000 people. Japan's emperor told Japan's military leaders to surrender. Japan finally surrendered on September 2, 1945. World War II finally ended

## The Results of World War II

World War II caused terrible destruction. Much of Europe, Japan, China, North Africa, and the Soviet Union had to be rebuilt. About 50 million people died. Many of these people were soldiers, but large numbers were civilians. About 300,000 American soldiers died in the war.

After the war some Nazi leaders went on trial in Nuremberg, Germany, for their crimes during the Holocaust. Some Nazis were executed for their crimes; others were sent to prison.

The bombing of Hiroshima started the atomic age. Atomic bombs could now be used to destroy cities in only seconds. People were afraid that another world war could end civilization. As a result, in 1945 the United States began to work with other nations to create the United Nations. This organization would work to keep peace among the world's nations.

133

# The Radio Broadcasts of Edward R. Murrow

Edward R. Murrow, an American reporter, spent most of World War II reporting from Great Britain. During the Battle of Britain, Murrow spoke about the courage of the British people. The Battle of Britain lasted from July 1940 until about May 1941.

### August 18, 1940

"I spent five hours . . . on the outskirts of London. Bombs fell. . . . But I found that one bombed house looks pretty much like another. . . . It's about the people I'd like to talk. . . . To me those people were incredibly brave. . . . They are the unknown heroes of this war. . . ."

### December 13, 1942

"Millions of human beings, most of them Jews, are being gathered up. . . . Let me tell you a little about what's happened in the Warsaw ghetto. . . . Ten thousand people were . . . shipped off. Those who survived the journey were dumped out at one of three camps, where they were killed. . . . The Jews are being systematically exterminated [killed] throughout all Poland. . . ."

### December 27, 1942

"Here in Britain the first year of global war has produced many changes. Civilian consumer goods have gradually disappeared from the shops; more millions of women have gone into industry or into the armed forces; the draft age has been lowered to eighteen. . . ."

### May 8, 1945

[Victory Day in Europe after Germany surrendered.]

"As you walk down the street you hear singing that comes from open windows; sometimes it's a chorus, sometimes it's just a single voice raised in song. . . . London is celebrating today. . . . The scars of war are all about."

## Write Your Answers

**Answer these questions in the assignment section of your social studies notebook.**

1. What happened in London on August 18, 1940?

2. How did the war change life in England?

3. **Think and Respond** Why do you think Edward R. Murrow had such a high opinion of the British people?

# A Japanese American Remembers Pearl Harbor

Daniel K. Inouye, a Japanese American, was a high school student when the Japanese bombed Pearl Harbor. He later fought in World War II, where he lost an arm in combat. In 1962, Inouye became a United States Senator, serving for more than 40 years.

## December 7, 1941

. . . I automatically clicked on the little radio that stood on the shelf above my bed. . . . "This is no test," the voice cried out. "Pearl Harbor is being bombed by the Japanese. . . ."

. . . Now my father was standing in the doorway listening, caught by the special horror instantly sensed by Americans of Japanese descent as the nightmare began to unfold. . . .

"Come outside!" my father said to me. . . . We stood in the warm sunshine . . . and stared out toward Pearl Harbor. . . . The dirty gray smoke of a great fire billowed up [covered] Pearl [Harbor]. . . . We could hear the soft crrump of the bombs. . . .

We went back into the house and the telephone was ringing. It was the secretary of the Red Cross aid station where I taught. "How soon can you be here, Dan?" he said tensely.

"I'm on my way," I told him. . . .

It would be five days, a lifetime before I came back. . . .

My eyes blurred with tears for all these frightened people [Japanese Americans]. . . . They had wanted so desperately to be accepted, to be good Americans. . . . I knew there was only deep trouble ahead. . . .

I reported in at the aid station. . . . Nearby a building caught fire and as the survivors came stumbling out, we patched their wounds as best we could. . . .

. . . There was so much to be done—broken bodies to be mended, temporary shelter to be found for bombed-out families . . . food for the hungry. We worked on into the following night and through the day after that. . . . Soon there was no dividing line between day and night at all.

## Write Your Answers

**Write the answers to these questions in your social studies notebook.**

1. What happened on December 7, 1941?

2. Why did Japanese Americans, such as Daniel Inouye, react with a "special horror" to the attack on Pearl Harbor?

3. **Think and Respond** Compare the Battle of Britain with the attack on Pearl Harbor. In what ways were they the same? In what ways were they different?

# Albert Einstein 1879–1955

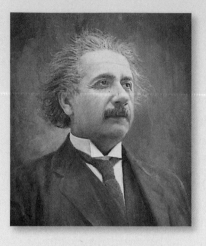

Albert Einstein was one of the world's greatest scientists. From 1902 to 1909, Einstein developed important scientific theories. His famous theory of relativity changed the way scientists looked at the universe. One part of the theory said that all things are made of atoms. If atoms were split open, they would release huge amounts of energy. This theory was used to develop the atomic bomb.

In 1913 Einstein became the director of the physics department at a university in Berlin, Germany. In 1921 Einstein received the Nobel Prize for his work in physics.

Einstein worked for two other important causes. The first was **Zionism**. Zionism is the belief that Jews should have their own country in Palestine, or present-day Israel. The second cause was **pacifism**, the belief that wars are wrong and that people should work for peace. Einstein spoke out against Germany's actions during World War I.

Einstein's life changed in 1933 when Hitler became the dictator of Germany. Because Einstein was Jewish, the government took away his property, his job, and his right to be a German citizen. Einstein had been traveling in the United States. He stayed and became a professor at Princeton University.

While living in America, Einstein used his own money to help Jews escape from Germany. He visited several foreign countries and spoke about the dangers faced by Jews.

In 1939 Einstein wrote a letter to President Roosevelt. He warned FDR that Germany was probably building an atomic bomb and that the United States should try to build this dangerous weapon first. Because of Einstein's advice, Roosevelt started a secret group, "The Manhattan Project," that built the first atomic bomb.

Einstein was an immigrant who made valuable contributions to the United States. He is remembered as one of the world's greatest scientists.

## In Your Own Words

Write a paragraph in the journal section of your notebook that tells how Albert Einstein helped the United States during World War II.

## CHAPTER 12 MAIN IDEAS

- Millions of American men served in the armed forces during World War II. Women worked in factories, building weapons and supplies for the war.

- Shortages of food and consumer goods led to rationing and recycling.

- About 112,000 Japanese Americans living on the West Coast were ordered to move to internment camps.

- The D-Day invasion started on June 6, 1944. Germany's last major attack against the Allies was the Battle of the Bulge. Germany finally surrendered on May 8, 1945.

- During the Holocaust the Nazis killed six million Jews and millions of other people.

- Japan surrendered on September 2, 1945, after the United States dropped atomic bombs on the Japanese cities of Hiroshima and Nagasaki.

## VOCABULARY

**Finish the Sentence** ■ Choose one of the words or phrases from the box that best completes each sentence. You will not use all the words in the box.

1. _____ built warplanes, tanks, and other equipment for World War II.

2. During the war about 112,000 Japanese Americans were forced to live as prisoners in _____ .

3. During the _____ the Nazis killed six million Jews and millions of other people.

4. The Allies _____ , or set free, people who had been held as prisoners in concentration camps.

5. During the war items such as soap, shoes, gasoline, and meat were limited, or _____ , in the United States.

rationed
defense industries
Holocaust
liberated
internment camps
aircraft carriers

## USING INFORMATION

**Writing an Opinion** ■ Some people risked their lives to help Jews hide or escape from the Nazis. Write a paragraph that explains what you would have done if you had been living in Europe during World War II.

## USING GRAPHIC ORGANIZERS

**Create an Information Chart** ■ Complete the graphic organizer below about important battles that were fought during World War II. Part of the chart has already been done for you.

| Name of Battle | Year Fought | Location of Battle | Significance of Battle |
| --- | --- | --- | --- |
| Battles in North Africa | 1943 | North Africa | Axis armies in North Africa surrendered |
| D-Day | | | |
| Battle of Stalingrad | | | |
| Battle of Midway | | | |
| Iwo Jima | | | |
| Hiroshima and Nagasaki | | | |

## CRITICAL THINKING

**Making Predictions** ■ Read the paragraph below about the end of World War II. Then check three sentences that predict what will happen after the war.

After years of fighting, World War II finally came to an end. The war that started with the German attack on Poland on September 1, 1939, ended with the surrender of Japan on September 2, 1945. About 50 million people died during the war, and many cities in Europe and Asia were destroyed. During the time they had ruled Germany, the Nazis had killed millions of Jews and other people whom the Nazis had held as prisoners in concentration camps. The end of World War II also brought about the beginning of the atomic age.

_____ 1. European countries would rebuild their cities.

_____ 2. A peace treaty would be signed by the Axis Powers and the Allies.

_____ 3. Germans would continue to persecute the Jewish people.

_____ 4. Nazi officers would stand trial for their acts during the war.

_____ 5. Germany would be allowed to keep its powerful military.

_____ 6. More countries would try to make atomic bombs.

# Comparing Circle Graphs

A circle graph, or pie graph, is a circle that has been divided into sections. Each section looks like a piece of pie. Often a circle graph shows a percent or part of 100. All the sections make up the whole circle or add up to 100 percent. The 2 circle graphs on this page compare the types of workers in the work force in 1940 and in 1944. These two different time periods show workers before and after the United States went to war.

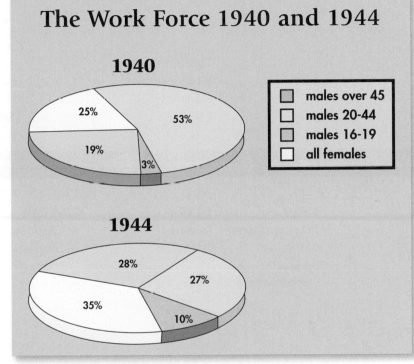

**The Work Force 1940 and 1944**

**1940**

25%  53%  19%  3%

☐ males over 45
☐ males 20-44
☐ males 16-19
☐ all females

**1944**

28%  27%  35%  10%

**Study the two graphs. Then answer the questions below.**

1.  What percent of the work force was female in 1944? _____

2.  What percent of men ages 20 to 44 were in the work force in 1940?

    _____

3.  What percent of men ages 20 to 44 were in the work force in 1944?

    _____

4.  How did the work force change for women, older men, and teenagers from 1940 to 1944? _____

5.  How did the work force change from 1940 to 1944 for men between the ages of 20 and 44? Explain why. _____

Study the time line on this page. You may want to read parts of Unit 3 again. Then use the words and the dates in the box to finish the paragraphs. There is one possible answer you will not use.

**Adolf Hitler becomes dictator of Germany. 1933**

**Congress passes the Lend-Lease Act. 1941**

**Allies invade France on D-Day. 1944**

**Japan surrenders. 1945**

1925 • • 1935 • • • 1945

**1929 The stock market crashes, and the Great Depression begins.**

**1933 The New Deal begins.**

**1939 World War II begins in Europe.**

**1941 Japan attacks Pearl Harbor.**

**1945 Germany surrenders.**

| | | |
|---|---|---|
| depression | overproduction | Lend-Lease Act |
| 1929 | Adolf Hitler | Germany |
| appeasement | farmers | atomic bombs |
| Roosevelt | New Deal | D-Day |
| Czechoslovakia | Social Security Act | Pearl Harbor |

The stock market crash in **1** _____ was the start of the Great Depression.

Some of the causes of the Great Depression were bank failures, **2** _____ , and

difficult years for **3** _____ in the 1920s. After Franklin D. **4** _____

became President in 1933, he started a program to end the depression called the

**5**_____ . In 1935 Congress passed the **6**_____ to give pensions to retired people.

While Americans struggled with the depression at home, there were serious problems in Europe. In 1933 **7**_____ became the dictator of Germany. In 1938 Hitler took control of Austria and the German region of **8**_____ . Great Britain and France used a policy called **9**_____ to avoid a war with Germany.

World War II began in Europe when Germany invaded Poland. In 1941 Congress passed the **10**_____ so the United States could give weapons and supplies to Great Britain. The United States entered World War II after Japan attacked **11**_____ on December 7, 1941. Thousands of Allied soldiers invaded France on **12**_____ on June 6, 1944. On May 8, 1945, **13**_____ surrendered and the war ended in Europe. After the United States dropped two **14**_____ on Japan, that nation surrendered.

---

## Looking Ahead to Unit 4

The United States and the Soviet Union, the two most powerful nations after World War II, became enemies after the war. The struggle between Communists and non-Communists took place in Eastern Europe, Africa, Asia, and Latin America.

Many changes took place in the United States after World War II. African Americans fought to win equal rights. Americans worried about poverty at home, energy problems, and war in Vietnam.

As you read Unit 4, think about the ways the United States tried to stop the spread of communism. Find out about the work of Martin Luther King, Jr. Explore the reasons why Americans fought in the Vietnam War. Learn about the nation's problems and successes after World War II.

The Marshall Plan
is created to contain
communism.
**1947**

Western
nations form
NATO.
**1949**

**1945**

**1955**

**1945**
The United
Nations begins.

**1948**
The Berlin
Airlift saves
West Berlin.

**1950**
The Korean
War begins.

**1954**
The Supreme Court rules in
*Brown* v. *Board of Education*
to end school segregation.

**1958**
The United States
sends its first
satellite into space.

# World War II

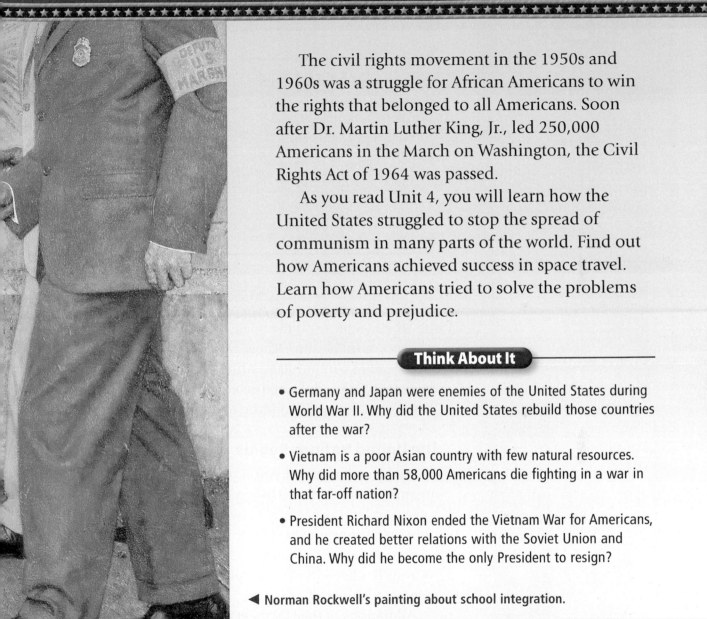

The civil rights movement in the 1950s and 1960s was a struggle for African Americans to win the rights that belonged to all Americans. Soon after Dr. Martin Luther King, Jr., led 250,000 Americans in the March on Washington, the Civil Rights Act of 1964 was passed.

As you read Unit 4, you will learn how the United States struggled to stop the spread of communism in many parts of the world. Find out how Americans achieved success in space travel. Learn how Americans tried to solve the problems of poverty and prejudice.

## Think About It

- Germany and Japan were enemies of the United States during World War II. Why did the United States rebuild those countries after the war?

- Vietnam is a poor Asian country with few natural resources. Why did more than 58,000 Americans die fighting in a war in that far-off nation?

- President Richard Nixon ended the Vietnam War for Americans, and he created better relations with the Soviet Union and China. Why did he become the only President to resign?

◀ Norman Rockwell's painting about school integration.

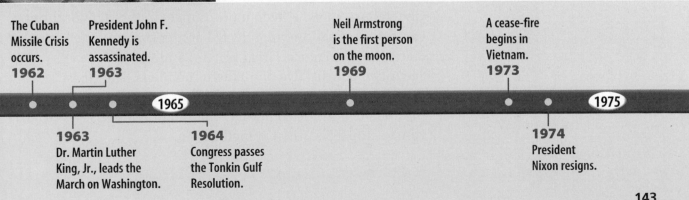

The Cuban Missile Crisis occurs.
**1962**

President John F. Kennedy is assassinated.
**1963**

Neil Armstrong is the first person on the moon.
**1969**

A cease-fire begins in Vietnam.
**1973**

**1965**

**1975**

**1963**
Dr. Martin Luther King, Jr., leads the March on Washington.

**1964**
Congress passes the Tonkin Gulf Resolution.

**1974**
President Nixon resigns.

**CHAPTER 13**

## PEOPLE

- George C. Marshall
- Mao Zedong
- Chiang Kai-shek
- Alger Hiss
- Joseph McCarthy
- Margaret Chase Smith
- Fidel Castro

## PLACES

- San Francisco
- Taiwan
- Korea

## NEW VOCABULARY

- Cold War
- superpowers
- iron curtain
- containment
- Berlin Airlift
- arms race
- truce
- McCarthyism
- satellite

# The Cold War Begins

## Focus on Main Ideas

1. How did the Cold War develop between the United States and the Soviet Union?

2. How did Senator McCarthy affect the United States?

3. How did the Cold War affect Europe, Asia, Africa, and Latin America?

▲ The flag of the United Nations

In 1945 a new type of war, the **Cold War**, began between the United States and the Soviet Union, two of the world's most powerful nations. These two **superpowers** struggled over the spread of communism. Although the United States and the Soviet Union did not directly fight each other, the Cold War brought fear and fighting to many parts of the world.

## The United Nations Begins

At the end of World War II, the Allies started an organization called the United Nations, or UN. Its goal was to solve problems peacefully between nations. Representatives from 50 nations met for the first time in April 1945 in San Francisco, California. Since 1952 the home for the United Nations has been in New York City. Today 191 nations are members of the UN.

All nations of the UN meet at least once a year in the General Assembly. Fifteen nations meet in the UN's Security Council. Ten nations are selected at random, and the United States, Russia, France, Great Britain, and China are the Security Council's five permanent members. The UN's Security Council can send UN soldiers to keep peace in troubled regions. Each permanent member can use a veto to vote to stop a Security Council action.

## Why Did the Cold War Begin?

The Cold War developed because the two superpowers wanted to spread different political and economic systems throughout the world. The United States wanted to spread its democratic form of government and its capitalist economy. Under capitalism, all people can own property and businesses to earn profits. By spreading capitalism to other countries, the United States could have more trading partners and earn more money.

The Soviet economic system was based on communism. Under communism, the government owned all businesses and property. The government decided what factories could produce, what farmers could grow, and what salaries people could earn. The Soviets had a totalitarian government led by a powerful dictator. Most people in the Soviet Union had little freedom.

Towards the end of World War II, Churchill, Roosevelt, and Stalin met at Yalta. During the meeting Stalin agreed to allow free elections in countries captured by the Soviet Union in Eastern Europe. Stalin broke this promise.

The Cold War began when the Soviet Union supported Communist

▲ After World War II, the Soviet Union controlled the countries of Eastern Europe. The Soviets often used their military to maintain control. In this photograph, tanks and soldiers from the Soviet Army are in Prague, the capital of Czechoslovakia.

▲ President Truman developed a policy against communism. George C. Marshall, at right, helped carry out that policy.

## President Truman and Communism

Harry S Truman was President at the start of the Cold War. In order to stop communism from spreading from Eastern Europe to other areas, Truman developed a policy of **containment**. He stated that the United States must support nations that were fighting to remain free from communism. His ideas were called the Truman Doctrine. Truman used this doctrine for the first time with Greece and Turkey. Americans believed Communist rebels were trying to take control of those countries. To prevent this, Truman asked Congress to give aid to Greece and Turkey. Congress voted to give these countries $400 million to fight Communist rebels. As a result, Greece and Turkey remained free from communism.

To carry out the Truman Doctrine, Secretary of State George C. Marshall devised a plan. Under the Marshall Plan, the United States agreed to rebuild the war-damaged nations of Europe. All European nations, including the Soviet Union, could receive American aid. By helping these nations build strong economies, Marshall and Truman believed the nations would not turn to communism. The nations of Western Europe accepted American aid. The United States gave billions of dollars to Germany and other nations in Western Europe. These nations became democracies with capitalist economies.

The United States also helped rebuild Japan. American troops, led by General Douglas MacArthur, controlled Japan after the war. MacArthur helped the Japanese

governments in Poland and in other Eastern European countries. The Soviets said they needed to control Poland so other nations would not march through Poland to attack the Soviet Union. But Soviet troops remained in other countries in Eastern Europe, not just in Poland. The United States was angry that the Soviet Union was spreading communism into the countries of Eastern Europe.

Soon after the Cold War began, Winston Churchill called the Soviet Union's control over Eastern Europe an **iron curtain**. The term described the tough, invisible wall that surrounded the Communist countries. The iron curtain kept the people of the Communist countries separated from the rest of Europe.

write a democratic constitution. Japan built a strong capitalist economy and became a democracy.

## A Divided Germany and the Berlin Airlift

After World War II ended, the four allies agreed to divide Germany into four zones, or areas. The United States, Great Britain, and France controlled the western part of Germany, while the Soviet Union controlled the eastern part. The German capital, Berlin, was in the Soviet zone. Berlin was also divided into four zones controlled by the same four countries.

In 1948 the United States, Britain, and France united their three zones to form an independent nation called the Republic of West Germany. The Soviets had lost 20 million people during the war, and they were angry that West Germany was becoming a strong, united nation. They decided to force the Allies to give up control of West Berlin.

Trains and trucks from West Germany had been bringing food and supplies through the Soviet zone into West Berlin. The Soviet Union started a blockade. All highways and railroads that carried supplies were closed. To save West Berlin, Truman ordered American planes to fly

▲ When Soviet troops stopped supplies from reaching West Berlin, President Truman ordered the American Air Force to fly them into the city. Every day for almost a year, planes landed with supplies about every 90 seconds.

supplies into the city. The British Air Force also helped. Together they carried out the **Berlin Airlift** that began in June 1948. In May 1949 Stalin ended the blockade. The Soviet zone in Germany became the Communist country of East Germany. West Berlin remained a free city inside East Germany.

## The United States and NATO

An **arms race**, or a race to build the largest military forces, began between the United States and the Soviet Union. The Soviet Union tested its first atomic bomb in 1949. After that test, each nation tried to build more powerful weapons and atomic bombs.

President Truman believed Western Europe needed a strong army in order to contain communism. So the United States and Canada formed a military alliance with ten nations in Western Europe. The alliance was called the North Atlantic Treaty Organization (NATO). NATO members agreed to protect any member that was attacked. In 1955 the Soviet Union started a military alliance with Eastern European nations. That military alliance was called the Warsaw Pact.

## China Becomes a Communist Nation

During World War II, China fought with the Allies against Japan. After the war the Chinese continued to fight in a civil war.

NATO and Warsaw Pact Countries

**MAP STUDY**

During the Cold War, most of the countries of Europe were members of either NATO or the Warsaw Pact. How many countries belonged to the Warsaw Pact?

(Geography Theme: region)

During the Chinese civil war, Mao Zedong led the Communists and tried to take control of the government. Mao received help from the Soviet Union. The Communists fought against the Chinese Nationalists. A dictator named Chiang Kai-shek led the Nationalists. The United States helped Chiang Kai-shek and the Nationalists because they were against communism.

Millions of poor people in China helped the Communists win the civil war in 1949. Chiang Kai-shek and the Nationalists escaped to the small island of Taiwan. The nation was called Nationalist China. Communist China was called the People's Republic of China. Mao Zedong became the dictator of the People's Republic of China. The country became a Soviet ally and also worked to spread communism. The United States refused to recognize, or deal with, China's government until 1978.

## The Korean War

The Cold War became a "hot" war in the east Asian country of Korea. In 1945 the Allies divided Korea at the 38th parallel. North Korea became a Communist country. The Korean War began when soldiers from North Korea invaded South Korea in 1950. The North Koreans wanted to unite the entire nation under one Communist government. In three days, North Korea won control of most of South Korea.

The United States called for an emergency meeting of the UN Security Council. The Security Council voted to send UN troops to help South Korea.

More than half of the UN soldiers were Americans.

Truman asked General MacArthur to lead the UN troops in Korea. MacArthur forced the North Koreans to leave from most of South Korea. Then he captured most of North Korea. However, about 200,000 soldiers from China helped North Korea. Once again Communists won control of North Korea.

General MacArthur wanted to attack Communist China. President Truman refused to allow MacArthur to attack China. When MacArthur continued to criticize the President, Truman fired him.

The Korean War ended when a **truce**, or an agreement to stop fighting, was reached in 1953. By that time Dwight D. Eisenhower was President of the United States. About 34,000 American soldiers had died during the Korean War. Korea is still divided at the 38th parallel. American and UN troops protect the dividing line between the two Koreas to this day.

## The Red Scare and McCarthyism

The fear of communism was strong in the United States in the early 1920s and again after World War II. Because of the fear of communism, Truman had the loyalty of three million federal workers checked. Freedom of speech and freedom of the press were in danger of being lost.

The House of Representatives formed the House Committee on Un-American Activities (HUAC) to find Communists in the government. In 1948 the Committee investigated Alger Hiss, an important person in the State Department. Hiss was accused of being a Communist spy. Hiss said he was innocent. The HUAC did not

▲ Senator Joseph McCarthy of Wisconsin accused many members of the government of being Communists.

prove that Hiss was guilty of spying, but he was found guilty of lying during his trial.

Senator Joseph McCarthy spread the fear of communism to every part of the nation. In 1950 McCarthy made a speech in which he said he had the names of 205 Communists in the State Department. McCarthy never named the people on his list nor did he prove they were guilty. But he continued to accuse many Americans of being Communists, and he ruined many of their careers. Even Presidents Truman and Eisenhower were called traitors. Most senators and representatives were afraid to speak out against McCarthy. They feared that they, too, would be accused of being Communists. However, Senator Margaret Chase Smith and six other senators did have the courage to speak out against McCarthy. Edward R. Murrow made television shows that reported how McCarthy had falsely accused people.

In 1954 McCarthy lost his power after he attacked the army for being filled with Communists. The Senate took action and made a statement against McCarthy. The fear of communism remained strong through the 1980s. **McCarthyism** now means the policy of falsely accusing people of working against the government.

## The Cold War Around the World

During the 1950s, 24 African colonies became independent nations. These nations were poor because they lacked industry, education, good farming methods, and modern transportation. The Soviet Union and the United States gave millions of dollars in foreign aid to win African nations to their sides.

The Cold War also came to Latin America. In 1959 Fidel Castro took control of Cuba's government. Cuba became a Communist country and a Soviet ally. The United States ended its relations and trade with Cuba. Americans worried that Castro would spread communism and revolutions to other Latin American nations. To prevent the spread of communism, President Eisenhower agreed to give $500 million in foreign aid to Latin America. However, Communist revolutions spread through parts of Central America.

The "space race" became part of the Cold War in 1957 when the Soviet Union sent *Sputnik*, the world's first **satellite**, into space. Not until 1958 did Americans send their first satellite into space.

The Cold War would continue to cause tension between the United States and the Soviet Union for more than forty years.

# Harry S Truman 1884–1972

Harry S Truman was President during the early years of the Cold War. He grew up in Missouri, and learned to read at an early age. Although he was an excellent student, his family was too poor to send him to college. He spent 13 years working on his family's farm. During World War I, he served as an army captain in France.

In 1934 Truman was elected to the United States Senate. He soon had a reputation for being very honest and hardworking. During World War II, Senator Truman led a committee that checked whether defense money was being wasted. Due to Truman's efforts, $15 billion of defense money was saved for the nation.

During the election for President in 1944, Roosevelt chose Truman to run as Vice President. The two men were elected easily. Truman had been Vice President for less than three months when Roosevelt died and Truman became President.

One of President Truman's first decisions was to use atomic bombs on Japan. Truman's goals were to save the lives of American soldiers and to end the war with Japan quickly.

After the war Truman made other difficult decisions. Truman helped create the Marshall Plan and NATO in order to contain communism. He joined all three branches of the armed forces together under one secretary of defense. He also ended segregation in the armed forces.

When North Korea invaded South Korea, Truman decided to send American troops to South Korea. His decision to send troops to fight with UN forces saved South Korea from communism.

At home Truman presented a 21-point program to Congress known as the Fair Deal. In it, Truman asked Congress to expand Social Security, create work for all who wanted it, and build public housing. In 1949 Congress raised the minimum wage, agreed to help clear the slums, and gave old-age benefits to more people. However, Congress refused to pass other parts of the Fair Deal.

Truman did not run for re–election in 1952. Instead he campaigned for Adlai Stevenson. The popular Republican general, Dwight D. Eisenhower, won the election.

Harry S Truman is remembered as a President who made tough decisions during World War II and the Cold War.

**In Your Own Words**

President Truman made several difficult decisions. Write a paragraph that tells which Truman decision you think was most important and why.

## CHAPTER 13 MAIN IDEAS

- During the Cold War, the United States and the Soviet Union struggled over the spread of communism.

- The United Nations was formed to solve problems peacefully between nations.

- The Truman Doctrine supported nations that were trying to remain free from communism. Under the Marshall Plan, the United States agreed to rebuild the war-damaged nations of Europe.

- In 1949 China became a Communist country.

- The Korean War was fought between 1950 and 1953. The United States and UN troops helped South Korea fight Communist North Korea.

- The Cold War spread to Africa, Latin America, and even into a space race.

## VOCABULARY

**Matching** ■ Match the vocabulary word or phrase in Group B with a definition in Group A. Write the letter of the correct answer on the line. You will not use all the words in Group B.

| Group A | Group B |
|---|---|
| _____ 1. falsely accusing people of working against the government | A. superpowers |
| _____ 2. an agreement to stop fighting | B. satellite |
| _____ 3. *Sputnik* was the first one to be sent into space | C. McCarthyism |
| _____ 4. a policy to stop the spread of communism | D. containment |
| _____ 5. a build-up of military forces between the United States and the Soviet Union | E. truce |
| | F. arms race |

## USING INFORMATION

**Writing an Opinion** ■ In 1950 Senator Joseph McCarthy accused many people of being Communists. At the time, many senators and representatives were afraid to speak out against McCarthy. Imagine that you were living in 1950. In your social studies notebook, write a letter to your state's representatives in Congress urging them to take a stand against Senator McCarthy. Your letter should follow the rules of good letter writing.

## COMPREHENSION CHECK

**Choose the Answer** ■ Write the letter of the word or phrase that best answers each question.

_____ 1. Who first used the term "iron curtain"?

    **a.** Harry Truman
    **b.** Joseph Stalin
    **c.** Winston Churchill

_____ 2. What was the purpose of NATO?

    **a.** to provide members with trading partners
    **b.** to stop communism in China
    **a.** to protect members that were attacked

_____ 3. What line of latitude divides the countries of North and South Korea?

    **a.** the 38th parallel
    **b.** the 17th parallel
    **c.** the equator

_____ 4. Who was the communist leader that came to power in Cuba in 1959?

    **a.** Alger Hiss
    **b.** Fidel Castro
    **c.** Mao Zedong

## CRITICAL THINKING

**Comparing and Contrasting** ■ In this chapter, you read about the differences between the United States and the Soviet Union that led to the Cold War. Compare and contrast the United States and the Soviet Union by completing the chart below.

|  | United States | Soviet Union |
| --- | --- | --- |
| Economic system |  |  |
| Type of government |  |  |
| Relationship with Germany |  |  |
| Relationship with Cuba |  |  |
| The Space Race |  |  |

**CHAPTER 14**

### PEOPLE

- Linda Brown
- Thurgood Marshall
- Earl Warren
- Rosa Parks
- Martin Luther King, Jr.
- John F. Kennedy
- James Meredith
- Lyndon B. Johnson
- Mohandas Gandhi
- Malcolm X

### PLACES

- Little Rock
- Montgomery
- Birmingham
- Los Angeles
- Newark
- Detroit

### NEW VOCABULARY

- civil rights movement
- facilities
- discrimination
- integration
- nonviolent resistance
- civil disobedience
- sit-ins
- affirmative action
- race riots

# The Civil Rights Movement

## Focus on Main Ideas

1. How did the Supreme Court's decision in *Brown v. Board of Education of Topeka, Kansas* help end segregation?

2. What laws were passed in the 1960s to protect the civil rights of African Americans?

3. What events in the civil rights movement helped African Americans end segregation?

▲ Linda Brown

The **civil rights movement** took place during the 1950s and 1960s. During this time African Americans and other minorities struggled to win the equal rights that were guaranteed in the Constitution and in the Bill of Rights.

## Segregation

After the Civil War, African Americans who had been enslaved were freed. The Thirteenth, Fourteenth, and Fifteenth Amendments ended slavery and gave African Americans equal rights. The Constitution and the Bill of Rights had been written to protect the rights of all Americans. But after Reconstruction ended, southern states passed segregation laws, or Jim Crow laws, to keep African American and white people apart in public places. These state laws took away the rights of African Americans. For almost 100 years, African Americans in the South had to use separate schools, water fountains, hospitals, restaurants, and beaches.

In 1896 the Supreme Court's decision in the case of *Plessy v. Ferguson* protected segregation. That decision said there could be segregation as long as places for African Americans were "separate but equal" to those for whites. In fact most of the **facilities** for whites were better than those for African Americans.

Throughout the nation African Americans faced **discrimination**, or unfair treatment, because of the color of their skin. They had fewer opportunities to get good jobs, and they earned lower salaries. Although there were no Jim Crow laws in the North, most African Americans still faced discrimination there. Often they could not live in white neighborhoods because homes would not be sold to them. In many northern cities, African American children went to neighborhood schools that did not have white children.

## Goals of the Civil Rights Movement

One of the goals of the civil rights movement that began in the 1950s was to end segregation. To end segregation, people called for the **integration** of public places. First, Jim Crow laws would have to be repealed. Then, new laws would have to be passed to protect the civil rights of all Americans. However, the people who struggled for civil rights knew that economic changes were also needed. African Americans needed the opportunity to have better jobs and to go to better schools.

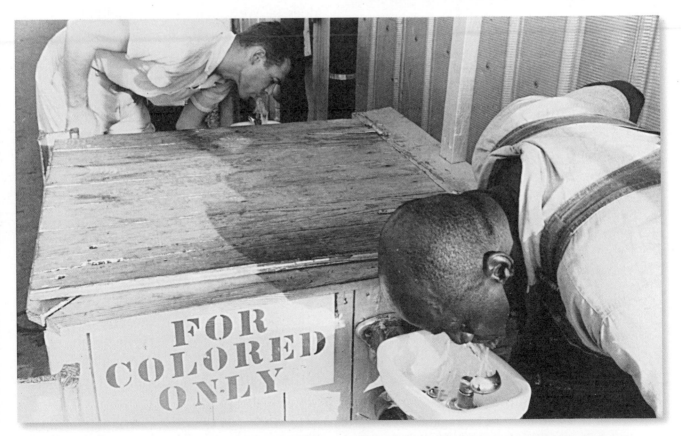

▲ Jim Crow laws kept African Americans and whites segregated. The policy that was created by Supreme Court decisions was that facilities could be "separate but equal." Signs identified which facilities, such as water fountains, rest rooms, restaurants, and schools, could be used.

155

▲ Thurgood Marshall, center, was the NAACP lawyer who argued that schools should not be segregated.

During the 1950s and 1960s, segregation ended because of Supreme Court decisions, actions of Presidents, and laws passed by Congress. Some states refused to follow these federal laws and Supreme Court decisions. This led to new arguments about how to share power between state governments and the federal government. What actions would be taken by the federal government if states refused to carry out federal laws and Supreme Court decisions?

## Brown v. Board of Education

In 1954 the Supreme Court made a decision to end school segregation. The decision was based on a case called *Brown v. Board of Education of Topeka, Kansas*. The case began when Linda Brown's father wanted her to attend the white elementary school that was near their home. The school refused to accept Linda because she was black. The National Association for the Advancement of Colored People, or the NAACP, took Brown's case to the Supreme Court. Thurgood Marshall, an NAACP lawyer, handled the case. Marshall later became a Supreme Court justice.

In 1954 the Supreme Court ruled in favor of Brown. Chief Justice Earl Warren wrote the decision:

"Does segregation of children in public schools solely on the basis of race . . . deprive the children of the minority group of equal educational opportunities? We believe that it does. . . .We conclude in the field of public education the doctrine [idea] of separate but equal has no place. . . ."

The *Brown* decision overturned the decision of *Plessy* v. *Ferguson*. Now all public schools had to end segregation because of the *Brown* decision. The Supreme Court had ruled to end segregation, but state governments had to carry out plans to end it. Southerners were furious and refused to integrate their schools.

## Integration at Central High School

Central High School in Little Rock, Arkansas, became a battleground for integration in 1957. The battle began when nine African American students tried to start school at the all-white high school. The governor of Arkansas refused to integrate the school although President Eisenhower had ordered him to do so. The governor said that the Constitution gave states the power to make education laws. Therefore, as governor he had the right to protect segregation of the schools in his state. The governor sent guards to prevent the African American students from entering Central High School. Angry crowds of white people surrounded the high school and threatened to attack the nine students.

President Eisenhower believed that states must obey Supreme Court decisions. He sent 1,000 soldiers to Little Rock to protect the African American students. On September 25, 1957, the black students entered the high school for the first time.

For the entire school year, the African American students needed guards to protect them. They were attacked daily by many white students. The following year, Central High School closed for the year in order to prevent integration.

School segregation ended slowly. However, most schools eventually were integrated. The nine brave students who attended Central High School had a reunion thirty years later in 1987. By that time an African American was president of Central High's student organization.

## The Montgomery Bus Boycott

In December 1955 Rosa Parks, an African American woman, was sitting down on a bus in Montgomery, Alabama.

▲ In 1957 Central High School in Little Rock, Arkansas, was a battleground in the fight to end school segregation. Arkansas's governor sent guards to the school so that nine African American children could not enter. President Eisenhower then sent troops so that the children could attend the school.

▲ Rosa Parks started a protest when she was arrested for boycotting buses in Montgomery, Alabama.

She was arrested when she refused to give her seat to a white man. The law required African Americans to sit in the back of public buses. Parks was arrested when she refused to give up her seat.

The African American community in Montgomery grew angry about the arrest of Rosa Parks. Led by a minister, Dr. Martin Luther King, Jr., they began to boycott, or stop using, the city's buses. They wanted the unfair law changed. Dr. King believed that **nonviolent resistance** was the best way to end segregation.

During the boycott African Americans refused to ride on the city's buses. Many people walked to work even in cold, rainy weather. The boycott lasted almost a year. The bus company lost money because before the boycott more than half of the bus riders had been African Americans.

In November 1956 the Supreme Court declared that segregation on public transportation was illegal. African Americans were allowed to sit anywhere on buses. The bus boycott ended. The boycott made Dr. King the most famous African American leader in the nation.

## More Battles for Civil Rights

In the early 1960s, **civil disobedience**, or disobeying unfair laws, became a weapon against segregation. African Americans and white people began **sit-ins** at lunch counters in the South. Although waiters refused to serve them, the protesters remained at the lunch counters until the restaurants closed. Sit-ins also took place in parks, libraries, and other public places. Often protesters were arrested and sent to jail. But many public places began to integrate.

In 1960 John F. Kennedy was elected President. During his campaign he had promised to help African Americans win equal rights.

In 1962 James Meredith, an African American, ended segregation at the University of Mississippi. The governor of Mississippi refused to allow Meredith to attend the university. President Kennedy sent federal troops to protect Meredith so he could attend school. Meredith became the first African American to graduate from the University of Mississippi.

In April 1963 Dr. King led protest marches to end segregation in Birmingham, Alabama. The city's police violently attacked the marchers. They arrested Dr. King and sent him to jail. Many Americans watched the violence in Birmingham on television. People in many states were convinced that segregation was wrong.

Many civil rights protests occurred during the early Cold War years. People in other nations wondered how Americans could work for democracy in other countries when they did not allow equal rights for African Americans in the United States.

## The March on Washington

In June 1963 President Kennedy sent a civil rights bill to Congress. Congress had to pass the bill for it to become a law. To win support for the civil rights bill, in August 1963, Dr. King led 250,000 people in a March on Washington, D.C. African Americans and whites stood together in front of the Lincoln Memorial. Millions of Americans watched the event on television and listened to Dr. King give his now-famous "I Have a Dream" speech.

". . . I have a dream that one day . . . little black boys and black girls will be able to join hands with little white boys and white girls as sisters and brothers. . . .

"With this faith we will be able to work together . . . to stand up for freedom together, knowing that we will be free one day. . . ."

## New Laws Help Civil Rights

President Kennedy was assassinated in November 1963 before the civil rights law was passed. After he died, Congress passed the Civil Rights Act of 1964.

▲ Dr. Martin Luther King, Jr., led more than 250,000 people in the March on Washington. Leaders of many civil rights groups were present and gave speeches that day. But the speech given by Dr. King is among the greatest speeches in American history.

▲ Malcolm X was a strong speaker who believed that African Americans and whites should be separated.

African Americans equal opportunities in education and jobs. Affirmative action required colleges and businesses to set aside places for African Americans. Affirmative action also helped women and other minority groups to have more opportunities. The Supreme Court later ruled that affirmative action programs cannot discriminate against whites in order to help minorities.

## Changes in the Civil Rights Movement

During the 1960s other civil rights leaders began to move away from Dr. King's ideas of nonviolence and integration. They stressed the need for "black power." People who believed in black power said African Americans should defend themselves if they were attacked. They wanted more rights and more power immediately. They also stressed learning about their African heritage. Some African Americans wore African-style clothing and hairstyles and changed their names to African names.

Many African Americans became frustrated that change was not taking place fast enough. That frustration led to **race riots** in large cities such as Los Angeles, California; Newark, New Jersey; and Detroit, Michigan. Then in April 1968, Dr. King was assassinated. Riots spread to more than 100 cities across the country. Millions of dollars worth of property was destroyed.

By 1970 the civil rights movement had ended all Jim Crow laws and had helped Congress pass new civil rights laws. These laws would continue to help many Americans win equal rights.

President Lyndon B. Johnson signed the bill and it became law. The new law made segregation and job discrimination because of race, sex, or religion against the law. To carry out the law, Congress created the Equal Employment Opportunity Commission.

In 1964 the Twenty-fourth Amendment was ratified. It ended poll taxes in the South. These taxes had prevented many African Americans from voting in elections.

The next year the Voting Rights Act of 1965 was passed. This law said it was illegal to require people to pass literacy tests in order to vote. Many more African Americans were able to vote in elections. Voting rights gave African Americans more power in the government.

In 1965 President Johnson created **affirmative action** programs to give

# Martin Luther King, Jr. 1929–1968

Martin Luther King, Jr., was a minister who became the civil rights movement's greatest leader.

King was born in Atlanta, Georgia. His grandfather and his father were ministers. To earn money while he was in college, King picked tobacco during the summer in Connecticut. As he watched African Americans and whites work together in the tobacco fields, King started to believe that the two races could live and work together everywhere.

King studied in Pennsylvania to become a minister. After earning his Ph.D. at Boston University, he was called Dr. King.

King studied the work of Mohandas Gandhi, the Indian leader who helped India win independence from Great Britain. Gandhi used nonviolent resistance to defeat the British. King decided to use nonviolent resistance to end segregation. Dr. King would continue to use nonviolence even when he became a victim of violence when bombs were thrown at his home.

Martin Luther King, Jr., was working as a minister in Montgomery, Alabama, when Rosa Parks was arrested. He became the leader of the boycott to end segregation on buses. The success of the boycott made Dr. King famous.

In 1964, the new Civil Rights Act was passed, and Dr. King received the Nobel Peace Prize.

Dr. King continued working for equal rights and better economic opportunities for African Americans. He stressed the importance of peace between all Americans.

In 1968 Dr. King was assassinated, and millions of Americans mourned for him. King's birthday became a national holiday.

Dr. Martin Luther King, Jr., is remembered as a great civil rights leader who wanted freedom for all Americans. The last lines from King's "I Have a Dream" speech were written on his tombstone: "Free at last! Free at last! Thank God Almighty, we are free at last."

## In Your Own Words

Write a paragraph in your journal that tells two ways that Dr. King worked to win equal rights.

# Rosa Parks and the Civil Rights Movement

**In 1955, Rosa Parks helped spark the Civil Rights Movement. She refused to give her seat on a Montgomery, Alabama, bus to a white man. In a 1995 interview, she spoke about the events leading to her arrest.**

I was arrested on December 1st, 1955, for refusing to stand up on the order of the bus driver, after the white seats had been occupied in the front. And of course, I was not in the front of the bus as many people have written and spoken that I was—that I got on the bus and took a front seat, but I did not. I took a seat that was just back of where the white people were sitting, in fact, the last seat. A man was next to the window, and I took an aisle seat and there were two women across.

We went on undisturbed until about the second or third stop when some white people boarded the bus and left one man standing. And when the driver noticed him standing, he told us to stand up and let him have those seats. . . .

And when the other three people . . . stood up, he wanted to know if I was going to stand up, and I was not. And he told me he would have me arrested. And I told him he may do that. And of course, he did. . . .

Two policemen came on the bus and one asked me if the driver had told me to stand and I said yes. And he wanted to know why I didn't stand, and I told him I didn't think I should have to stand up.

And then I asked him, why did they push us around? And he said, and I quote him, "I don't know, but the law is the law and you are under arrest." And with that, I got off the bus, under arrest.

. . . I was arrested on Thursday evening and on Friday evening they had the meeting at the Dexter Avenue Baptist Church where Dr. Martin Luther King was pastor. . . .

My trial was December 5th, when they found me guilty. . . . The only thing that bothered me was that we waited so long to make this protest . . . and to let it be known . . . that all of us should be free and equal and have all the opportunities that others should have.

## Write Your Answers

**Write the answers to these questions in your social studies notebook.**

1. Why did Rosa Parks refuse to give up her seat on the bus?

2. What do you think Mrs. Parks might have said to the police officer when he arrested her?

3. **Think and Respond** Reread the last paragraph. What do you think Mrs. Parks meant when she said, "The only thing that bothered me was that we waited so long to make this protest?"

# *Warriors Don't Cry* by Melba Pattillo Beals

Melba Pattillo Beals was 15 years old when she became one of the nine students to integrate Central High School in Little Rock, Arkansas. The governor of Arkansas, Orval Faubus, was determined to keep the school segregated. Pattillo wrote about the difficulties she faced as she went to school with hostile white students.

On our first day at Central High, Governor Faubus dispatched [sent] gun-toting Arkansas National Guard soldiers to prevent us from entering. Three weeks later, having won a federal court order, we black children maneuvered our way past an angry mob to enter the side door of Central High. But by eleven that morning, hundreds of people outside were running wild, crashing through police barriers to get us out of school. . . . A few . . . brave members of the Little Rock police force saved our lives by spiriting us past the mob to safety. . . .

[Melba Pattillo finally entered Central High School with army troops on September 24. The following are two entries from her diary.]

## September 26, 1957

*It's Thursday, September 26, 1957. Now I have a bodyguard. I know very well that the*

*President didn't send those soldiers just to protect me but to show support for an idea—the idea that a governor can't ignore federal laws. Still, I feel specially cared about because the guard is there.*

## February 18, 1958

*A red-haired, freckle-faced girl . . . keeps trailing me in the hallway between classes. Today she spit on me, then slapped me. Later in the day as I came around a corner, she tripped me so that I fell down a flight of stairs. I picked myself up to face a group of boys who then chased me up the stairs. . . . I told a school official about it. . . . He asked me what did I expect when I came to a place where I knew I wasn't welcome.*

---

## Write Your Answers

Answer these questions in the assignment section of your notebook.

1. What happened on Melba Pattillo's first day at Central High School?

2. Why did Melba have a bodyguard?

3. **Think and Respond** Whom do you admire—Rosa Parks or Melba Patillo Beals? Why?

## CHAPTER 14 MAIN IDEAS

- During the civil rights movement, African Americans struggled to win equal rights, better jobs, and educational opportunities.

- In 1954 the Supreme Court ruled that school segregation was illegal in the case of *Brown* v. *Board of Education of Topeka, Kansas*.

- President Eisenhower sent soldiers to Little Rock, Arkansas, to protect nine African American students who began to attend Central High School.

- Rosa Parks, an African American woman, sparked a bus boycott in Montgomery, Alabama, when she was arrested for refusing to give her bus seat to a white man.

- The civil rights movement, led by Martin Luther King, Jr., used different methods to achieve its goals including boycotts, nonviolent resistance, civil disobedience, marches, and sit-ins.

- The Civil Rights Act of 1964 made segregation and job discrimination illegal. The Twenty-Fourth Amendment made poll taxes illegal.

- Martin Luther King, Jr., was assassinated in April 1968. As a result, race riots occurred in more than 100 cities across the United States.

## VOCABULARY

**Writing With Vocabulary Words** ■ Use six or more vocabulary terms below to write a paragraph that tells about the methods used in the civil rights movement. Write your paragraph in your social studies notebook.

| | |
|---|---|
| civil rights movement | discrimination |
| nonviolent resistance | integration |
| sit-ins | civil disobedience |
| race riots | affirmative action |

## USING INFORMATION

**Writing an Essay** ■ Choose two events that you feel best describe the goals of the civil rights movement in the 1950s and 1960s. Write a paragraph in the assignment section of your social studies notebook that describes each event. Start your paragraph with a topic sentence.

## USING GRAPHIC ORGANIZERS

**Creating an Information Chart** ■ Complete the graphic organizer below about the civil rights movement.

| Event | When It Happened | Why It Was Important |
|---|---|---|
| *Brown v. Bd. of Education,* Topeka, Kansas | | |
| Central High School | | |
| Montgomery Bus Boycott | | *Ended segregation of city buses* |
| March on Washington, D.C. | | |
| Civil Rights Act of 1964 | *1964* | |

## CRITICAL THINKING

**Drawing Conclusions** ■ Read the paragraph below and the sentences that follow it. Put a check in front of the conclusions that can be drawn from the paragraph. You should find three conclusions.

In a court case called *Brown* v. *Board of Education of Topeka, Kansas*, the Supreme Court ruled that separate schools for African Americans were illegal and ordered schools to become integrated. In 1957, the governor of Arkansas refused to allow nine African American students to attend classes at Central High School in Little Rock. The governor felt that the Constitution gave states the power to make laws about education. He also believed that segregation should continue. President Eisenhower sent troops to Little Rock to protect the African American students.

_____ **1.** Martin Luther King, Jr., was an important civil rights leader.

_____ **2.** The *Brown* v. *Board of Education of Topeka, Kansas* case would be used to end school segregation in the South.

_____ **3.** President Eisenhower wanted to prove that states must obey federal laws.

_____ **4.** The *Brown* decision helped James Meredith integrate the University of Mississippi.

# Place: Washington, D.C.

Landforms, climate, people, culture, and work in an area tell us what makes a place special. Washington, D.C., is the center of the federal government. Most people who work in Washington work for the federal government. Because so many important decisions are made in Washington, it is the place for many important rallies like the 1963 Civil Rights March on Washington.

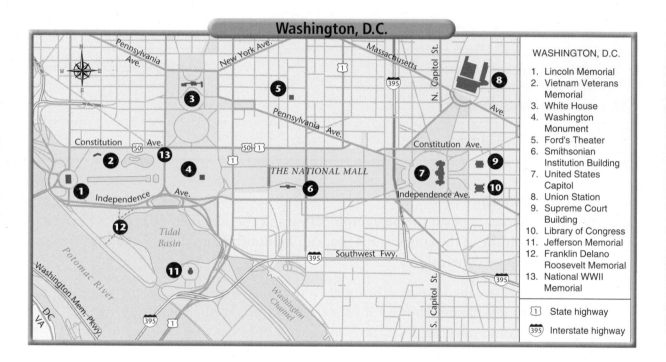

**Washington, D.C.**

WASHINGTON, D.C.

1. Lincoln Memorial
2. Vietnam Veterans Memorial
3. White House
4. Washington Monument
5. Ford's Theater
6. Smithsonian Institution Building
7. United States Capitol
8. Union Station
9. Supreme Court Building
10. Library of Congress
11. Jefferson Memorial
12. Franklin Delano Roosevelt Memorial
13. National WWII Memorial

State highway
Interstate highway

**Read the paragraph and study the map of Washington, D.C. Answer the questions below.**

1. Name three bodies of water in Washington, D.C. _____ , _____ , and _____

2. Which two buildings are near the United States Capitol? _____ , and _____

3. Name two memorials in Washington, D.C. _____ , and _____

4. Why are many protests and rallies held in Washington? _____
_____

# Americans Fight a War in Vietnam

## Focus on Main Ideas

1. Why did war begin in Vietnam?

2. Why did the United States become more involved in Vietnam?

3. How did the Vietnam War end?

4. How did the United States change because of the Vietnam War?

▲ POW/MIA emblem

Vietnam is a small country in Southeast Asia. For about twenty years, from the mid-1950s to 1975, the United States was involved in a war there. More than 58,000 Americans died in the Vietnam War. Today people continue to debate whether or not Americans should have fought and died in Vietnam.

### Vietnam Under French Rule

Vietnam had been part of a French colony called Indochina. The people of Vietnam wanted their independence. Ho Chi Minh led the fight for Vietnam's independence from France. From 1945 to 1954, Ho led the Vietminh, or Vietnamese Communists, in a war against the French.

Vietnam's northern neighbor, China, had become a Communist nation in 1949. To stop communism from spreading throughout Southeast Asia, the United States gave war supplies to the French in Vietnam. In 1954 the Vietminh defeated the French. Vietnam became independent.

### Vietnam Is Divided and War Begins

In 1954 Vietnam was divided at the 17th parallel. Ho Chi Minh became the leader of a Communist government in

▲ Ho Chi Minh was the Communist leader who defeated the French in 1954. Then he became the leader of North Vietnam.

North Vietnam. South Vietnam did not have a Communist government, but its government was not popular because it was dishonest. The president of South Vietnam ruled as a dictator.

In 1956 the North Vietnamese wanted to hold elections so people could vote to unite Vietnam under one government. South Vietnam's president refused to have elections. He said Communists would use the elections to control the entire country.

In order to unite all of Vietnam, Communists in the North sent weapons and additional soldiers to help the Viet Cong, the Communists living in the South. Many poor peasants in the South joined the Viet Cong. They joined because they were angry with South Vietnam's government, which did not help the nation's poor people. The government

also took away religious freedom from people who followed **Buddhism**, South Vietnam's main religion.

The Vietnam War began in 1957 when the Viet Cong revolted against South Vietnam's government. The Vietnam War began as a struggle between Communists and non-Communists for control of South Vietnam. North Vietnam and the Viet Cong wanted one united Communist nation. The non-Communist government in South Vietnam wanted to remain an independent nation.

## The United States Becomes Involved with Vietnam

President Eisenhower agreed with the Truman Doctrine of containing communism. Eisenhower also believed in the **domino theory**. He compared countries to dominoes. All the dominoes in a row fall when the first one is knocked down. According to the domino theory, if one nation in Southeast Asia fell to communism, all the others would fall, too. So Eisenhower sent money and weapons to South Vietnam.

President John F. Kennedy continued Eisenhower's policies. However, the United States gave greater amounts of weapons and money than before. President Kennedy also sent many advisers to South Vietnam.

Vice President Lyndon B. Johnson became President when Kennedy was assassinated in November 1963. At first, Johnson continued Kennedy's policy and sent money, weapons, and advisers to South Vietnam. Johnson was worried because in 1963 and 1964 North Vietnam sent its own soldiers to South Vietnam to win control of the country. By the end of

1964, the Viet Cong controlled about three quarters of South Vietnam's people.

President Johnson believed in the domino theory, and he wanted to save South Vietnam. He did not want to be known as the President who lost South Vietnam to the Communists.

In August 1964, President Johnson said North Vietnam's ships had attacked two American ships in North Vietnam's Gulf of Tonkin. Johnson asked Congress for power to take all necessary military action against North Vietnam. Congress quickly passed the Tonkin Gulf Resolution, which gave President Johnson the power to go to war against North Vietnam.

After the Tonkin Gulf Resolution of 1964, the United States was at war with North Vietnam. However, Congress never declared war as the Constitution requires.

## President Johnson and the Vietnam War

After winning the election in November 1964, Johnson began to **escalate**, or increase, America's war effort. To stop the North Vietnamese from sending soldiers and supplies to the Viet Cong, American planes bombed North Vietnam's supply routes. In 1965 the first American soldiers and marines were sent to fight in the South.

Each year more American soldiers were sent to Vietnam. In 1965 almost 200,000 troops were there. By 1968 there were more than 500,000 American soldiers there. The number of **casualties**, people killed or injured, increased as thousands of Americans were killed or wounded each year.

**The Vietnam War**

## MAP STUDY

The war in Vietnam spread to Laos and Cambodia. What did the Americans attack in those countries?

(Geography Theme: region)

To defeat the Communists, the United States bombed North Vietnam. The American Air Force dropped more bombs during the Vietnam War than it had dropped in World War II.

Helicopters were important in the war. Helicopters were used to carry away wounded soldiers for treatment. They were used during "search and destroy" missions. During these missions, Americans in helicopters searched for Viet Cong soldiers who were hiding in villages, jungles, and mountains. Then Americans destroyed their hiding places.

**169**

▲ Helicopters were used in "search and destroy" missions, and they were used to carry wounded soldiers away from the battlefield.

Americans used a chemical called Agent Orange to destroy plants and trees in jungles and on mountains, so the Viet Cong had fewer places to hide. Agent Orange made many American soldiers and the Vietnamese very sick.

## The Tet Offensive

Early in January 1968, Americans were told they were winning the war in Vietnam. So on January 30, 1968, Americans were shocked when the North Vietnamese army and the Viet Cong began to attack cities throughout South Vietnam. These attacks were called the Tet Offensive because they began during the Tet holiday. During this holiday the Vietnamese celebrate the New Year. American and South Vietnamese forces fought back. They recaptured the cities, but they lost many soldiers.

The Tet Offensive upset Americans at home. Americans had sent their best

soldiers and weapons to Vietnam. But after two years of fighting, the Communists still had the power to attack the South. It was clear that many people in South Vietnam supported the Communists. They admired Ho Chi Minh, and they did not like South Vietnam's dishonest government.

Many Americans began to believe that the United States would not be able to defeat the Communists in Vietnam. The Communists fought a dangerous **guerrilla war**. In a guerrilla war, soldiers do not wear uniforms or fight openly. So the Viet Cong soldiers hid in villages and jungles. They would use sneak attacks on American and South Vietnamese forces. It was impossible to know which people in a village were Viet Cong soldiers. Also, Americans were not used to the land and the climate. Much of South Vietnam was covered with mountains and hot, rainy jungles.

In March 1968 President Johnson announced that he would start peace talks to end the war. He also surprised the nation when he said he would not run for President again. Peace talks with North Vietnam began in May, but they failed to end the war.

## The Protest Movement

Many Americans supported the war in Vietnam. People who supported the war were called "hawks." Many hawks wanted the United States to declare war against North Vietnam and then destroy the enemy. They did not agree with Johnson's limited efforts to defeat the Communists.

After the Tet Offensive, large numbers of Americans became "doves," or people who wanted to end the Vietnam War. Hundreds of thousands of people across the nation held protest marches. Their goal was to pressure the United States government to leave Vietnam. Many protests turned into violent riots.

Many important leaders became doves. Robert F. Kennedy, President Kennedy's brother, spoke out against the war. Martin Luther King, Jr., also criticized the war. He said the United States was spending billions of dollars on a war that had nothing to do with our nation. He wanted the United States to spend that money on programs to help African Americans and other minority groups.

The protest movement against the war grew stronger each year. It divided Americans against each other. Thousands of men moved to Canada in order to avoid serving in Vietnam.

American soldiers in Vietnam learned about the war protests. It was painful for them to fight in a war that so many Americans did not support.

## President Nixon and the Vietnam War

In 1968 Richard Nixon, a Republican, won the election for President. During his campaign, he promised "peace with honor" to end the Vietnam War.

President Nixon began a program called **Vietnamization**. Its goal was to train South Vietnam's soldiers to fight the Communists by themselves. As the South Vietnamese army grew stronger, the American army started a **withdrawal**, leaving Vietnam and returning home. In July 1969, American soldiers began returning home. The peace talks continued in Paris, but they failed to end the war.

In April 1970 Nixon ordered the air force to bomb Vietnam's western neighbor, Cambodia. The Viet Cong had weapons and bases in Cambodia that they used for attacking South Vietnam. Americans were furious that the war was spreading to Cambodia. There were protests and riots in hundreds of universities across the nation.

Kent State University had one of the worst riots. Students destroyed property to show their anger about the war. The National Guard was called to stop the riots. Four students were shot to death as the National Guard tried to end the riots.

At last Congress took action to end the war. In December 1970 Congress repealed

▲ Vietnamese try to escape the fighting in Saigon during the Tet Offensive. The Vietnam War created thousands of refugees.

▲ Four students were killed when National Guard troops tried to stop a Vietnam War protest at Kent State University in Ohio.

▲ Americans left the American embassy in Saigon by helicopter as North Vietnamese troops captured the city.

the Tonkin Gulf Resolution. The President no longer had full power to fight a war in Vietnam.

The United States continued to withdraw American soldiers from Vietnam. After many Americans left, North Vietnamese soldiers invaded the South in 1972. Nixon tried to stop the invasion by bombing North Vietnam.

## The End of the Vietnam War

In 1969 President Nixon had sent Henry Kissinger, his security adviser, to lead secret peace talks with North Vietnam. Kissinger, a Jewish American, was born in Germany. He had come to the United States at age 15 to escape the Holocaust.

Kissinger **negotiated** secretly with North Vietnamese leaders for several years. At last, in January 1973, a **cease-fire** agreement was signed in Paris. The agreement required all American forces to leave Vietnam in two months. The warring nations agreed to return all prisoners of war, or POWs. Two months later, all American soldiers had returned home.

The Vietnam War started again soon after the American forces left. North Vietnam's troops invaded South Vietnam. The South Vietnamese could not stop the North Vietnamese forces. Saigon, the capital of South Vietnam, was captured by the North Vietnamese. The last Americans left the American **embassy** by helicopter. Finally on April 30, 1975, South Vietnam surrendered to North Vietnam. All of Vietnam became one Communist nation.

Many non-Communists were afraid to remain in Vietnam after 1975. More than one million Vietnamese people fled from their country. Thousands escaped in small boats and became known as boat people. Many boat people have settled in the United States.

## Results of the Vietnam War

The Vietnam War became the first war the United States ever lost. Almost three million Americans served in the Vietnam War. More than 58,000 soldiers died. The war cost $150 billion.

North Vietnam returned hundreds of POWs to the United States. Many of them had lived through years of cruel treatment in North Vietnamese prisons. But about 4,000 soldiers never returned from Vietnam. Since there was no proof that they were dead, they were listed as "missing in action," or MIA.

The war changed the United States. The nation moved closer to its old policy of isolationism. Americans no longer felt they had to protect all nations in the world from communism.

In 1973 Congress passed a law called the War Powers Act, which limits a President's power to make war. A President must now have permission from Congress to send American troops into battles that are expected to last more than a few months.

Americans learned important lessons because of the war in Vietnam. One lesson was that the domino theory was wrong. Communists did not win control of all of Southeast Asia. Another lesson was that when we fight in a war, we must really believe in the cause for which we are fighting. Then all Americans must unite and do everything possible to win.

## The Vietnam Veterans Memorial

Many Americans felt the nation needed a memorial to honor the men and women who died in the Vietnam War. Maya Lin, a Chinese American, designed the memorial. Money to build the memorial was contributed by Americans from every part of the nation.

The Vietnam Veterans Memorial is in Washington, D.C. On its two long, black walls are the names of more than 58,000 soldiers who died in the war. It also has the names of people who are still missing in action. In 1993 the Vietnam Women's Memorial was built nearby to honor thousands of women who served in the war. Millions of Americans have visited the memorials. Honoring the people who served in Vietnam has helped heal the anger from this long, bitter war.

▲ The names of more than 58,000 soldiers killed or missing in action during the Vietnam War are listed on this memorial.

# Everett Alvarez, Jr. 1937–

Everett Alvarez, Jr., became the first American pilot to be shot down while flying over North Vietnam. He spent more time as a prisoner of war than any other American soldier.

Alvarez was born in California to a Mexican American family. He became the first person in his family to graduate from college. After college he joined the navy. He became a fighter pilot and was sent to Vietnam. In August 1964, Alvarez's plane was shot down over North Vietnam. He was captured and he became a prisoner of war, or POW.

For more than eight years, Alvarez suffered terribly in a filthy North Vietnamese prison. He was beaten and tortured. He was given very little to eat, and the food that he was given was often full of bugs. Alvarez's hardest time in prison was when he learned that his wife had divorced him and had married another man.

The North Vietnamese wanted Alvarez to publicly criticize the United States. However, the loyal pilot refused to speak out against America, even when he was being tortured.

After the cease-fire in 1973, Alvarez was returned to the United States. Upon landing, he spoke on television to the nation: "For years and years we dreamed of this day and we kept the faith. . . . We have come home. God bless the President and God bless you, Mr. and Mrs. America. You did not forget us."

Alvarez rebuilt his life. He became a lawyer, married again, and had two sons. After the Vietnam Veterans Memorial was completed, Alvarez spoke at its dedication ceremony in Washington, D.C.

In California there is a high school that is named for Everett Alvarez. From Alvarez's story students learn the importance of hard work, a good education, and loyalty to the United States.

## In Your Own Words

Everett Alvarez spent more time as a POW in North Vietnam than any other American. Write a paragraph in your journal that describes what happened to Alvarez after he became a POW in 1964.

# REVIEW AND APPLY

## CHAPTER 15 MAIN IDEAS

- In 1954 the country of Vietnam won its independence from France. Communist leader Ho Chi Minh led this fight for independence. After it became independent, Vietnam was divided at the 17th parallel.

- Communist North Vietnam attacked South Vietnam in hopes of making the entire country a Communist nation.

- At first the United States sent money and supplies to aid the South Vietnamese. By 1964 the United States was sending soldiers to fight there.

- By 1968 more than 500,000 American troops were in Vietnam, but the guerrilla warfare tactics of the Viet Cong made it difficult to defeat the Communists.

- Thousands of Americans protested the Vietnam War.

- In 1975 American troops finally left Vietnam. A short time later, South Vietnam surrendered, and Vietnam became a united Communist country.

## VOCABULARY

**Find the Meaning** ■ Write the word or phrase that best completes each sentence.

1. Soldiers do not wear uniforms or fight in the open in a _____ .
   **civil war**     **world war**     **guerrilla war**

2. An agreement is _____ when two or more parties discuss a settlement.
   **boycotted**     **negotiated**     **protested**

3. An agreement to stop fighting during a war is called a _____ .
   **contract**     **debate**     **cease-fire**

4. The belief that one country after another will become Communist if the spread of communism is not stopped is known as (the) _____ .
   **escalation**     **Vietnamization**     **domino theory**

5. The main religion in Vietnam is _____ .
   **Buddhism**     **Judaism**     **Islam**

6. President Johnson began to _____ , or increase, America's involvement in the war in 1964.
   **escalate**     **negotiate**     **involve**

## COMPREHENSION CHECK

**Write the Answer** ■ Write one or more sentences to answer each question.

1. Why did North Vietnam attack South Vietnam in 1957?

_____

2. Who were the Viet Cong, and what did they want?

_____

3. What was the importance of the Tonkin Gulf Resolution?

_____

4. Why did Americans protest the Vietnam War?

_____

5. How did American involvement in the Vietnam War come to an end?

_____


## CRITICAL THINKING

**Sequencing Information** ■ Write the numbers 1, 2, 3, 4, 5, and 6 next to these sentences to show the correct order.

_____ Communists attack cities in South Vietnam during the Tet Offensive.

_____ A cease-fire is signed and all American troops leave Vietnam.

_____ Ho Chi Minh helps the Vietnamese gain their independence from the French.

_____ South Vietnam surrenders to North Vietnam, and Vietnam becomes a united, Communist country.

_____ Vietnam is divided at the 17th parallel.

_____ President Nixon starts his plan of Vietnamization.


## USING INFORMATION

**Writing an Opinion** ■ The United States fought for nine years in Vietnam, and over 58,000 Americans died there. Write a paragraph in your social studies notebook in which you describe how you would thank a Vietnam veteran for his or her efforts during the war. Start your paragraph with a topic sentence.

# Applying a Statistics Table

The **statistics table** on this page provides information about the number of soldiers who were killed or wounded in the Vietnam War. The table shows us that after the Tonkin Gulf Resolution in 1964, the number of casualties, people killed or injured, greatly increased. It also shows us that casualties began to decrease during the period of Vietnamization that began after 1969.

## American Casualties in the Vietnam War 1960-1973

| Year | Number of American Troops | Combat Deaths | Wounded |
|------|---------------------------|---------------|---------|
| 1960 | 900 | — | — |
| 1961 | 3,200 | — | 14 |
| 1962 | 11,000 | 14 | 95 |
| 1963 | 16,500 | 76 | 413 |
| 1964 | 23,000 | 140 | 1,138 |
| 1965 | 180,000 | 1,350 | 5,300 |
| 1966 | 280,000 | 5,008 | 30,093 |
| 1967 | 500,000 | 9,353 | 99,742 |
| 1968 | 500,000 | 14,592 | 100,000 |
| 1969 | 479,000 | 9,414 | 60,000 |
| 1970 | 280,000 | 4,204 | 9,000 |
| 1971 | 159,000 | 1,386 | 2,000 |
| 1972 | 24,000 | 4,300 | 5,800 |
| 1973 | last troops withdrawn | 12 | 21 |

**Study the table. Then answer the questions below.**

1. In which year were there no casualties? _____

2. Which two years had the most casualties? _____

3. Which two years had the most troops? _____

4. Why did the number of casualties increase from 1960 to 1968?

   _____

5. Which two years had the smallest number of wounded men? _____

6. Which year between 1968 and 1973 had the fewest casualties? _____

7. How many combat deaths took place in 1972? _____

8. When the number of troops increased, how did casualty figures change?

   _____

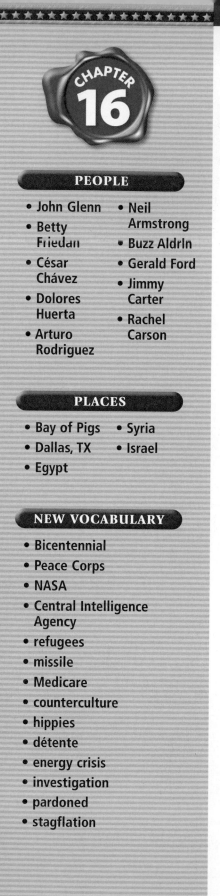

# Successes and Troubles in the 1960s and 1970s

▲ Peace Symbol

## Focus on Main Ideas

1. What were some of the nation's successes in the 1960s and 1970s?

2. What problems troubled the nation in the 1960s and 1970s?

3. What was the Watergate scandal?

On July 4, 1976, Americans celebrated the nation's **Bicentennial** with great pride. But they were also troubled about serious problems facing the nation on its 200th birthday. The 1960s and 1970s were years of troubles and successes.

## John F. Kennedy Becomes President

In 1960 John F. Kennedy ran for President and defeated Richard Nixon, a Republican. Kennedy was the first Catholic to become President.

Kennedy inspired Americans to feel that they could improve their country. In his inaugural speech he said, ". . . And so, my fellow Americans: ask not what your country can do for you—ask what you can do for your country."

Kennedy's program for the nation was called the New Frontier. The program included plans for a strong civil rights law as well as laws to help the poor, improve the nation's schools, and improve health care. Congress did not pass most of Kennedy's programs. Kennedy did create the **Peace Corps**. Peace Corps volunteers went to Asia, Africa, and Latin America to work with people in different countries to improve health care, farming, and education.

The space race began in 1957 when the Soviet Union sent *Sputnik* into space. To win the space race, Kennedy promised that the United States would land people on the moon by 1970. To accomplish this goal, Congress created the space agency called **NASA**. In 1962 Americans were thrilled when John Glenn became the first American astronaut to circle Earth.

## Kennedy and the Cold War

Like Truman and Eisenhower, Kennedy tried to stop the spread of communism. Kennedy worried that Fidel Castro, Cuba's dictator, would spread communism throughout Latin America.

Because of this concern, Kennedy allowed the **Central Intelligence Agency**, or CIA, to secretly train about 1,000 Cuban **refugees** to attack Cuba and capture Castro. In April 1961 the Cuban refugees invaded Cuba. The invasion occurred at the Bay of Pigs, in southern Cuba. Castro's army quickly attacked, and most of the invaders were captured or killed. Americans learned about the attack after it had failed. Many people criticized Kennedy for the Bay of Pigs invasion.

In October 1962 the United States learned that the Soviet Union had built **missile** bases in Cuba. The Soviets had given Cuba missiles armed with nuclear weapons. If those missiles were fired at

▲ When President Kennedy learned that the Soviets had placed missiles in Cuba that could attack the United States, he demanded that the missiles be removed. Americans feared that nuclear war would begin. After three tense days, the Soviets agreed to remove the missiles.

▲ President Lyndon B. Johnson tried to help the nation's poor by launching the War on Poverty to end hunger and poverty in America.

Berlin Wall in 1961 to separate East and West Berlin. East German police shot people who tried to climb over the wall. President Kennedy visited West Berlin in 1963. He told the cheering crowd of Germans, "I am a Berliner." With those words Kennedy showed the Germans that he admired their struggle against communism. The wall divided Berlin until 1989.

## Johnson's Great Society

On November 22, 1963, President Kennedy was shot and killed during a visit to Dallas, Texas. Vice President Lyndon B. Johnson immediately became President.

President Johnson's program for the nation was called the Great Society. His goal was to improve life for all Americans.

Johnson had been a member of Congress for almost 25 years, so he knew how to work with Congress to get laws passed. Many laws that Kennedy had wanted were passed soon after Johnson became President. Congress passed the Civil Rights Act of 1964. New laws increased federal aid to the nation's schools. **Medicare**, a health care program for older Americans, was created.

Johnson started the "War on Poverty" to end hunger and poverty. About one fourth of the nation was living in poverty. Johnson's program included job training and food stamps to help poor people have a healthy diet. By 1969 there was much less poverty in America.

While President Johnson planned the Great Society, he needed millions of dollars to pay for the war in Vietnam. To get money for the war, Johnson took money away from Great Society programs.

the United States, they could quickly destroy American cities. Kennedy decided that the Soviet Union must remove the missiles, but he wanted to avoid a war. On October 22, 1962, he announced that American ships would blockade Cuba and stop Soviet ships from delivering more missiles. Kennedy told the Soviet Union to destroy the Cuban missile bases and to remove all missiles that were there.

For three days Americans lived in fear that a war would start. Finally, the Soviets agreed to destroy the bases and to remove all the missiles. In return, the United States promised not to invade Cuba. President Kennedy became a hero for solving the crisis without a war.

In Europe thousands of East Germans escaped from communism by moving to the free city of West Berlin. To stop people from moving there, the Soviets built the

Because of the Vietnam War, the Great Society did not have as much success as Johnson wanted.

## The Revolt Against American Culture

During the 1960s and 1970s, many young adults were angry that their government was sending some of them off to fight in Vietnam. Angry young adults did not want to live like their parents. They did not want to think about getting married, having a career, and working to earn a lot of money. They spoke about a new society based on peace, love, and total freedom. To protest against their parents' way of life, they formed their own culture, which became known as the **counterculture**. Many members of the counterculture became **hippies** who dressed in old clothes. They created their own form of music.

The counterculture slowly ended at the end of the 1970s. Many hippies began to get married, wear regular clothes, and start families and careers.

## Working for Equal Rights

The civil rights movement encouraged women and minority groups to work for equal rights and equal opportunities. The Civil Rights Act of 1964 and affirmative action programs helped these groups.

At this time few women were doctors, lawyers, or other kinds of professionals. Most women earned far less money than men. Betty Friedan wrote about these problems in her book, *The Feminine Mystique*. She also worked with other women to start the National Organization for Women, or NOW. NOW worked with Congress to pass laws that gave women equal job and educational opportunities. One law required equal pay for men and women doing the same job.

Minority groups also worked for equal rights. Many Mexican Americans worked as migrant farm workers. They received very low salaries and were not protected by job contracts. César Chávez and Dolores Huerta started a union called the United Farm Workers (UFW) to help migrant workers. Chávez and Huerta used strikes and boycotts to peacefully help migrant workers. After Chávez died in 1993, Arturo Rodriguez became president of the union. Today the UFW workers enjoy better pay, medical benefits, and paid vacations.

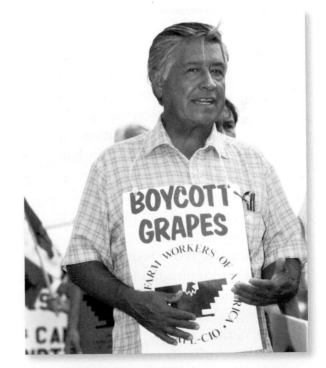

▲ César Chávez led the United Farm Workers, which helped migrant farm workers win better working conditions.

▲ On July 20, 1969, astronauts Neil Armstrong and Buzz Aldrin became the first people to walk on the moon.

Native Americans also demanded equal rights and more control over their reservations. Native Americans faced poverty because their reservations did not have good schools, transportation, or places to work. Most reservations had poor soil for farming. In 1968 Native Americans started the American Indian Movement, or AIM. They succeeded in winning more control over their reservations. They also wanted the government to return lands that had been taken unfairly. They had success in Maine when a federal court agreed to pay two Native American groups $25 billion for land that was unfairly taken from them.

### The Nixon Years

Richard Nixon became President in 1969. Nixon succeeded in improving American relations with China and the Soviet Union. He hated communism, but he became the first President to visit Communist China. He also visited Moscow, the Soviet capital. Nixon worked with the Soviets for a peaceful relationship that was called **détente**. Since the Soviets did not have enough food, President Nixon agreed to sell American wheat to them.

In 1973 the nation faced an **energy crisis**. During the energy crisis, the nation did not have enough oil for its needs. The United States depended on oil from the Middle East. The energy crisis began because of a war in the Middle East. The war began when two Arab nations, Egypt and Syria, attacked Israel. Because Israel was America's ally, the United States sent large amounts of weapons to help defend Israel. Israel won the war. Several Arab nations started an oil embargo against the United States and other countries that had helped Israel.

As less oil was available, the energy crisis became worse. Americans needed oil to make electricity, to heat their homes, and to make gasoline for cars, trucks, and planes. Nixon encouraged Americans to use less electricity and heat. Many people saved energy by using public transportation instead of driving their cars. In some areas nuclear power plants were built to make electricity. After several accidents in nuclear power plants, Americans stopped building them.

### Watergate

In 1972 President Nixon was running for reelection. Most people believed Nixon would easily win the election.

However, some people took illegal actions to help Nixon win. They decided to steal the Democrats' campaign plans. On June 17, 1972, five men were caught breaking into the Democrats' headquarters in the Watergate building in Washington, D.C.

Members of Congress tried to find out what had happened at Watergate and who had sent the men to steal campaign plans. Several people who worked for President Nixon tried to cover up, or keep secret, what had happened. During the **investigation** they learned that Nixon had recorded all conversations in his office. Congress asked to listen to the tapes about Watergate. Nixon refused to allow Congress to hear the Watergate tapes. The Supreme Court ordered Nixon to give the tapes to Congress. The Supreme Court said a President cannot use his power to cover up crimes.

The Watergate tapes proved that Nixon had helped plan the cover–up. He had broken the law. He had lied to Congress, to the courts, and to the American people.

The House of Representatives prepared to impeach Nixon. If the representatives impeached Nixon, he would have to go on trial in the Senate. If the senators found Nixon guilty, he would no longer be President. To avoid the trial, Nixon resigned on August 9, 1974. Vice President Gerald Ford immediately became the nation's President.

A few weeks later, Ford **pardoned**, or forgave, Nixon for any crimes he might have committed. Nixon was never punished. Many other people who were involved with Watergate spent time in jail. Watergate proved that American democracy was strong and could survive crises and scandals.

## Presidents Ford and Carter

Inflation and unemployment were serious problems when Gerald Ford became President. He could not solve these problems in two years, and he lost the 1976 election to Jimmy Carter, a Democrat.

Inflation and unemployment continued to be serious problems. The problem was called **stagflation**. President Carter worked with Congress to create jobs. Unemployment began to drop, but inflation grew worse as oil became more expensive. As the 1970s came to an end, Americans hoped that the next decade would bring better times to a troubled nation.

▲ On August 9, 1974, President Richard Nixon resigned because of the Watergate cover–up. Nixon is the only President to have resigned from office.

# Rachel Carson 1907–1964

Rachel Carson was one of the first people to make Americans aware of the dangers of pollution.

As a college student, Carson discovered that she loved studying science and biology. She was especially interested in ocean life. Carson studied for a Master of Arts degree in marine zoology, the study of animal life in the sea.

The United States Fish and Wildlife Service hired Carson to write radio programs about marine life. Carson's work quickly became popular. She was promoted to an important position in the Fish and Wildlife Service. Few women at that time held such important jobs. She worked for this agency for most of her life.

In 1951 she wrote *The Sea Around Us.* In her book Carson explained how all living things depended on each other to survive. She taught the importance of taking care of the environment. The book became a best seller and Carson became famous.

In 1962 Carson wrote *Silent Spring.* In *Silent Spring* Carson wrote about the dangers of pesticides, powerful chemicals that are used to kill insects. Farmers depended on pesticides to kill the insect population so they could grow food. Carson explained that pesticides were a danger to plant and animal life. They could also cause cancer in humans. Carson explained other methods that could be used to control the insect population. She wanted pesticides to be used less often and more carefully. President Kennedy started a committee to study the effects of pesticides. The committee found that Carson's work was correct. Efforts were made to limit the use of pesticides.

Rachel Carson proved that women could make important contributions in science. She helped Americans learn to protect their air, land, and water.

## In Your Own Words

Through her work as a scientist and a writer, Rachel Carson helped the United States. Write a paragraph in the journal section of your social studies notebook that explains how Carson's work helped the nation.

★★★★★★★★★★★★★★★★★★★★★★★★★★★★★★★★★★★★★★★★★★★★★★★★★★★★★★★★★

## CHAPTER 16 MAIN IDEAS

■ John F. Kennedy, who became President in 1960, started a volunteer group called the Peace Corps that taught people in Asia, Africa, and Latin America how to improve their lives.

■ President Kennedy used different methods for trying to stop the spread of communism including the Bay of Pigs invasion, the Cuban Missile Crisis, and his visit to West Berlin in 1963.

■ Lyndon B. Johnson became President when President Kennedy was assassinated on November 22, 1963.

■ President Johnson's program to improve the life of all Americans was called the Great Society.

■ During the 1960s and 1970s, many young adults rejected the values of their parents and started a counterculture.

■ In 1973, Americans faced an energy crisis because Arab nations started an oil embargo against the United States and other countries.

■ President Nixon resigned from office on August 9, 1974, as a result of the Watergate scandal.

■ Under Presidents Ford and Carter, inflation and unemployment were serious problems.

## VOCABULARY

**Defining and Using Vocabulary** ■ Use the glossary to find the meaning of each word or phrase listed below. Write each word's definition in your social studies notebook. Then use each word in a sentence.

| | |
|---|---|
| missile | energy crisis |
| Medicare | pardon |
| hippies | stagflation |
| détente | |

## USING INFORMATION

**Journal Writing** ■ Imagine if you lived through the energy crisis in the early 1970s. What would you have done about long gas lines? What would you have done to save energy? Write a paragraph in your social studies notebook that tells what you would have done during this time in our country's history. Start your paragraph with a topic sentence.

## USING GRAPHIC ORGANIZERS

**Problem/Solution Chart** ■ Complete the graphic organizer by explaining the problem each person faced and one or two ways he or she tried to solve the problem.

| Name | Problem | Solution |
|---|---|---|
| President Lyndon B. Johnson | | |
| Betty Friedan | | |
| César Chávez | | |
| President Jimmy Carter | | |

## CRITICAL THINKING

**Fact or Opinion** ■ Write **F** on the blank next to each statement that is a fact. Write **O** on the blank if the statement is an opinion. If the statement gives both a fact and an opinion, write **FO**. Then draw a line under the part of the sentence that is an opinion.

_____ 1. The United States had great success in its space program, but the money used for *Apollo 11* should have been used to help the poor.

_____ 2. The Soviet Union built missile bases in Cuba.

_____ 3. President Kennedy should have sent American soldiers to destroy the Berlin Wall.

_____ 4. The United States should have built more nuclear power plants.

_____ 5. President Ford pardoned Richard Nixon for his Watergate crimes, but Nixon should have spent time in jail for his actions.

# Interpreting a Political Cartoon

Political cartoons are drawn by artists to express opinions about events. The cartoons below were drawn by two different artists. In Cartoon A, from 1948, the artist shows how Russia is trying to force the United States, France, and Britain from Berlin. In Cartoon B, from 1940, the artist shows ducks that represent France, Holland, and Denmark. Hitler and Mussolini have shot three ducks. But Uncle Sam is reminding Hitler and Mussolini about the Monroe Doctrine, which says that they cannot take control of territories in Latin America (Western Hemisphere).

**CARTOON A**          **CARTOON B**

**Study the cartoons. Then write the answer to each question.**

1. In Cartoon A, what animal does the artist use to show Russia?

   _____

2. In Cartoon A, how does the artist show that Russia wants to control Berlin?

   _____

3. In Cartoon B, what is the United States doing to stop Hitler and Mussolini?

   _____

4. How do these cartoons help you to understand history?

   _____

Study the time line on this page. You may want to read parts of Unit 4 again. Then use the words and dates in the box to finish the paragraphs. The box has one possible answer you will not use.

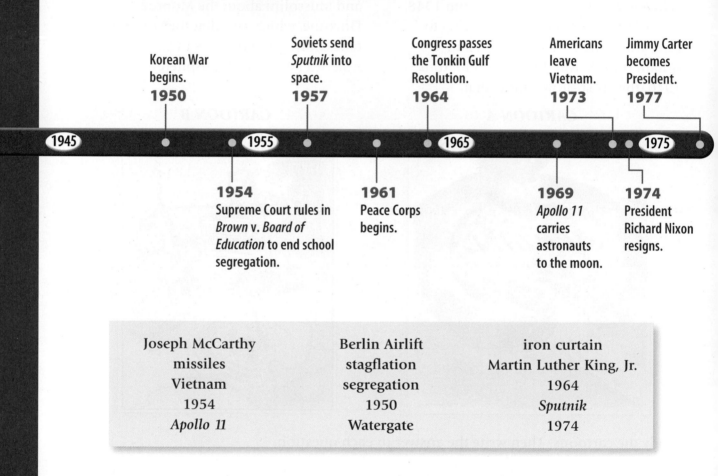

Korean War begins.
**1950**

Soviets send *Sputnik* into space.
**1957**

Congress passes the Tonkin Gulf Resolution.
**1964**

Americans leave Vietnam.
**1973**

Jimmy Carter becomes President.
**1977**

1945    1955    1965    1975

**1954**
Supreme Court rules in *Brown* v. *Board of Education* to end school segregation.

**1961**
Peace Corps begins.

**1969**
*Apollo 11* carries astronauts to the moon.

**1974**
President Richard Nixon resigns.

| Joseph McCarthy | Berlin Airlift | iron curtain |
| missiles | stagflation | Martin Luther King, Jr. |
| Vietnam | segregation | 1964 |
| 1954 | 1950 | *Sputnik* |
| *Apollo 11* | Watergate | 1974 |

After Communists took control of Eastern Europe, Winston Churchill said there was a wall like an **1**_____ around that region. During the Soviet Union's blockade of West Berlin, the United States and Great Britain saved the city with the **2**_____ . The Cold War became a hot war in Korea in **3**_____ . The space race became part of the Cold War after the Soviets sent the **4**_____ satellite into space in 1957. The United States won the space race in 1969 when

**5**_____ carried American astronauts to the moon. The Cold War almost

became a hot war when the Soviet Union sent **6**_____ to Cuba in 1962.

After Congress passed the Tonkin Gulf Resolution in **7**_____ , thousands of

American troops were sent to fight in **8**_____ .

In the early 1950s, **9**_____ falsely accused many Americans of being

Communists. In **10**_____ the Supreme Court decided in the case called *Brown*

v. *Board of Education of Topeka, Kansas*, that school segregation was illegal. After Rosa

Parks was arrested for not giving up her seat on a bus, **11**_____ led the

Montgomery bus boycott. The boycott ended in 1956 after the Supreme Court ruled

that **12**_____ on public transportation was against the law.

Richard Nixon helped plan the **13**_____ cover up, and he became the first

President to resign. While Jimmy Carter was President, unemployment and inflation

led to **14**_____ .

## Looking Ahead to Unit 5

At the end of the 1980s, the nations of Eastern Europe moved away from communism. The Berlin Wall was torn down, and the Soviet Union broke apart. The Cold War ended, and the United States became the world's most powerful nation. The United States fought two wars with Iraq. Americans also began a war against terrorism, both at home and abroad.

Americans continued to face many problems at home, such as poverty, discrimination, pollution, and terrorism. As technology improves, Americans will have new tools for solving these problems.

As you read Unit 5, think about how the United States has worked for peace. Find out what Americans are doing to protect the environment. Read on to learn how Americans are building a brighter and safer future at home and around the world.

Sally Ride becomes
the first American
woman in space.
**1983**

Germany
becomes a
united nation.
**1990**

**1975**

**1985**

**1979**
The leaders of Israel and Egypt sign
the Camp David Accords. An Islamic
revolution occurs in Iran.

**1989**
Communism ends
in Eastern Europe.

# Today and Tomorrow

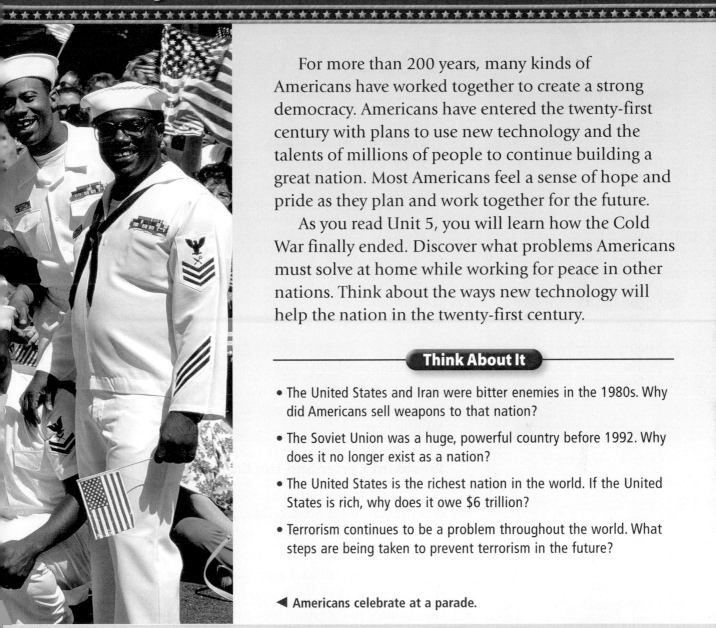

For more than 200 years, many kinds of Americans have worked together to create a strong democracy. Americans have entered the twenty-first century with plans to use new technology and the talents of millions of people to continue building a great nation. Most Americans feel a sense of hope and pride as they plan and work together for the future.

As you read Unit 5, you will learn how the Cold War finally ended. Discover what problems Americans must solve at home while working for peace in other nations. Think about the ways new technology will help the nation in the twenty-first century.

## Think About It

- The United States and Iran were bitter enemies in the 1980s. Why did Americans sell weapons to that nation?

- The Soviet Union was a huge, powerful country before 1992. Why does it no longer exist as a nation?

- The United States is the richest nation in the world. If the United States is rich, why does it owe $6 trillion?

- Terrorism continues to be a problem throughout the world. What steps are being taken to prevent terrorism in the future?

◀ Americans celebrate at a parade.

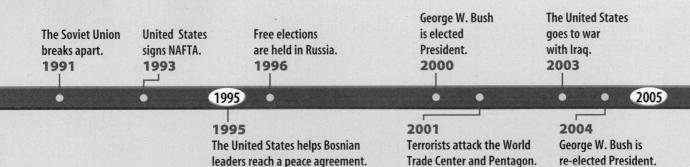

The Soviet Union breaks apart.
**1991**

United States signs NAFTA.
**1993**

Free elections are held in Russia.
**1996**

George W. Bush is elected President.
**2000**

The United States goes to war with Iraq.
**2003**

1995

2005

**1995**
The United States helps Bosnian leaders reach a peace agreement.

**2001**
Terrorists attack the World Trade Center and Pentagon.

**2004**
George W. Bush is re-elected President.

# The United States Faces World Problems

## Focus on Main Ideas

1. How did President Carter help Israel and Egypt create a peace treaty?
2. What caused the hostage crisis in Iran and how did it end?
3. What was the Iran-contra scandal, and why did it happen?
4. How did the Cold War end?

▲ An American held hostage in Iran

During the 1970s and 1980s, the United States continued to fight the spread of communism. The United States also tried to bring peace to troubled areas of the world, such as the Middle East.

### President Carter and the Camp David Accords

One of Jimmy Carter's greatest achievements as President was the **Camp David Accords**, a peace treaty between Egypt and Israel. The peace treaty ended 30 years of war between two enemy nations in the Middle East.

Wars between Israel and Arab nations in the Middle East first began in 1948. In that year the United Nations divided the country of Palestine into two nations, Israel and Jordan. Israel was created as a Jewish homeland. The land had been the home of the Jews thousands of years ago when their religion first began.

The Arab nations in the Middle East refused to recognize the Jewish state of Israel. So they fought four wars against Israel in 1948, 1956, 1967, and 1973. After each war Israel remained a free nation. Many Palestinians became refugees when they left Israel during the 1948 war. During the 1967 war, Israel captured lands that had belonged to Egypt, Syria, and Jordan. Some of that captured land is still controlled by Israel.

The United States has been Israel's ally since it became a nation in 1948. The United States gave aid to Israel because that country was a democracy and it was against communism. The Arab nations have also been important to the United States because Americans buy oil from them.

In 1978 President Carter invited Egypt's president, Anwar Sadat, and Israel's prime minister, Menachem Begin, to peace talks in the United States. The three leaders met at the President's vacation home at Camp David, Maryland. After two weeks of hard work, the three leaders reached an agreement. Israel agreed to return land it had captured from Egypt in 1967. In return Egypt agreed to recognize Israel as a nation and to sign a peace treaty with Israel. In 1979 Begin and Sadat signed the Camp David Accords, the first peace treaty between Israel and an Arab nation. The two leaders later received the Nobel Peace Prize. President Carter played an important role in creating the Camp David Accords. In 1981 President Sadat was assassinated by people in Egypt who opposed the peace treaty.

▲ Egypt's President Anwar Sadat, President Jimmy Carter, and Israel's Prime Minister Menachem Begin signed the Camp David Accords. This agreement was the first peace treaty between Israel and an Arab nation. President Carter played a major role in bringing these former enemies together.

▲ This protest in Iran was one of many during the Iran hostage crisis. Iranians were angry at the United States for giving the former Shah medical treatment.

## Other Foreign Affairs Under Carter

The United States had controlled the Panama Canal since it opened in 1914. President Carter believed Panama should control the Panama Canal. In 1977 the United States and Panama signed a treaty that gave Panama complete control of the Canal on December 31, 1999.

Carter also worked to protect **human rights**, the right to personal freedom, in many nations. When the Soviet Union refused to allow Jews to practice their religion, Carter protested strongly.

Carter took action when the Soviet Union invaded the Muslim nation of

Afghanistan in 1979. He stopped American wheat sales to the Soviets. Americans did not take part in the 1980 Olympic Games that were held in Moscow, the Soviet capital. The United States Senate did not pass an agreement called SALT II, which required both nations to limit nuclear weapons. The period of détente, or better relations with the Soviets, came to an end.

## The Hostage Crisis in Iran

The most difficult problem that President Carter faced in foreign affairs occurred in the Middle East nation of Iran. Iran is a Muslim nation with a large oil supply. In 1953 the CIA helped Mohammed Reza Pahlavi become **shah**, or king, of Iran. The Shah worked to make Iran more like the western nations of the United States and Europe. New industries were started, new schools were built, and women had the right to vote. Many Iranians were angry with the Shah because he moved the country away from the teachings of Islam. Other Iranians hated the Shah because he was a dictator who allowed very little freedom.

In the late 1970s, a revolution began in Iran. In 1979 the Shah fled from Iran. The Ayatollah Ruhollah Khomeini, a Muslim religious leader, won control of the government. A new government was started that was based on the laws of Islam.

The new government wanted the Shah to return to Iran to be put on trial. When the Shah became ill, he went to the United States for medical treatment. Iranians were furious when President Carter refused to send the Shah back to Iran. On April 4, 1979, angry Iranians took control of the American embassy in Iran's capital, Teheran. For the next 444 days, 52 Americans were held as **hostages** in Iran.

President Carter was not able to win the release of the hostages. To pressure Iran, Carter stopped importing oil from that country. Before long the United States had a new energy crisis.

In April 1980 Carter decided to use military force to free the hostages. Unfortunately, several helicopters crashed, eight members of the rescue team were killed, and the mission failed.

The Shah died in July 1980, but the Iranians refused to release the American hostages. Many Americans were upset that Carter could not get the hostages released. In 1980 Carter lost the presidential election to Ronald Reagan. The Iran hostage crisis was one of several problems that led to Carter's defeat. Finally, on January 20, 1981, the day Reagan became President, Iran released the American hostages.

## Civil Wars in Central America

President Ronald Reagan strongly believed that communism was a serious threat to the United States. In 1982 when Communists won control of Grenada, a tiny island located in the Caribbean Sea, Reagan sent American troops to defeat the Communists. A new government that was friendly to the United States was started in Grenada.

The United States also became involved in Nicaragua, a country in Central America. There had been a civil war in Nicaragua. As a result, a group

called the **Sandinistas** ruled Nicaragua. The civil war continued because people who opposed the Sandinistas, the **contras**, fought to control Nicaragua. The Soviets sent aid to the Sandinistas to help them fight the contras. In 1981 Congress agreed to send weapons and aid to the contras. Reagan wanted more aid for the contras, but in 1984 Congress passed a law that ended American aid. After years of fighting, the Sandinista leader of Nicaragua, Daniel Ortega, agreed to hold elections. A non-Communist leader was elected president of Nicaragua.

▲ These Sandinista soldiers helped fight the contras in Nicaragua. The United States supported the contra rebels, who continued to fight the Sandinistas after Nicaragua's civil war.

El Salvador, a Central American nation near Nicaragua, also had a civil war. Communist guerrilla fighters tried to win control of the government. Because there was terrible poverty in El Salvador, many people favored the Communists. The Sandinistas in Nicaragua sent aid to the Communist rebels. President Reagan sent aid to the ruling non-Communist government. The war ended and a peace treaty was signed in 1992. Since then El Salvador has elected a non-Communist government.

## The Dangers of Terrorism

Since the late 1970s, **terrorism** has been a problem in many parts of the world. Terrorism is the use of dangerous acts against innocent people to force an enemy to give in to terrorists' demands. The policy of the United States has been to refuse to give terrorists what they demand.

In 1985 terrorists bombed a restaurant in Spain near an American air force base. A few months later other terrorists bombed an American military base in Germany. That same year terrorists attacked Americans in planes and airports in a few other countries.

One of the worst acts of terrorism occurred in 1988. Terrorists placed a bomb on an American plane. It exploded as it flew over Scotland. All 270 passengers, including 38 American students, were killed.

▲ In 1988 a terrorist bomb blew up this plane as it flew over Scotland. All of the passengers and crew were killed, including many Americans. Police and government officials looked for clues and eventually charged two Libyans with the crime.

## The Iran-Contra Scandal

The Iran-contra scandal developed because President Reagan wanted to find a way to release seven American hostages who were being held by terrorists in Lebanon. He also wanted to help the contras in Nicaragua even though Congress had stopped American aid.

To reach Reagan's goals, members of his staff carried out secret plans. They secretly and illegally sold arms, or weapons, to America's enemy, Iran. In return Iran agreed to work for the release of the seven American hostages. Profits from the arms sale to Iran were sent to the contras in Nicaragua.

Americans were shocked when they learned about the Iran-contra deal. It was against American policy to deal with terrorists and to sell weapons to America's enemies. It was also illegal to help the contras.

Congress investigated the scandal in 1987. Several members of Reagan's staff were found guilty. President Reagan denied that he knew about the secret deals. However, many people criticized the President for not knowing what was happening among his staff members.

## President Reagan and the Soviet Union

President Reagan believed that the Soviet Union was a threat to the security of the United States. To protect the United States from the Soviet Union, Reagan spent billions of dollars building up the military strength of the nation. The increase in military spending helped cause

▲ President Reagan hated communism, but he developed a good relationship with Mikhail Gorbachev, the leader of the Soviet Union.

the nation's **deficit**, or shortage of money, to grow larger.

Reagan wanted the nation to build a new defense system called the **Strategic Defense Initiative**. People also called the system Star Wars. The system would have space satellites that would shoot down nuclear missiles that were fired at the United States. However, changing events in the Soviet Union made Star Wars less necessary for the United States.

In 1985 Mikhail Gorbachev became the new leader of the Soviet Union. He decided to try to solve the country's serious economic problems by allowing some private control of business and industry. These changes in the Communist system were given the Russian name **perestroika**.

Gorbachev also allowed more freedoms for the Soviet people. There was more freedom of speech, freedom of the press,

▲ Since the time it was built in 1961, the Berlin Wall had become a symbol of the Cold War. In November 1989 Germans celebrated as the Berlin Wall was opened, allowing travel between East and West. Thousands of Germans helped tear down the hated wall.

and freedom of religion. These new freedoms and more openness were given the Russian name **glasnost**.

By 1987 President Reagan believed the Soviet Union was no longer America's most dangerous enemy. In that year Reagan and Gorbachev signed the INF Treaty. In the treaty, both nations agreed to destroy thousands of nuclear missiles.

## The End of the Cold War

Since 1945 the nations of Eastern Europe had been controlled by the Soviet Union. The changes Mikhail Gorbachev made in the Soviet Union quickly spread to Eastern Europe and communism grew weaker.

In 1989 Poland became the first nation in Eastern Europe to hold free elections. Lech Walesa was the leader of

the **Solidarity** labor union. He was elected President of a non-Communist Polish government. During the next few months, the other nations of Eastern Europe started non-Communist governments.

As freedom spread through Eastern Europe, East Germans wanted to travel to West Berlin. In November 1989 the Berlin Wall was opened and people could once again travel between East Berlin and West Berlin. Germans on both sides quickly tore down the hated wall. In 1990 all of Berlin became one city again. East Germany and West Germany rejoined and formed a united Germany in 1990.

For more than forty years, Americans had feared the Soviet Union and communism. Once communism was no longer a threat, the Berlin Wall was torn down, and the long years of the Cold War ended.

# Ronald Reagan 1911–2004

Ronald Reagan was one of the most popular Presidents in American history. Reagan grew up in Illinois. Reagan's family was so poor that he wore his brother's old clothes and was often hungry from the lack of food. Reagan became an actor after finishing college. He starred in many movies and several television shows from 1937 to 1965.

Reagan was also interested in politics. In 1966 he was elected governor of California. He served two terms. Then in 1976, and again in 1980, he ran for President. During his campaign against Jimmy Carter in 1980, Reagan promised to cut taxes, lower inflation, and improve the economy. Reagan won the election.

As President, Reagan carried out an idea called **supply-side economics**. The idea was later called Reaganomics. Reagan believed that the economy would improve if the amount of goods produced could increase. Therefore, he cut taxes so that businesses could invest money in hiring workers and producing goods. Once businesses earned larger profits, they would pay more taxes.

Reagan also believed the federal government should be less involved in the lives of the people. So he cut programs for education and welfare. Some people said that these cuts hurt poor Americans, but Reagan insisted that a strong economy would help everyone.

By the end of Reagan's second term, the economy had improved. But the nation had also borrowed large amounts of money to pay for defense spending and social programs.

By 1989, most Americans were happy with the improved economy and the new friendship with the Soviet Union. Even the Iran-contra scandal could not destroy Reagan's popularity. When his second term ended, Reagan was one of the most popular Presidents in American history. Reagan retired to California where he died in 2004 from Alzheimer's Disease.

## In Your Own Words

Write a paragraph that tells why Reagan was a very popular President.

## CHAPTER 17 MAIN IDEAS

- The Camp David Accords, a peace treaty between Egypt and Israel, was one of President Carter's greatest achievements.

- On April 4, 1979, Iranians took control of the American embassy in Teheran and held 52 Americans hostage for the next 444 days.

- President Reagan fought the spread of communism in Central America.

- Terrorist acts throughout the world have killed many innocent people.

- In 1985 Mikhail Gorbachev became the new leader of the Soviet Union.

- In 1989 the Berlin Wall was torn down, and the Cold War came to an end.

## VOCABULARY

**Finish the Sentence** ■ **Choose one of the words or phrases from the box to complete each sentence. Write the word or phrase on the correct line. You will not use all the words in the box.**

1. The _____ was a peace treaty between the countries of Israel and Egypt.

2. President Carter worked to protect the _____, or personal freedoms, of people around the world.

3. Nicaragua's Communists were called _____.

4. President Reagan sent aid to the Nicaraguan rebels called _____.

5. The name of the Polish labor union headed by Lech Walesa was _____.

Sandinistas
Camp David Accords
Solidarity
hostages
human rights
contras
shah

## USING INFORMATION

**Writing an Opinion** ■ **Both President Carter and President Reagan were successful in foreign affairs. Write a paragraph in your social studies notebook explaining which President you think was more successful in foreign affairs and why. Start your paragraph with a topic sentence.**

## COMPREHENSION CHECK

**Who Said It?** ■ Read each statement in Group A. Then look at the names in Group B for the person who might have said it. Write the letter of the correct answer on the blank. There is one name you will not use.

### Group A

_____ 1. "I stopped Americans from participating in the 1980 Olympic Games."

_____ 2. "I led a new government in Iran that wanted to put the Shah on trial."

_____ 3. "I believed that the Soviet Union was a threat to the security of the United States."

_____ 4. "I wanted to give the Soviet people more personal freedom."

_____ 5. "I was the Egyptian President who signed a peace treaty with Israel."

_____ 6. "I was elected President of Poland."

### Group B

**A.** Daniel Ortega

**B.** Ronald Reagan

**C.** Jimmy Carter

**D.** Lech Walesa

**E.** Mikhail Gorbachev

**F.** Anwar Sadat

**G.** Ayatollah Khomeini

## CRITICAL THINKING

**Categories** ■ Read the words in each group. Write a title for each group on the line above each group. There is one title that you will not use.

| Iran-Contra Scandal | End of the Cold War | Terrorist Acts |
| The Carter Presidency | Sandinistas | |

1. _____

could not get Americans freed from Iran
held meetings with leaders of Egypt and Israel
stopped American wheat sales to the Soviet Union

2. _____

led by Daniel Ortega
sent aid to Communists in El Salvador
given aid by the Soviet Union

3. _____

bombing a restaurant in Spain
placing a bomb on a plane
a problem in many parts of the world

4. _____

took place during the Reagan administration
American weapons were sold to Iran
Iran agreed to work for the release of American hostages

# The United States in Today's World

▲ American soldier in the Persian Gulf War

## Focus on Main Ideas

1. Why did the United States fight in the Persian Gulf War?

2. Why is the Soviet Union no longer a nation?

3. How has the United States worked for peace in the Middle East, Bosnia, and Africa?

4. How has the United States worked with Canada and Mexico?

During the 1990s the United States often acted as a leader and a peacemaker in the world's trouble spots.

## The Persian Gulf War

In August 1990 Iraq captured the neighboring nation of Kuwait. Both Kuwait and Iraq are oil-rich nations on the Persian Gulf. Iraq wanted to rule Kuwait in order to control its oil fields. After winning control of Kuwait, Saddam Hussein, the dictator of Iraq, threatened to attack Saudi Arabia, Kuwait's oil-rich neighbor. Since Americans imported oil from Kuwait and Saudi Arabia, the United States decided to stop Iraq from controlling their oil fields.

President George Bush acted quickly with other UN nations to organize a **coalition** of 28 nations that were willing to use military force against Iraq. War began in the Persian Gulf on January 16, 1991. The war was called the Persian Gulf War. General H. Norman Schwarzkopf and General Colin Powell led American forces during the war. The United States and other coalition members, such as Britain and France, bombed Iraq for five weeks.

Then American soldiers began fighting in Iraq and Kuwait. After four days Kuwait became a free nation. The war ended on February 28, 1991. About 85,000 Iraqis and 146 Americans had been killed.

The quick victory made President Bush popular after the war. However, Saddam Hussein remained Iraq's dictator.

## The Soviet Union Falls Apart

During the forty years after World War II, Americans feared the power of the Soviet Union. But by 1992 the Soviet Union would no longer be one nation.

After becoming the leader of the Soviet Union in 1985, Mikhail Gorbachev made important changes. He ended communism in Eastern Europe and the Cold War. He also encouraged peace with the United States. In 1991 Gorbachev and President Bush signed START, the Strategic Arms Reduction Treaty, a treaty to limit nuclear weapons.

Gorbachev also brought more freedom to the Soviet Union than any Soviet leader had ever allowed before. This freedom encouraged nationalism to grow in the 15 republics that made up the Soviet Union. The republics wanted to be independent nations like they had been before the Soviet Union began in 1922.

By 1991 many people in the Soviet Union were unhappy with Gorbachev. Some did not like the changes he had made in the government. Millions of people were upset because there were shortages of all types of food and goods. Gorbachev's enemies tried to **overthrow** him. On December 25, 1991, Gorbachev resigned, and the Soviet Union was no longer a nation. The 15 republics became independent countries.

Russia was the largest republic in the Soviet Union. Russia and 11 republics

▲ American forces stopped Iraqi forces that were trying to leave Kuwait. Thousands of Iraqi trucks were destroyed on this highway.

▲ The land battle lasted only four days during the Persian Gulf War. Troops from 28 nations, including the United States, defeated the Iraqi forces.

from the former Soviet Union formed an organization called the Commonwealth of Independent States, or CIS. The CIS tries to help republics control their nuclear weapons and it encourages trade.

In 1996 the first free elections for president were held in Russia. Boris Yeltsin, a non-Communist, defeated a Communist candidate to win the election.

Yeltsin tried to help Russia become more democratic. However, many Russians were unhappy because millions of people were poor. On December 31, 1999, Boris Yeltsin resigned as president. Vladimir Putin was elected as the new president. Putin promised to build democracy in Russia.

President Putin leads a country that is made of 21 states that are called republics. One very poor republic is Chechnya. Unlike most Russians, people in Chechnya are **Muslims**. They follow the religion of **Islam**. In 1991, Chechnya said it was an independent nation. The Russian army has fought against the Chechens for many years. Chechnya has remained a part of Russia.

Putin was reelected as president in 2004. He is working to improve relations with the United States, Europe and NATO.

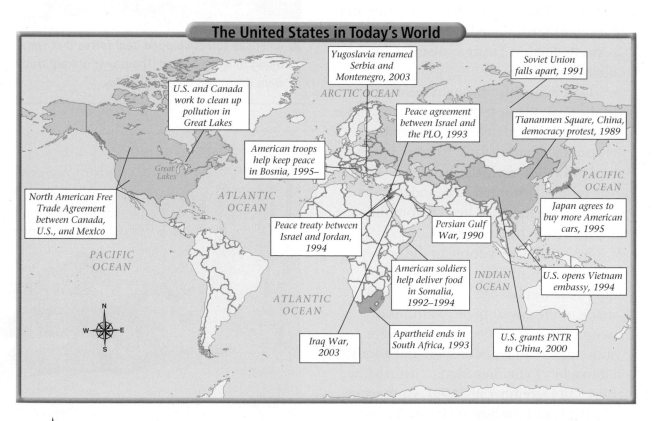

**The United States in Today's World**

Yugoslavia renamed Serbia and Montenegro, 2003

Soviet Union falls apart, 1991

ARCTIC OCEAN

U.S. and Canada work to clean up pollution in Great Lakes

Peace agreement between Israel and the PLO, 1993

Tiananmen Square, China, democracy protest, 1989

American troops help keep peace in Bosnia, 1995–

Great Lakes

ATLANTIC OCEAN

PACIFIC OCEAN

North American Free Trade Agreement between Canada, U.S., and Mexico

Japan agrees to buy more American cars, 1995

Peace treaty between Israel and Jordan, 1994

Persian Gulf War, 1990

PACIFIC OCEAN

American soldiers help deliver food in Somalia, 1992–1994

INDIAN OCEAN

U.S. opens Vietnam embassy, 1994

ATLANTIC OCEAN

N W E S

Iraq War, 2003

Apartheid ends in South Africa, 1993

U.S. grants PNTR to China, 2000

### ✦ MAP STUDY

The United States is a world leader because it participates in events around the world. The United States supports peace talks and human rights efforts. In what ways does the United States act with other countries around the world? (Geography Theme: movement)

## The United States and Africa

In 1992 President Bush used American money and soldiers to help the East African nation of Somalia. Due to a civil war and a long drought, the nation had a **famine**, or a severe food shortage. To save more than one million people from starving, American troops went to Somalia in 1992. They helped the UN deliver food and supplies to Somalians. About 28,000 American soldiers served in Somalia. In March 1994 they returned home.

The United States also helped South Africa. For many years **apartheid** laws kept different racial groups apart in all public places in South Africa. Although black people made up 75 percent of South Africa's population, white South Africans controlled the country until 1993. The United States pressured South Africa to end apartheid. Along with European nations, the United States placed **sanctions** on certain kinds of trade with South Africa.

In 1993 South Africans wrote a new constitution. It gave all racial groups equal rights. In April 1994 national elections were held, and for the first time, all South African adults could vote. Nelson Mandela was elected president, the nation's first black person to hold that office. Mandela won the Nobel Peace Prize for his work in South Africa. In 1999 South Africans elected Thabo Mbeki as the second black president.

The African continent faces a serious health crisis. A disease called **AIDS**, acquired immune deficiency syndrome, causes the crisis. A virus that destroys the immune system causes AIDS. This virus is now the number one killer in African countries south of the Sahara Desert. By 2004, about 10 million African children had lost both of their parents to AIDS.

AIDS is serious because it is spreading fast. It hurts poor families, leaves millions of children as orphans, and destroys the workforce.

The United States and world health organizations are working to prevent and treat the virus that causes AIDS. The United States is providing medicine for AIDS in many villages. But more effort is needed to control this disease.

## The United States and the Middle East

For years the Palestine Liberation Organization, or PLO, had said its goal was to destroy Israel and create a Palestinian state instead. In 1993 President Bill Clinton helped Israel reach an agreement with the PLO. The agreement stated that some of the land Israel had captured in 1967 would be controlled by the PLO. The PLO agreed to recognize Israel's right to exist as a nation.

Clinton also encouraged Israel's eastern neighbor, Jordan, to sign a peace treaty. In October 1994 Jordan's King Hussein and Israel's Yitzhak Rabin signed a peace treaty. It was the second peace treaty between an Arab nation and Israel.

The United States continued to work for peace between Palestinians and Israelis throughout the 1990s. In 2003, the United States and other countries proposed a "road map" for peace between Israelis and Palestinians. The road map lists steps that would lead to the creation of an independent country for the Palestinians. In return, Palestine would work to end violence and terror against Israel. The goal of the plan was to end the conflict by 2005.

## The United States and Yugoslavia

The six republics of Yugoslavia broke up into separate independent nations when communism ended in that country in 1990. Only Serbia and Montenegro remained part of Yugoslavia. Civil war broke out in the new country called Bosnia and Herzegovina. It is often called Bosnia.

Bosnia's civil war began in 1992 among three ethnic groups in the nation. Those groups—Muslims, Croats, and Serbs—fought for control of Bosnia. Serbs captured about two thirds of the country. Then they began killing thousands of Muslims in order to remove them from the region the Serbs controlled.

In September 1995 American leaders met in Dayton, Ohio, with the leaders of Bosnia's three ethnic groups. The United States created a peace plan that the leaders signed. Under that plan Bosnia became a nation with two states. The Serbs control one state, and the Muslims and the Croats control the other state.

In 1997 fighting began in the Serbian state of Kosovo. Many people in Kosovo began fighting for indepence from Serbia. The Serbian army fought against Kosovo and refused to end fighting. In 1999, NATO planes attacked Serbia and stopped the fighting in Kosovo. The state has remained part of Serbia but United Nations soldiers have worked to keep peace in Kosovo.

**Yugoslavia**

Yugoslavia 1946 to 1991
Yugoslavia 1991 to 2003

## ★ MAP STUDY

Communism ended in Yugoslavia in 1990. A year later, in 1991, four of Yugoslavia's six republics broke away to form independent nations. Name the four new countries that were formed when Yugoslavia broke up.

(Geography Theme: region)

In 2003 the leaders of Serbia and Montenegro agreed to be part of a **federation**. The federation is in charge of defense, foreign policy, and money for both countries. At the same time, each country has its own government. As part of the agreement, the county of Yugoslavia was renamed Serbia and Montenegro.

## The United States and Asia

After World War II, the United States helped the Japanese rebuild their nation. Today Japan is the fourth largest trading partner of the United States. Americans **import** large numbers of cars, cameras, and electronic equipment from Japan. But Japan limits the amount it imports from the United States. In 1995 Japan agreed to buy more American cars.

China is the third largest trading partner of the United States. Unlike the Soviet Union, China has remained a powerful Communist nation. In 1989 thousands of Chinese students protested that they wanted freedom and democracy. They gathered in a place called Tiananmen Square in the capital city of Beijing. The protests spread to more than twenty Chinese cities.

The Chinese government sent army troops and tanks to attack the protesting students. At least 5,000 protesters were killed. The United States criticized China's actions but did not try to punish China.

In 2000 the United States granted Permanent Normal Trade Relations, or **PNTR**, to China. There are lower tariffs on goods traded with nations that are given PNTR. This greatly increased trade between the United States and China. Many American businesses now own

▲ In 1989 thousands of Chinese protested in Tiananmen Square in Beijing. They were protesting for freedom and democracy in Communist China.

factories in China. The United States hopes that China will move closer to democracy.

One of the United States' trading partners in Asia is Vietnam. After the Vietnam War, the United States ended all trade and relations with Vietnam. After 19 years President Clinton allowed trade to start again between the two nations. The United States now has an ambassador and an embassy in Vietnam. Vietnam opened an embassy with government representatives in the United States.

## The United States, Mexico, and Canada

The United States trades with many nations around the world. To improve trade with Canada and Mexico, the United States signed **NAFTA**, or the North American Free Trade Agreement. By the year 2009, NAFTA will end most tariffs on products traded between the United States and its neighbors. NAFTA has made it easier for one nation to start businesses and industries in the other nations. It is easier for workers from one nation to get jobs in the other nations.

Many members of Congress did not want to vote for NAFTA because they thought it would cause unemployment in the United States. They feared that American businesses would move to Mexico where they could pay lower salaries to Mexican workers. However, Congress passed the agreement in 1993.

Mexico has large supplies of mineral resources such as silver, gold, copper, iron, and petroleum. Mexico is now the second largest trading partner of the United States.

Although Mexico is working to become a modern industrial nation, it has many problems. Almost one half of the population is poor, and its cities are very crowded. Unemployment and inflation rates are high. Salaries for workers are very low, and Mexico has a huge national debt.

At the end of 1994, Mexico faced an economic crisis. It had an enormous deficit because it had imported far more goods than it had sold to other countries. Mexico owed other nations huge amounts of money. Mexican money, the **peso**, lost its value. To save Mexico's economy, President Clinton agreed to lend $20 billion to that nation. Mexico's president created a six-year plan to improve the economy. Mexico has repaid its debt to the United States, and its economy is improving.

Each year many Mexicans move to the United States in search of better-paying jobs. Although most move legally, many arrive as **illegal aliens**. They come without permission from the United States. As a result, the United States has increased the number of agents that patrol the border between the United States and Mexico. The United States also wants Mexico to do more to stop illegal aliens from entering the United States.

The United States and Canada share the world's longest unguarded border. Although Canada is much larger in size, its population is much smaller. The United States has more trade with Canada than it has with any other nation.

Pollution has been a problem between the United States and Canada. Winds blow American air pollution into Canada where it mixes with rain or snow and becomes **acid rain**. Acid rain has damaged plants, forests, lakes, and animal life in both nations. To reduce the problem of pollution and acid rain, Congress passed the Clean Air Act. The law requires cars and factories to send less pollution into the air.

Both nations have also worked together to clean up pollution in the Great Lakes. The two nations share four of the five Great Lakes. By working together, the water in these lakes has become cleaner. However, it is still not safe to eat certain fish from some of the Great Lakes.

The United States will continue to be a world leader in the twenty-first century.

## Colin Powell 1937–

Colin Powell became a popular war hero during the Persian Gulf War.

Powell grew up in the South Bronx of New York City. Powell's parents were immigrants from the Caribbean island of Jamaica. His parents stressed the importance of a college education, so after high school he attended City College in New York City. There he joined the Reserve Officers Training Corps, or ROTC. The ROTC prepares students to become army officers. After graduating from college in 1958, Powell began his military career in the United States Army at Fort Benning, Georgia.

Powell won a medal for courage while serving in the Vietnam War from 1968 to 1969. He was in a helicopter that crashed. Powell escaped and returned to the burning helicopter to rescue the other soldiers.

While Ronald Reagan was President, Powell became a four-star general. President George Bush appointed Powell to be chairman of the Joint Chiefs of Staff. The Joint Chiefs of Staff are the leaders of the army, the air force, the marines, and the navy. As chairman, Powell was in charge of all the branches of the military. He was America's highest officer. Powell was the first African American to hold this position.

As chairman of the Joint Chiefs of Staff, he made battle plans during the Persian Gulf War. Due to his excellent plans and the work of General H. Norman Schwarzkopf, Iraq was defeated, with a low number of American casualties.

After the war ended, Powell retired from the military. Powell wrote a book, his autobiography, called *My American Journey*. His book tells how a New York City boy became one of the nation's great military leaders. After George W. Bush was elected President in 2000, he asked Powell to be Secretary of State in his Cabinet. Powell became the first African American to hold this important position.

### In Your Own Words

Write in the journal section of your social studies notebook a paragraph that tells about Powell's success as a leader.

## CHAPTER 18 MAIN IDEAS

- The Persian Gulf War started after Iraq invaded the country of Kuwait. The United States, along with other UN nations, brought a quick end to the war. The fighting ended on February 28, 1991.

- On December 25, 1991, Mikhail Gorbachev resigned as leader of the Soviet Union, and the country divided into 15 independent countries. Russia was the largest of these independent countries. Since 1999 Vladimir Putin has been Russia's president.

- President Bush sent money and soldiers to help the East African nation of Somalia, which was suffering through severe drought and famine.

- The United States pressured South Africa to end its policy of apartheid.

- In 1994 President Bill Clinton helped Israel and Jordan sign a peace agreement.

- In September 1995 American leaders helped the leaders of Bosnia's ethnic groups stop the war in that country.

- In 2003 the country of Yugoslavia was renamed Serbia and Montenegro.

- The NAFTA treaty was signed to help increase trade and reduce most tariffs between the United States, Canada, and Mexico by 2009.

## VOCABULARY

**Defining and Using Vocabulary** ■ In the assignment section of your social studies notebook, write the meaning of each word. Then write a sentence for each word.

| | | | | |
|---|---|---|---|---|
| coalition | sanctions | acid rain | AIDS | import |
| apartheid | NAFTA | famine | overthrow | peso |

## USING INFORMATION

**Writing an Opinion** ■ In what region of the world do you think the United States had the most impact as a world leader? Write in your social studies notebook a paragraph that uses facts from the text to support your opinion. Start your paragraph with a topic sentence.

## USING GRAPHIC ORGANIZERS

**Concept Web** ■ Complete the graphic organizer below with information about the United States' role as a world leader.

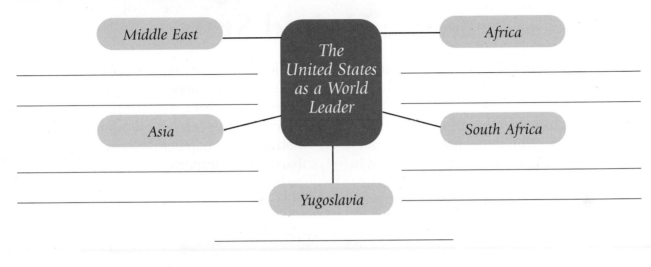

## CRITICAL THINKING

**Cause and Effect** ■ Choose a cause or an effect from Group B to complete each sentence in Group A. Write the letter of the correct answer on the blank. Group B has one more answer than you need.

### Group A

_____ 1. _____ , so Iraq wanted to rule Kuwait to control Kuwait's oil fields.

_____ 2. Many people in the Soviet Union were unhappy with the leadership of Mikhail Gorbachev, so _____

_____ 3. In 1994, all South Africans could vote in a national election, so _____

_____ 4. _____ , so today Japan is the fourth largest trading partner of the United States.

_____ 5. In 1994 Mexico's peso lost its value, so _____

### Group B

A. After World War II, the United States helped the Japanese rebuild their nation

B. Kuwait is an oil-rich country

C. apartheid came to an end.

D. Gorbachev resigned on December 25, 1991.

E. President Clinton agreed to lend Mexico $20 billion.

F. the country elected its first black president, Nelson Mandela.

# Movement: Foreign Oil to the United States

Movement tells how people, resources, ideas, and goods move from one place to another.

The United States imports oil, or petroleum, from many nations in order to meet its energy needs. Oil is measured in barrels. A barrel contains 42 gallons. In 2003 the United States imported 3.5 billion barrels of oil. That oil was brought to the United States on ships from many parts of the world. About eighty–six percent of this foreign oil came from nine nations. The map below shows how many barrels were imported from those nine nations.

**Foreign Oil to the United States, 2003**

**Study the map. Then answer the questions.**

1. From which nation did the United States buy the most oil? _____

2. How much oil did the United States buy from Canada? _____

3. Name a nation in Europe that exports oil to the United States.

   _____

4. Name two Latin American nations that sell oil to the United States.

   _____

5. How much oil did the United States buy from Mexico? _____

# Interpreting a Political Cartoon

Political cartoons are drawn by an artist to express an opinion about an event. The political cartoon on this page shows the changes that were taking place in the Soviet Union in September 1991. Three Soviet republics—Latvia, Lithuania, and Estonia—had declared their independence. Those three republics started the breakup of the Soviet Union. At the time no one knew that by 1992 the Soviet Union would no longer exist.

Read pages 197–198 and pages 203–204 again and study the political cartoon. Then answer the questions.

1. How did the Soviet Union shrink in September 1991?

   _____

2. How did the artist show the cause of the shrinking of the Soviet Union?

   _____

3. What, do you think, was the artist's opinion of the change in the Soviet Union?

   _____

4. What kind of cartoon about the Soviet Union would this artist draw after December 1991? _____

   _____

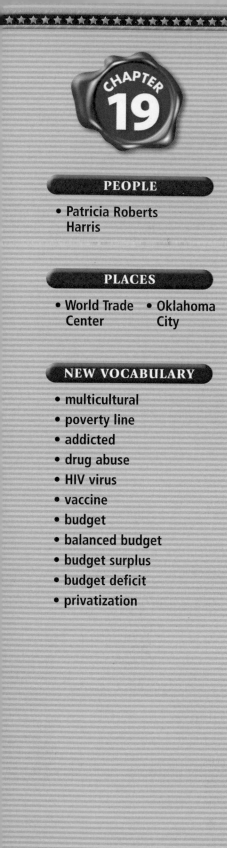

CHAPTER
19

## PEOPLE

- Patricia Roberts Harris

## PLACES

- World Trade Center
- Oklahoma City

## NEW VOCABULARY

- multicultural
- poverty line
- addicted
- drug abuse
- HIV virus
- vaccine
- budget
- balanced budget
- budget surplus
- budget deficit
- privatization

# Challenges Facing American Society

## Focus on Main Ideas

1. How is American society changing?

2. How is immigration to the United States changing?

3. What are some ways that Americans are dealing with the difficult problems of poverty, crimes, drugs, and terrorism in the United States?

4. How can the United States solve its problems?

▲ Social Security card

Americans have solved many difficult problems since the nation first began in 1776. The twenty-first century has brought new problems that Americans will work to solve.

## Changes in American Society

American society is quickly changing in many ways. First, the nation's African American, Asian, and Hispanic populations are growing faster than the white population. For example, today less than half of the students in California schools are white. Because immigrants are coming to the United States from many nations and cultures, the society is becoming more **multicultural**. America's schools must teach children who come from many different cultures and speak many languages other than English.

Second, the American family is changing. Today about one fourth of all children come from homes with only one parent. Most of the time that single parent is the mother.

Third, Americans have more education than ever before. About 80 percent of all Americans finish high school, and many students attend college. People with more education usually earn higher salaries.

Fourth, more women are working at jobs outside of their homes. Women are working in many jobs that in the past were only done by men.

Fifth, American society has more elderly people than ever before. About 35 million people are age 65 and over. The elderly population continues to grow larger each year. Many older citizens depend on Social Security pensions and health care through Medicare. But some government leaders believe the Social Security system will not have enough money to care for the growing population of older citizens. New ways must be found to provide money for the Social Security system.

Sixth, more Americans are now settling in the South and the West. California now has the largest population, and Texas has the second largest. As states gain or lose population, they also gain or lose representatives in Congress. In 2002 California had eight more representatives than it had in 1984. Those extra representatives gave California more power in Congress. Also, since 1964, every President except Gerald Ford has come from the South or the West.

## Changes in Immigration

The United States has always been a nation of immigrants. Yet immigration has

▲ The nation's work force continues to change as more women work at jobs outside their homes. Many women are working at jobs that had once been done only by men. More women today are working as construction workers, doctors, lawyers, and military officers than ever before.

been a debated issue throughout the nation's history. Some people in the United States criticize immigrants for taking jobs away from other Americans. Others complain that immigrants use government benefits that only citizens should receive.

Most immigrants today still come to the United States for better opportunities. Many work hard at low-paying jobs. They earn money and pay their share of taxes. Some immigrants are refugees who have escaped from danger and wars.

Until 1965 immigration laws favored people from northern and western Europe. Immigration laws since 1965 have favored people from Asia and Latin America. A new law passed in 1990 made it easier for people who have special skills to move to America. Today many scientists bring their talents to America. The law also helped people with families already living in this country to become immigrants. In 2003, 455,000 immigrants settled in the United States.

## The Problems of Poverty, Crime, and Drugs

Many Americans now live better than ever before. Since 1995 most American families have earned higher incomes than at any time in history. In 2002 the number

▲ Many of the nation's poor are homeless. They often live in public parks or on city streets. No one knows how many people are homeless, but the number may be as high as seven million. There are many private and public organizations that try to help homeless people.

of poor Americans was about 35 million people. There is still too much poverty in the United States, and more than one third of the poor are children. These children need quality schools and training to give them equal opportunities for success.

The federal government measures how much poverty exists in the nation by creating a **poverty line**. People who have incomes that fall below the line are considered poor. The poverty line changes every year. In 2002, the poverty line for a family with four people was $18,392. A family with four people who earned less than $18,392 was counted as poor. To end poverty, more job training programs are needed. New job opportunities must be created. More housing is also needed for people with low incomes.

The nation's homeless population is another problem. Many of the nation's poor often live in bus and train stations or on city streets. To solve this problem, city and state governments are trying to create more low-income housing as well as emergency shelters.

Crime is another American problem. There are more murders in the United States than in other nations such as Canada or Japan. Crime is sometimes caused by unemployment and a lack of education. Violent television shows and movies may also encourage crime. Because handguns are often used to commit crimes, some people argue that stricter gun control laws may help solve the crime problem.

Much of the nation's crime is caused by the sale and use of illegal drugs. People who use illegal drugs, such as marijuana, cocaine, and heroin, become **addicted** to

▲ Many illegal drugs are smuggled into the country. Federal agencies work to stop illegal drugs from entering the United States.

them. These drug addicts must have the drugs in order to feel normal. Drug addicts often commit crimes to get money to buy more drugs.

The federal government has fought "a War on Drugs" to end the problem of **drug abuse**. Drug abuse means using a drug in a way that is not correct. The War on Drugs costs the nation $19 billion each year, including money spent on treatment and prevention. However, the War on Drugs has failed to solve the drug problem.

### The AIDS Epidemic

Americans first learned about the disease called AIDS in 1981. In 2002, more than 880,000 Americans had the disease. But many more carry the **HIV virus** that

▲ In 1993 terrorists exploded a large bomb in the garage under New York City's World Trade Center. Six people were killed and more than 1,000 were hurt.

▲ In April 1995, 168 people were killed when a terrorist bomb blew up a federal building in Oklahoma City. Most of the building was destroyed by the bomb blast.

causes the disease. People can carry and spread the virus for 10 years before becoming sick with AIDS. Many people who have AIDS die after long periods of illness. There is no cure for AIDS. However, powerful new medicines are helping people with AIDS to live much longer. Pregnant women with AIDS can give the HIV virus to their babies. But if these women take medicines their babies usually do not get AIDS.

AIDS is a serious problem because it is spreading so rapidly. Millions of dollars have been spent on AIDS research around the world. Scientists continue trying to create a **vaccine** to prevent the disease.

## The Problem of Terrorism

If you had visited the United States Capitol in 1986, you would have simply entered and toured the building. If you made that same visit in 2004, you would have been stopped at the door by a security guard. That guard would have checked to make sure you were not carrying a weapon or a bomb. Security guards are needed because of the threat of terrorism.

Terrorism is a growing threat in the United States. In 1993 terrorists bombed the garage under New York City's World Trade Center. In April 1995 terrorists blew up a federal building in Oklahoma City. In 1998 American embassies were bombed in Kenya and Tanzania.

In 2000, terrorists bombed the American Navy ship, the *USS Cole*, in the Middle East country of Yemen. Seventeen American sailors died and many were hurt. You will read more about terrorism in Chapter 21.

## Budget Problems and the National Debt

Every year the President must plan the nation's **budget**. The budget is the plan for how the government will spend tax money to pay for government programs. The budget includes money for defense, Social Security programs, the War on Drugs, and all other expenses of the federal government. The President's budget cannot be put into action until it is passed by Congress.

For many years our nation has not had a **balanced budget**. In a balanced budget, there is enough money from taxes to pay for all government expenses. Instead there has been a budget deficit, or shortage of money, so the government borrowed money to pay for its many programs. To borrow money the government sold bonds. The national debt, the money that the federal government borrows and must repay, grows larger each year. In 2004 the national debt was about $6 trillion. The government used 20 percent of its budget just to repay the interest on the national debt. That money could be used for many other programs.

During President Clinton's first term, Congress passed a bill to reduce the amount of money government could spend. Then in 1997 Congress passed the Balanced Budget Act. This law required the federal government to pay for all items in the budget with tax money. The government could no longer borrow money to pay for its budget. One year later, for the first time in many years, the federal government had a balanced budget and a **budget surplus**. That year the government had $70 billion more than it needed to pay for everything in the budget. During the next three years, President Clinton wrote balanced budgets and Congress passed them.

The budget surplus grew larger each year. The United States had a long period of economic growth. Most people had jobs and the money to buy what they needed. However, in the early 2000s, the government once again began spending more money than it raised in taxes. By 2004, the **budget deficit** had reached a record high of $477 billion. The national debt has grown larger each year.

Since the days when the New Deal tried to end the Great Depression, Americans have depended on the federal government to solve many problems. The federal government now plays a larger role in the lives of Americans than it did before the New Deal. All these services cost money.

Today Americans continue to argue about who should solve the nation's problems and how to pay for them. Some believe the federal government should spend money to end poverty, terrorism, drug abuse, and crime. Other people want state and local governments to solve these problems. Still other people feel these problems may be solved by individuals and by private businesses. Some states have started **privatization** by allowing private companies to run government programs such as issuing driver's licenses. If privatization succeeds, other state governments may have private companies take control of public schools, public hospitals, and public transportation.

As the United States grows and changes, it will continue to try different ways to solve old and new problems.

# Patricia Roberts Harris 1924–1985

Patricia Roberts Harris was the first African American woman to be a United States ambassador. She was also the first African American to serve as a cabinet member to a United States president.

Patricia Roberts was born in Illinois to a railroad dining car waiter and his wife. She received a scholarship to Howard University in Washington, D.C. While in college, she worked for civil rights. In 1943 she took part in a student protest against a cafeteria that would not serve African Americans.

While at Howard, she also met her husband, a professor of law at the university. They were married in 1955.

Harris received a law degree from George Washington University, graduating at the top of her class. After working for a short time at the United States Department of Justice, she became a professor at the Howard University School of Law.

Throughout her career Harris continued to work for the rights of all people. In 1963, President John F. Kennedy made her co-chair of the National Women's Committee for Civil Rights. Then in 1965 President Lyndon B. Johnson asked her to be the United States Ambassador to Luxembourg.

She returned to Howard University in 1967 to teach at the law school. In 1969 she served as the law school's dean.

In 1977 President Jimmy Carter asked Harris to be his Secretary of Housing and Urban Development (HUD). Some senators did not want Harris to take the job. They asked how she could speak for poor people who needed housing.

She replied, "You do not seem to understand who I am. I am a black woman, the daughter of a dining car waiter. I am a black woman who could not buy a house eight years ago in parts of the District of Columbia. I didn't start out as a member of a prestigious [important] law firm, but as a woman who needed a scholarship to go to school. If you think that I have forgotten that, you are wrong."

Harris received the appointment. As Secretary of HUD, she worked for fairness and equal housing for all Americans. In 1980, President Carter appointed her Secretary of the Department of Health, Education and Welfare.

Patricia Roberts Harris died of cancer in 1985. She had worked hard for the rights of all Americans. In 2000 the United States Postal Service issued a Black Heritage stamp in her honor.

## In Your Own Words

Write a paragraph in your notebook that explains why Patricia Roberts Harris deserved to be honored by a Black Heritage stamp.

# REVIEW AND APPLY

## CHAPTER 19 MAIN IDEAS

- American society is quickly changing in many ways.

- Major problems facing the United States are poverty, crime, drugs, and the national debt.

- AIDS is a serious health problem in the United States because it is spreading so rapidly and no cure has yet been found for this disease.

- Terrorist acts are a growing threat to the United States.

- There is disagreement among our leaders in Washington about the best way to solve the nation's problems.

## VOCABULARY

**Find the Meaning** ■ Write the word or phrase that best completes each sentence on the blank.

1. As more people come to the United States from many different countries, American society is becoming more _____ .
   **privatized**        **multicultural**        **addicted**

2. People whose income falls below the _____ are considered poor.
   **budget**        **depression**        **poverty line**

3. Using drugs in a way that is not correct is known as _____ .
   **drug abuse**        **addiction**        **disease**

4. The _____ causes the AIDS disease.
   **cocaine**        **HIV virus**        **drug abuse**

5. The _____ is a plan for how the government will spend tax money to pay for government programs.
   **budget**        **budget surplus**        **national debt**

6. _____ allows private companies to run government programs.
   **Monopolies**        **Budget cuts**        **Privatization**

7. Scientists are trying to create a _____ to prevent AIDS.
   **virus**        **vaccine**        **security**

## USING INFORMATION

**Writing an Essay** ■ There are six reasons why American society is changing so quickly. Explain four of these reasons. Start your essay with a topic sentence.

## COMPREHENSION CHECK

**Choose the Answer** ■ Write the letter of the sentence or phrase that best answers each question.

_____ 1. In what way is the American family changing?

    a. Families are becoming larger.

    b. There are more one-parent families.

    c. All children are more educated.

_____ 2. In what way is American society changing?

    a. American society is becoming more multicultural.

    b. American society is becoming poorer.

    c. American society has fewer elderly people.

_____ 3. What is the government's "War on Drugs" trying to accomplish?

    a. to legalize marijuana

    b. to end drug abuse

    c. to sell drugs in stores

_____ 4. What must happen before a President's budget can be put into action?

    a. It must be approved by Congress.

    b. It must be passed by the Supreme Court.

    c. It must be voted on by the people.

## CRITICAL THINKING

**Distinguishing Relevant Information** ■ Imagine that you are telling your friend about the difficult challenges facing American society today. Read each sentence below. Decide which sentences are relevant to what you will say. Put a check in front of the relevant sentences. There are four relevant sentences.

_____ 1. More women are working at jobs that in the past were done only by men.

_____ 2. Many Americans criticize immigrants.

_____ 3. There are more murders in the United States than in other nations.

_____ 4. Bill Clinton was elected President in 1992.

_____ 5. There are millions of poor children.

_____ 6. Terrorism is a growing threat in the United States.

## PEOPLE

- Mae Carol Jemison
- Ellen Ochoa
- Ben Nighthorse Campbell
- Carol Moseley Braun
- Sally Ride
- Guion Bluford, Jr.
- Christa McAuliffe
- George W. Bush
- Al Gore

## NEW VOCABULARY

- rovers
- orbit
- environmental pollution
- emissions
- global warming
- microchip
- microsurgery
- Internet
- electronic mail
- personal digital assistant
- cell phones
- camera phones
- DNA

# America in the New Century

▲ A computer chip

## Focus on Main Ideas

1. What progress has been made in the field of equal rights and opportunities?

2. How has technology improved life in America?

3. How have Americans harmed their environment and resources?

In 1992 Mae Carol Jemison became the first African American woman in space. The next year Ellen Ochoa, the first Hispanic woman in space, took part in a ten-day space mission. Progress in technology made these exciting space flights possible. In the twenty-first century, women and minorities will continue to win equal rights and opportunities.

## Equal Rights and Opportunities

Prejudice and racism still exist in the United States, but great progress has been made in allowing equal rights and opportunities for all Americans. In 1993 Ben Nighthorse Campbell became the first Native American to be elected to the United States Senate in more than 60 years. That same year Carol Moseley Braun became the first African American woman in the Senate. In 2002, thirty-nine African Americans were elected to the House of Representatives. Sixty-two members of the House were women.

The fight for civil rights has also helped Americans with disabilities. In the past, they were unable to use public transportation, and they faced discrimination when they applied for jobs. The Civil Rights Act of 1964 was the first law

▲ The Americans with Disabilities Act requires that public transportation, businesses, and other public facilities be designed so that all people can use them.

to help people with disabilities. In 1990 Congress passed the Americans with Disabilities Act, or ADA. This law makes it illegal to discriminate when a person with a disability applies for a job. It requires public transportation and public places to be designed so that all people can use them. To help children with disabilities get a better education, Congress passed laws in 1975 and 1997. The 1997 Individuals with Disabilities Education Act, or IDEA, helps all children get a good public school education.

## Progress in Space

After *Apollo 11* went to the moon in 1969, there were other *Apollo* space missions to the moon. New technology made further space exploration possible. In 1981 the first reusable spaceship, the space shuttle, was sent into space. Two years later Sally Ride traveled in the space shuttle when she became America's first woman astronaut. The next year Guion Bluford, Jr., became the first African American astronaut.

In January 1986 Americans were shocked when the *Challenger* space shuttle exploded after takeoff. All seven crew members died, including a teacher named Christa McAuliffe. She was the first civilian to travel in space. All space shuttle missions were stopped for two years.

Shuttle flights started again in 1988. There were many successful flights. Then on February 1, 2003, the *Columbia* space shuttle broke apart as it returned to Earth. Again, all seven crew members were lost, including six Americans and an astronaut from Israel.

Scientists believe the disaster was caused by damage to the panels on *Columbia*'s left wing. Engineers at NASA, America's space agency, are working to find ways to avoid future accidents.

During the 1990s the United States worked with Russia and many other countries to build the International Space Station. This space station is about 250 miles above Earth. It is the most powerful spacecraft ever built. Astronauts can live in the space station for many months while doing space experiments.

In 2000 an American and two Russians became the first people to live and work on the space station. Since that time, more crews have come and gone. Each crew stays in the space station for six months.

▲ *Opportunity* was one of two rovers to explore Mars in 2004.

Scientists at NASA are also studying the Solar System. In 2004 two **rovers** reached Mars. Rovers are spacecraft that can travel on a planet.

Once on the ground, the rovers took photos which were sent back to Earth. Instruments on board the rovers studied samples of rock and soil from Mars. The rovers made an exciting discovery. At one time, there was water on Mars. This could mean that life once existed on the planet.

Then in July of 2004, the *Cassini* spacecraft went into **orbit** around Saturn, a planet far from Earth. The spacecraft traveled almost seven years to reach Saturn. Once there, it took photos of Saturn's rings and moons. The photos were sent by radio signals back to Earth. By studying Saturn's rings, scientists hope to learn more about how the Solar System was formed.

## Protecting Our Environment and Resources

Cars, airplanes, and modern factories are some of the modern inventions that have created **environmental pollution**. Environmental pollution occurs when human activities harm the environment. Factory smoke, car **emissions**, traffic noise, and crop pesticides are some of the things that damage Earth's air, soil, and water.

▲ Recycling is an example of how to use resources wisely.

Some scientists believe that air pollution is causing **global warming**, or a rise in Earth's temperature. Global warming is said to be caused by the burning of oil, gasoline, and coal in order to make energy. To help prevent global warming, scientists will need to find cleaner ways to burn fuels.

The United States is fortunate to have many kinds of resources. America has some renewable resources, such as trees and animals, which can be replaced. Conservation helps us save our renewable resources. To save America's forests, new trees must be planted when forests are chopped down.

Nonrenewable resources, such as coal and oil, can never be replaced if they are used up. As we use up America's supply of oil and natural gas, we become more dependent on other nations to meet our energy needs. This dependence may lead to another energy crisis. We save nonrenewable resources by using less energy.

Scientists are also inventing new ways to produce energy. Wind farms now produce electricity in some states. Solar energy, or energy from the sun, is producing electricity, heating homes, and making hot water.

Recycling is one of the best ways to protect our natural resources. Recycling means reusing old products to create new ones. Glass, newspapers, plastic, and metal products can be recycled and made into new products. Many communities now have facilities or collection places for recycling.

## Technology Improves the Nation

Modern technology can help us care for our environment and resources. Technology has also improved the nation in other ways. Computers are now used in almost every school, business, airport, and hospital. The invention of the **microchip** made it possible to build smaller, cheaper, and more powerful computers.

Technology has improved medical care. Doctors have learned to perform operations by using **microsurgery**, surgery done with microscopes and special tiny instruments. Many types of operations are now done with powerful beams of light called lasers. The lasers can cut without causing damage to surrounding areas.

Technology has also changed the way we communicate. Millions of people use the **Internet**. The Internet is a system that links computers to each other. The

Internet allows people to gather information from other computers around the world. Computer users can also communicate with each other through **electronic mail**, or e-mail.

With a hand-held computer called a **personal digital assistant**, or PDA, you can keep track of appointments, addresses, and phone numbers. You can also use a PDA to check and send your e-mail and play music.

People also communicate with **cell phones**. Cell phones use radio signals to send and receive voices. The newest cell phones are **camera phones**. They can take pictures that can be sent to other camera phones or computers anywhere in the world.

Scientists have also found a way to use **DNA** to help solve crimes. DNA is a molecule that is found in every cell of living things. It contains information about you, such as your eye and hair color. Your DNA is special to you. Unless you are an identical twin, no one else has your exact DNA.

Scientists have learned to collect DNA at crime scenes. They can use the DNA to find out if a person has committed a crime. People who commit crimes often leave skin, blood, or other body cells at a crime scene. The DNA in these cells can be used to link a person to the crime.

Technology is helping to improve the lives of people in the United States and around the world.

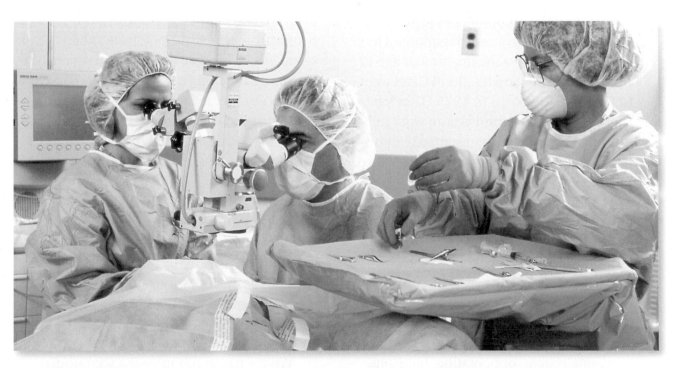

▲ Technology has improved medical care. Many operations that in the past were difficult or impossible to do have become easier. Powerful microscopes allow doctors to see in great detail and to use tiny instruments in surgery. Technology has also helped develop medicines that sometimes make surgery unnecessary.

# Bill Gates 1955–

Bill Gates created Microsoft, the world's largest computer software company. When Gates was a boy, computers were not yet being used in homes and classrooms. He used a computer for the first time at age 12.

After finishing high school, Gates went to Harvard University. In 1975 Gates left Harvard during his third year to work full-time at a company he had started with his friend, Paul Allen. The company was called Microsoft. Their goal was to create computer software for the popular new PCs, or personal computers, that were beginning to be sold. A computer needs different kinds of software in order to do jobs such as typing a report, writing a check, storing information, or making a poster.

In 1980 IBM, an important computer company, asked Gates to create a new operating system, or operating directions, for all of its PC computers. Gates created a new system called the Microsoft Disc Operating System, or MS-DOS. All IBM PCs and similar computers needed MS-DOS to run other software programs. Soon the Microsoft company was earning millions of dollars.

In 1985 Microsoft introduced a new software program called Windows. Windows makes it possible to do several jobs on a computer at the same time.

Microsoft programs are now being used around the world. However, with Microsoft's success have come challenges. In 1998, the United States government took Microsoft to court. The Department of Justice said that Microsoft tried to stop people from using software from other companies. This gave Microsoft an unfair advantage in selling its software. The legal charges were settled in 2004 when Microsoft agreed to allow more competition.

In 1999 Bill Gates and his wife started the Gates Foundation. This organization works to improve health and education in many parts of the world. In 2003 the foundation donated more than $1 billion.

Bill Gates was able to build a giant company because of his own talents and willingness to work very hard.

## In Your Own Words

Write a paragraph in your social studies journal that tells how Bill Gates has helped computer technology.

★★★★★★★★★★★★★★★★★★★★★★★★★★★★★★★★★★★★★★★★★★★★★★★★

## CHAPTER 20 MAIN IDEAS

- Although prejudice and racism still exist in the United States, great progress has been made in allowing equal rights and opportunities for all Americans.

- The United States continues to study space through space shuttles and other spacecraft and was one of the countries that built the International Space Station.

- Technology such as the computer, microsurgery, and lasers have improved the nation.

- Scientists have found ways to use DNA to help solve crimes.

- Environmental pollution caused by factory smoke, car emissions, traffic noise, and crop pesticides is damaging the environment.

## VOCABULARY

**Finish the Sentence** ■ **Choose one of the words or phrases from the box to complete each sentence. Write the word or phrase on the correct line. You will not use all the words in the box.**

| |
|---|
| **electronic mail** |
| **DNA** |
| **ballots** |
| **global warming** |
| **microchip** |
| **microsurgery** |
| **Internet** |
| **emissions** |
| **environmental pollution** |

1. Car _____ damage Earth's air.

2. The _____ made it possible to build smaller, cheaper, and more powerful computers.

3. The _____ is a system that links millions of computers to each other.

4. _____ allows computer users to communicate with each other.

5. _____ occurs when human activities harm the environment.

6. _____ is a rise in the earth's temperature.

7. Doctors use microscopes and tiny instruments to perform _____ .

8. Scientists can use _____ to link a person to a crime.

## USING GRAPHIC ORGANIZERS

**Create an Information Chart** ■ Complete the graphic organizer by listing at least two ways in which Americans have made progress in the areas of equal rights, technology, and the environment.

| Area | How Americans Have Made Progress |
|---|---|
| Equal Rights | |
| Environment | |
| Technology | |

## CRITICAL THINKING

**Making Predictions** ■ Read the paragraph below about America. Then check three sentences that predict what will happen during the twenty-first century.

Many changes are taking place in American society during the twenty-first century. More American women and minorities are gaining equal rights. These Americans are working as doctors, lawyers, and military officers. Technology is also changing the ways Americans live. Personal computers have become a part of many Americans' lives. Also, more Americans are becoming concerned about saving Earth's environment and natural resources.

_____ 1. All the best jobs in the twenty-first century will be held by women.

_____ 2. More Americans in the twenty-first century will use computers.

_____ 3. Recycling will mean more natural resources will be available in the twenty-first century.

_____ 4. New technology will continue to change the lives of Americans.

_____ 5. Fewer people will drive cars in the twenty-first century.

## USING INFORMATION

**Writing an Opinion** ■ How does technology help to improve your life? Write a paragraph in your social studies notebook that uses facts from the text to support your opinion. Start your paragraph with a topic sentence.

# Reading a Flow Chart

A flow chart is used to show a sequence of events. One event follows another on a flow chart.

The flow chart on this page shows the steps that are needed to recycle newspapers and turn them into new paper products. Notice that there are seven events or steps in this flow chart. The steps are numbered, and Step 1 is in the upper left-hand corner of the flow chart.

**The Process of Recycling Newspaper**

1. Newspaper is separated from garbage.

2. Newspaper is sent to a recycling plant.

3. Cardboard and magazine paper are removed.

4. Newspapers are chopped and mixed with water and chemicals to make pulp.

5. Ink is removed from pulp.

6. Pulp is spread over a moving wire screen. Water drips out, leaving paper fibers. Rollers press fibers into a thin layer that becomes paper.

7. **RECYCLED PRODUCTS** Recycled paper is made into new products such as newspapers, paper towels, and egg cartons.

**Study the flow chart. Then write a sentence to answer each question.**

1. What happens in the first recycling step? _____

_____

2. What happens when newspaper reaches a recycling plant? _____

_____

3. What kinds of products are made from recycled newspapers? _____

_____

4. How does recycling newspaper protect the environment and conserve our resources?

_____

**CHAPTER 21**

### PEOPLE

- Al Gore
- George W. Bush
- Tom Ridge
- Osama bin Laden
- Rudolph Giuliani
- Muslim

### PLACES

- World Trade Center
- Pentagon
- Afghanistan
- Pakistan

### NEW VOCABULARY

- popular vote
- electoral vote
- ballots
- recount
- hijacked
- evacuate
- debris
- al Qaeda
- Taliban
- Northern Alliance
- Department of Homeland Security
- intelligence
- Federal Bureau of Investigation

# Americans Face Challenges and Terrorism

▲ Al Gore and George W. Bush were candidates in the 2000 presidential election.

## Focus on Main Ideas

1. How was the 2000 presidential election different from other elections?

2. How did terrorists attack the United States on September 11, 2001?

3. What did the United States do to protect the nation after September 11?

4. What was *The 9/11 Commission Report*?

George W. Bush became the first American President of the twenty-first century. However, his election victory was not easy, and it raised many questions. Less than nine months later, terrorists attacked the United States. Almost 3,000 people were killed, and Americans were stunned and outraged.

## The 2000 Election

The 2000 presidential election was different from most previous elections in the nation's history. More people voted for candidate Al Gore than for George Bush, but Gore lost the election. Gore had won the **popular vote**, or votes by the people. However, the Constitution requires that a candidate win the **electoral vote**.

Each state has an assigned number of electoral votes. This number equals the total number of representatives and senators a state has in Congress. A candidate must get 270 electoral votes to become President. In most states, the candidate who wins the state's popular vote gets all of its electoral votes.

Late on election night, George W. Bush had 246 electoral votes, and Al Gore had 266. Both candidates needed Florida's 25 electoral votes to win. Bush won the state's popular vote by only 537 votes. But Gore wanted many of Florida's **ballots** counted again. He believed there had been problems with the way the ballots were counted. For five weeks Americans waited to see who would become President. Finally, the United States Supreme Court ruled that the Florida **recount** was not fair to all of the state's citizens. The ruling stopped the recount process.

George W. Bush had won Florida's electoral votes. He became the forty-third President of the United States. His father, George H.W. Bush, had been President during the Persian Gulf War. The 2000 election was the first election in which the Supreme Court had ever become involved.

## Terrorists Attack America

Throughout the 1990s, terrorism had become a growing threat. In 1993 Islamic terrorists attacked the World Trade Center in New York City. In 1995 a terrorist bombed the federal building in Oklahoma City. In 1998 two Americans embassies in Africa were attacked. These attacks killed hundreds of people. They did not prepare anyone for the events of September 11, 2001. Terrorists spent years planning to attack America on September 11, 2001. That morning, nineteen terrorists **hijacked**, or took control of, four airplanes and used them as weapons to attack important places in the United States. The attacks killed more then 3,000 people, more than the number of people killed at Pearl Harbor in 1941.

▲ **The Twin Towers of the World Trade Center before September 11, 2001.**

One group of terrorists hijacked a plane that was flying from Boston to California. At 8:45 A.M. they crashed it into the North Tower of the World Trade Center in New York City. Eighteen minutes later, a second group of terrorists hijacked another plane in Boston and crashed it into the South Tower. The two skyscrapers, the tallest in New York City, had 110 floors each and were called the Twin Towers. Burning jet fuel from the plane created enormous fires in both towers.

Police officers and firefighters quickly rushed to the scene to help **evacuate** as many people as possible from the burning towers. The towers burned fiercely for about an hour and then collapsed within minutes of each other. Almost 3,000 workers were killed in the burning Twin Towers.

233

A third group of terrorists hijacked a plane heading for Washington, D.C. They forced it to crash into the Pentagon, the headquarters of the United States armed forces. It is a huge office building located just outside Washington, D.C. The attack on the Pentagon killed nearly 200 people.

A fourth group of terrorists hijacked a plane in New Jersey. They planned to crash it into the Capitol building or the White House in Washington, D.C. However, passengers on the plane learned of the attacks on the World Trade Center from cell phone conversations. They quickly learned that the terrorists were planning to crash their plane in Washington, D.C. The passengers fought the hijackers and tried to take control of the plane. In the struggle, the plane crashed into an empty field in Pennsylvania. Forty people died.

## America Reacts

When President Bush realized that America was being attacked, he ordered the closing of every airport in the nation. No planes were allowed to take off or land. After a few days, airports reopened and planes began flying again.

In New York City, firefighters and police officers had quickly rushed to the World Trade Center. Many died trying to help others escape. Altogether, 343 firefighters and 60 police officers died as a result of the attacks. In the days that followed, rescue workers searched for

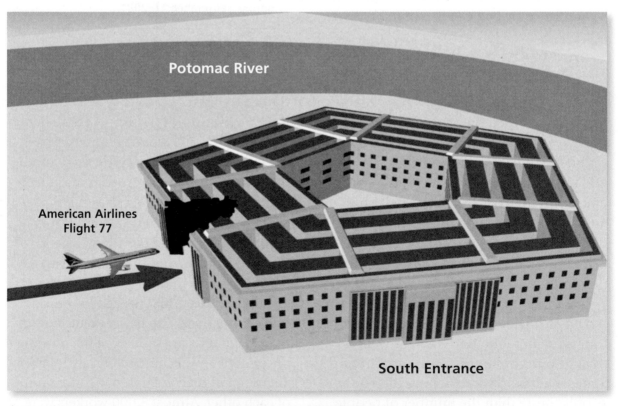

Potomac River

American Airlines Flight 77

South Entrance

▲ Terroists crashed a plane into the Pentagon in Washington, D.C. on September 11, 2001.

survivors. More than 300 specially trained dogs were used to help with the search. One police officer was rescued after being buried for 22 hours under 40 feet of **debris**.

Across the nation, Americans were angered and frightened by the attacks. People wanted to help the victims of September 11. People sent food, blankets, and clothing to the rescue workers. Americans gave blood for the injured. They also gave money to help people who lost family members.

## Al Qaeda and the September 11 Terrorists

Americans learned that the September 11 terrorists were Muslims from Arab countries in the Middle East. They were part of a large terrorist group called **al Qaeda**. Al Qaeda was formed in 1989 by Osama bin Laden, a billionaire from Saudi Arabia. Unlike the terrorists, most Muslims are against terrorism.

Osama bin Laden became a hero to many Muslims by fighting the Soviet Union in Afghanistan. Afghanistan is a Muslim country in Central Asia. The Soviet army took control of Afghanistan in 1978. Muslim fighters fought to free Afghanistan. In 1989 the Muslim fighters forced the Soviet Union out of Afghanistan.

Following the Soviet defeat, bin Laden formed al Qaeda. *Al Qaeda* means "the base." Bin Laden saw Afghanistan as a base to train terrorists. He wanted to overthrow the governments of some Muslim countries and start new governments that agreed with his ideas about Islam. He trained thousands of terrorists in Afghanistan.

▲ Osama bin Laden started al Qaeda and planned the September 11 attacks.

In 1996, bin Laden helped a group known as the **Taliban** take power in Afghanistan. Like bin Laden, the Taliban believed there should be no separation between religion and government. The Taliban forced the Afghan people to obey their ideas about Islam. They made laws that said girls could not go to school and women could not hold jobs. They made laws against watching television and movies. The Taliban protected bin Laden and his terrorist training camps. In return, bin Laden used his wealth and his fighters to help the Taliban stay in power. While he was in Afghanistan, bin Laden planned the September 11 attacks.

## The War on Terrorism

President Bush declared a War on Terrorism. He demanded that the Taliban arrest bin Laden and close all al Qaeda training camps. The Taliban refused. So in October 2001, the United States and some allies attacked Afghanistan. American soldiers captured parts of Afghanistan from the Taliban. A large Afghan rebel group called the **Northern Alliance** also fought against the Taliban. With American help, the Northern Alliance defeated the Taliban.

American soldiers searched Afghanistan for Osama bin Laden but failed to find him. Many people believe bin Laden and other al Qaeda terrorists escaped to Pakistan, Afghanistan's neighbor. Many people think that al Qaeda continues to train terrorists in Pakistan.

Following the war, the United States helped Afghanistan start a new government. The United States and other countries have also given Afghanistan billions of dollars in food and other aid. Hundreds of schools have been repaired and reopened. Millions of textbooks have been delivered to classrooms. In October 2004, free elections were held and the people of Afghanistan elected a new president. Girls have returned to school, and women have begun working again.

## Preventing Future Terrorist Attacks

To prevent future attacks, President Bush and Congress passed some new laws. The Patriot Act was passed in October 2001. This law gave the government more

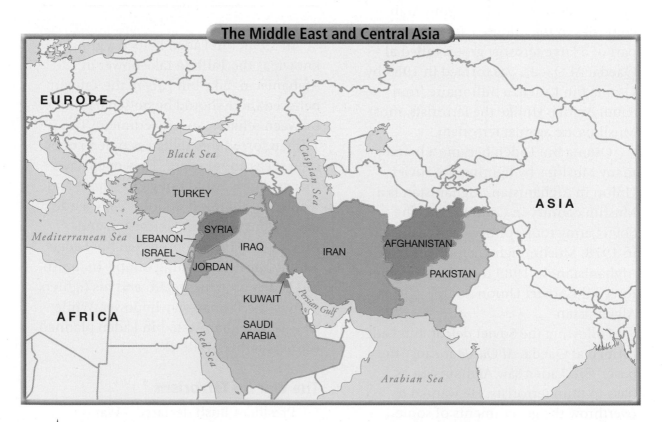

**The Middle East and Central Asia**

### ✴ MAP STUDY

In 2001 the United States began its first war on terrorism in Afghanistan. What countries are located to the west and east of Afghanistan? (Geography Theme: location)

power to search for terrorists. Some people believe the law gave the government so much power that it may threaten the rights of ordinary citizens.

In January 2002 Congress created the **Department of Homeland Security**. The department has the job of protecting America from another terrorist attack. It brings together 22 government agencies. These include the Coast Guard, the Secret Service, and the Border Patrol. In addition, it oversees a new federal agency, the Transportation Security Administration. The TSA protects the country's airports, ports, and railroads. Tom Ridge became the first person to lead the department. The Director of Homeland Security is part of the President's Cabinet.

Congress and the President also set up a special committee. It studied how the September 11 attacks happened and how to prevent future attacks. In July 2004 the committee published *The 9/11 Commission Report*. The report pointed out ways to reform the nation's **intelligence** services. Intelligence means secret information about possible enemies.

The **Federal Bureau of Investigation** and the Central Intelligence Agency are the country's main intelligence services. They have different responsibilities. The FBI gathers and studies intelligence in the United States. The CIA gathers and studies intelligence in other countries.

*The 9/11 Commission Report* said that the CIA needs more agents to collect intelligence in other countries. It also said that the FBI and the CIA must share their information with each other.

Despite these actions, many Americans still worry that there may be more terrorist attacks. Since September 11, 2001, terrorists have attacked several other countries. In October 2002 about 200 people were killed in a bomb attack in Bali, Indonesia. In March 2004 al Qaeda bombed four trains in Spain, a close ally of the United States. That attack killed 191 people.

In the United States, people worked to rebuild and to remember. Within a year of the September 11 attacks, the Pentagon was rebuilt. Plans have been made for new buildings to be built on the site of the World Trade Center. The new buildings will include a place to honor and remember those who died on September 11, 2001.

▲ **United States soldiers on a military base at a former airport in Afghanistan**

## President George W. Bush

On September 11, 2001, President George W. Bush was visiting a school in Florida when planes crashed into the World Trade Center and the Pentagon. He quickly returned to Washington, D.C. That night the President spoke to the nation. Here is part of his speech.

"Today, our fellow citizens, our way of life, our very freedom came under attack in a series of deliberate and deadly terrorist acts. The victims were in airplanes, or in their offices. . . .

The pictures of airplanes flying into buildings, fires burning, huge structures collapsing, have filled us with disbelief, terrible sadness, and a quiet, unyielding [determined] anger. . . .

A great people has been moved to defend a great nation. Terrorist attacks can shake the foundation of our biggest buildings, but they cannot touch the foundation of America. . . .

Today, our nation saw evil, the very worst of human nature. And we responded with the best of America—with the daring of our rescue workers, with the caring for strangers and neighbors who came to give blood and help in any way they could. . . .

Our military is powerful, and it's prepared. Our emergency teams are working in New York City and Washington, D.C., to help with local rescue efforts.

Our first priority [aim] is to get help to those who have been injured, and to take every precaution to protect our citizens at home and around the world from further attacks. . . .

The search is under way for those who are behind these evil acts. I've directed the full resources of our intelligence and law enforcement communities to find those responsible and to bring them to justice. . . .

America and our friends and allies join with all those who want peace and security in the world, and we stand together to win the war against terrorism."

---

### Write Your Answers

**Answer these questions in the assignment section of your social studies notebook.**

1. What did the President say was attacked on September 11, 2001?

2. What was the first priority that day?

3. **Think and Respond** Why do you think the President spoke to the nation that evening? Do you think he was successful?

# Firefighter Kenneth Escoffery's Experience on September 11, 2001

On the day of September 11, 2001, Kenneth Escoffery was a 43-year-old African American New York City firefighter. He was part of a company called Ladder 20. As soon as Escoffery learned about the World Trade Center attacks, he rushed to the scene to help rescue people. In an interview, Escoffery spoke about his experiences that day.

"We realized that the plane had hit the World Trade Center. . . . We decided to go see if we could help. . . . We pulled up in front of the North Tower. . . . We saw the devastation [destruction].

We went into the lobby, which was functioning as the command station. We were told our company was working its way up from the twenty-seventh floor. The chief asked us to check the elevators to make sure everybody was out of them.

We didn't have a radio. We didn't have equipment. We didn't have a mask. We didn't have a flashlight. We had nothing. But we stayed on the staircase for about 40 minutes trying to help evacuate people.

We got into the courtyard when a blast knocked us down. Later on we found out that it wasn't the North Tower but the South Tower that had collapsed then. We went back to look for our company, hoping they got out.

No one had seen Ladder 20. We waited the whole day hoping that we'd hear that the guys in our [fire]house were okay. I think that was the hardest part, when you had the loved ones calling and asking, "Did you see this person?" and you have to tell them, "No, I didn't". . . .

For the first week or two, we went back down to Ground Zero to dig and to search for survivors.

Out of the first sixteen [firefighters from the company] that responded down there, we lost fourteen. Only George and I made it, because the chief asked us to check the elevators and then check the second floor.

I've been to a lot of funerals, too many. Working with guys thirteen years . . . then you come in the firehouse and they're no longer there. . . . Sleeping was really rough the first few weeks."

## Write Your Answers

**Answer these questions in the assignment section of your social studies notebook.**

1. What did the chief ask Kenneth Escoffery to do at the World Trade Center? What was the rest of his company doing?

2. What happened to Escoffery's company, Ladder 20?

3. **Think and Respond** Compare the experiences and feelings of Kenneth Escoffery and those of President Bush on September 11, 2001.

# Rudolph Giuliani 1944–

Rudolph Giuliani was mayor of New York City on September 11, 2001. He led the city through the terrible days after the attacks. His strong leadership helped calm his city and the nation in a difficult time.

Guiliani was born in New York City. His mother and father were Italian immigrants who worked hard to earn a living. From his father he learned the importance of honesty. His father also taught him to love the New York Yankees baseball team. Giuliani went to law school and became a lawyer. He helped put important criminals in jail.

In 1989 Rudolph Giuliani ran for mayor of New York City. He lost to David Dinkins, the Democratic candidate. Dinkins became New York City's first African American mayor. In 1993 Giuliani ran against Dinkins again, and this time he won. Then he was reelected to a second term in 1997.

As mayor, Giuliani worked to reduce crime and make the city safer. He supported new park and building projects and a clean up of the subway. With a strong economy, new jobs and new businesses were created.

On the morning of September 11, 2001, Rudolph Giuliani rushed to the World Trade Center when he learned about the attacks. He spoke to New Yorkers on television at least six times that day, so they would know what was happening and remain calm.

In the days and weeks that followed, Giuliani worked to bring normal life back to the city. He told New Yorkers to go shopping, to eat in restaurants, and to visit theaters again. He asked Americans to begin visiting New York City again. But he never forgot the people who had been lost on September 11. He went to many of the funerals for police and firefighters who were killed on 9/11. He started the Twin Towers Fund, raising millions of dollars for the families of police and firefighters who died. On New York City's darkest day, Rudolph Guiliani was a strong leader.

## In Your Own Words

Write a paragraph in the journal section of your notebook that tells how Rudolph Giuliani helped New York City before and after September 11, 2001.

# REVIEW AND APPLY

## CHAPTER 21 MAIN IDEAS

- George W. Bush won the electoral vote but not the popular vote in the 2000 presidential election.

- On September 11, 2001, nineteen terrorists attacked the World Trade Center and the Pentagon. More than 3,000 people were killed that day.

- The North and South Towers of the World Trade Center burned fiercely for about an hour, and then they collapsed.

- The hijackers belonged to a terrorist organization called al Qaeda. Osama bin Laden started al Qaeda and planned the September 11 attacks.

- President George W. Bush declared a War on Terrorism.

- The United States attacked Afghanistan and defeated the Taliban. Osama bin Laden was not found.

- To protect Americans, Congress passed the Patriot Act of 2001 and a law that created the Department of Homeland Security.

## VOCABULARY

**Finish the Sentence** ■ Choose the word or phrase from the box to complete each sentence. Write the correct word or phrase on the blank.

1. Terrorists took control by force, or _____, four planes on September 11, 2001.

2. Firefighters tried to _____ people from the Twin Towers.

3. _____ is secret information about enemy plans.

4. Al Gore asked that the _____ be recounted in Florida.

5. The people in the _____ were Afghan rebels who fought against the Taliban.

ballots
evacuate
Northern
  Alliance
hijacked
intelligence

## COMPREHENSION CHECK
**Write the Answer** ■ Write one or more sentences to answer each question.

1. Why did the United States Supreme Court stop the recount of ballots in Florida?

   _____

   _____

2. What did terrorists do to the World Trade Center and the Pentagon on September 11, 2001?

   _____

3. About how many people were killed on September 11? _____

4. How does the Department of Homeland Security work to protect the United States?

   _____

5. Who is Osama bin Laden? _____

6. When and why did the United States attack Afghanistan? _____

   _____

## CRITICAL THINKING
**Sequencing Information** ■ Write the numbers 1, 2, 3, 4, and 5 next to these sentences to show the correct order..

_____ A special committee published *The 9/11 Commission Report.*

_____ Terrorists crashed planes into the World Trade Center and the Pentagon.

_____ It took five weeks to decide that George W. Bush won the 2000 election.

_____ The Department of Homeland Security was formed.

_____ The United States attacked the Taliban in Afghanistan but did not find sama bin Laden.

## USING INFORMATION
**Writing an Opinion** ■ What do you think the United States should do to prevent attacks by terrorists? Write a paragraph in your social studies notebook that explains your opinion. Start your paragraph with a topic sentence.

**CHAPTER 22**

### PEOPLE

- John F. Kerry

### PLACES

- Baghdad

### NEW VOCABULARY

- weapons of mass destruction
- inspectors
- World Trade Organization
- European Union
- trade deficit
- No Child Left Behind Act
- tutoring
- foreign oil
- ethanol
- wind energy
- solar energy
- conserve

# The United States in a Changing World

▲ UN inspector

## Focus on Main Ideas

1. Why did the United States go to war against Iraq?

2. What countries are a threat to the United States?

3. How is the United States improving trade with other nations?

4. What problems must Americans solve at home?

Americans worried about future terrorist attacks on their country after September 11, 2001. As the United States tried to work with nations in many parts of the world, it also tried to solve problems at home.

### The Iraq War

The Persian Gulf War of 1991 was fought to free Kuwait from invasion by Iraq. The quick victory brought freedom to Kuwait. However, Iraq's dictator, Saddam Hussein, continued to rule his country.

Under Saddam's rule, Iraq had produced **weapons of mass destruction** that could kill thousands of people at a time. Following the war, the United Nations Security Council ordered Iraq to turn over or destroy all of these dangerous weapons. The American government believed that Saddam was hiding some weapons and disobeying the UN order. So in 1998, President Clinton ordered American planes to bomb places in Iraq where weapons might be found.

After the September 11 attacks, intelligence reports said Iraq still had large amounts of the dangerous weapons. President George W. Bush feared Iraq might use them against the United States or give them to al Qaeda terrorists. In September 2002 Bush demanded that Saddam turn over any

▲ United States soldiers take down a statue of Saddam Hussein during the Iraq War.

weapons of mass destruction to the United Nations.

UN weapons **inspectors** went to Iraq but did not find any weapons. However, President Bush and many other people believed that Saddam was hiding the weapons in Iraq or in a nearby country. Bush thought the United States should go to war against Iraq in order to find and destroy the weapons. He also wanted to remove Saddam Hussein from power. In October 2002 Congress voted for the United States to attack Iraq if Saddam still did not cooperate. In December of 2002 Bush began sending American troops to Kuwait for a possible attack.

President Bush wanted America's allies in Europe to join the war against Iraq. Great Britain, Spain, Italy, and some other nations agreed. France, Germany, and Russia refused. They said they wanted to give the UN weapons inspectors more time to find Hussein's weapons.

On March 20, 2003, the Iraq War began. American and British planes and soldiers attacked Iraq. They captured Baghdad, the capital city, and defeated the Iraqi army. Major fighting ended on May 1, 2003. Saddam Hussein went into hiding. He was no longer Iraq's leader. On December 14, 2003, American soldiers captured him. In June 2004 they turned him over to the new Iraqi government for a criminal trial. As Iraq's dictator, Saddam was responsible for killing at least 300,000 people.

Most Iraqis were happy that Saddam was gone. But terrorists and people who were loyal to Saddam continued to fight. They attacked American and British soldiers and UN workers. They also attacked Iraqi citizens.

The United States and its allies controlled Iraq's government until the end of June 2004. They did not find any weapons of mass destruction. However, they did help Iraq write a new constitution giving the people more freedom. On June 28, 2004, new Iraqi leaders took control of their government. They promised to allow free elections for future leaders.

## Other Threats

Iraq was not the only country President Bush thought was a danger to the United States. In January of 2002 President Bush also said that Iran and North Korea are dangerous. The President said that these countries may have weapons of mass destruction. They may be building these terrible weapons. They may use these weapons against other nations or give them to terrorists.

North Korea is a very poor nation. The people there have little freedom. Despite its poverty, North Korea developed nuclear weapons and the missiles needed to carry the weapons. The United States and other countries pressured North Korea by refusing to trade with that nation. In 2004 North Korean leaders spoke about ending their nuclear weapons program if the United States would help North Korea build trade with other nations. The United States, however, wants UN inspectors to check that North Korea no longer has nuclear weapons.

Iran is a large, oil-rich Muslim nation in the Middle East. Many people believe Iran wants to build nuclear weapons. In addition, *The 9/11 Commission Report* of 2004 said that al Qaeda had used Iran as a place to train terrorists.

## The United States and Trade

The United States today is also working to increase world trade. It is a member of the **World Trade Organization**, which is part of the United Nations. This group of 147 nations makes rules that govern world trade. When there are problems between nations over trade, the WTO decides if rules have been broken.

The United States has trade with many nations. Canada, Mexico, China, and Japan are the largest trading partners of the United States. Trade with China has grown in the last 20 years. China is a communist nation. With more than one billion people, it has the world's largest population. China imports technology and many products from the United States.

Many American companies now have factories in China. Chinese workers earn much lower salaries than American

▲ Chinese factory workers producing goods sold in the United States

workers. By using Chinese workers, American companies save money and earn greater profits. However, American workers often lose their jobs when work is transferred to Chinese factories.

The United States also trades with the **European Union**, or EU. The European Union is a group of 25 European nations. They work together for peace and for trade. There are no tariffs on goods that member nations sell to each other. The United States is the largest trading partner of the EU.

In recent years, the United States has built up a huge **trade deficit**. That means the country imports more goods than it exports. The United States is buying more from other countries than it is selling to them. Some people believe this could be a problem for the economy.

## Solving Problems in the United States

At home, Americans are trying to solve four important problems. The first problem involves education. Many students in American schools are not doing well in reading and math. In 2001 Congress passed an education law called the **No Child Left Behind Act**, which President Bush signed. The law requires all students in grades three through eight to take reading and math tests each year. Students who score below their grade level must be given **tutoring**.

A second problem is that millions of Americans cannot afford health insurance.

**The European Union**

## MAP STUDY

In EU countries, cars and trucks can travel freely across borders within the EU. Which country is surrounded by EU nations?

(Geography Theme: place)

People need health insurance to pay for doctors and hospitals. New ways must be found to help all Americans have health insurance.

The third problem is that the population of the United States is growing older. Currently millions of older Americans receive Social Security money each month. They depend on this money to pay for the things they need. As more and more Americans retire, Social Security claims will increase. Some members of Congress fear that one day there will not be enough Social Security money in the federal budget for all of the nation's senior citizens.

The fourth problem is America's dependence on **foreign oil**. We use oil to make electricity, to heat homes, and to make gasoline for cars. Much of our foreign oil comes from the Middle East. When oil-producing nations there raised prices in 2004, many Americans struggled to pay for expensive gasoline and home heating oil.

The United States must find other ways to produce energy. One type of energy that can be used for cars is **ethanol**. Ethanol is a type of alcohol made from corn, sugar cane, and other plants. It can be used for fuel instead of gasoline. In Brazil, cars using ethanol save about 10 million gallons of gasoline each year.

**Wind energy** is being used to make electricity in parts of Florida, Iowa, and California. Energy from the sun, or **solar energy**, can be used to heat homes. Burning garbage can also produce electricity. In Japan, more than half of the country's garbage is burned to produce electricity.

Americans are also working to **conserve**, or save, energy. One way is to drive smaller cars that use less gasoline. Another way is to use less electricity. By conserving energy, Americans will depend less on foreign oil.

## Democracy in the Twenty-First Century

In 2004 Americans in every state used their right to vote to elect a new President. John F. Kerry, a Democrat, ran against Republican President George W. Bush. Americans re-elected George W. Bush as their President.

For more than 200 years, the United States has been a land of opportunity. Millions of people have built better lives in America. It is also a land where people believe they can improve their communities and build a better nation. Today, thousands of students in every part of the nation volunteer their time to help others. Some spend time helping senior citizens. Other students clean up parks, forests, and beaches. These people are improving their communities and helping their nation.

You can help the United States remain a great land of liberty. By reading newspapers and listening to news reports, you can form educated opinions about the actions our government leaders should take. You can influence members of Congress and the President by writing letters and e-mails to them. Most important, you will have a voice in American democracy by using your right to vote. As you work for America's future, you will be part of the next chapter of America's history.

# Antonia Novello 1944–

As a child, Antonia Novello dreamed about becoming a doctor. Through hard work, she succeeded. Antonia Novello became one of the most important doctors in the United States.

Antonia Novello was born in a small town in Puerto Rico. Life was hard for young Antonia. Her parents were divorced, and her father died when she was young. Antonia suffered from health problems. She spent part of each summer in the hospital. Because she spent so much time in hospitals, she decided to become a pediatrician, or a doctor for children.

Antonia's mother was a teacher and later became a principal. She encouraged Antonia to be an excellent student. Antonia graduated from college. Then she went on to medical school at the University of Puerto Rico in San Juan.

After two years as a pediatrician, Dr. Novello began studying public health issues. People who work in the field of public health try to improve the health of communities.

In 1989 President George H.W. Bush asked Dr. Novello to be the Surgeon General of the United States. The job of the Surgeon General is to provide important health information to all Americans. Dr. Novello was the first woman and the first Hispanic to be the Surgeon General.

As the Surgeon General, Dr. Novello worked hard to teach teenagers not to smoke cigarettes. She warned that smoking causes lung cancer. She spoke out against the dangers of teens drinking alcohol. Novello worked to end teenage drug abuse. She taught Americans that pregnant women with AIDS could give the terrible virus to their babies.

In 1999 the governor of New York asked Dr. Novello to be the New York State Health Commissioner. Dr. Novello created a program that provides health insurance for all poor families in New York.

Dr. Novello has become a role model to many young women and to many Hispanics. She proved that through hard work, people can reach their goals.

## In Your Own Words

Write a paragraph in the journal section of your notebook that explains how Dr. Antonia Novello has worked for better health for Americans. Tell why she is a role model for many people.

## CHAPTER 22 MAIN IDEAS

■ In 2003 the United States fought a short war against Iraq. Saddam Hussein was captured, but weapons of mass destruction were not found. Iraq now has a new constitution and a new government.

■ Iran and North Korea are two nations that are unfriendly to the United States. They may be building weapons of mass destruction.

■ The United States is a member of the World Trade Organization. Canada, Mexico, Japan, and China are the largest trading partners of the United States.

■ The No Child Left Behind Act aims to improve reading and math education in the nation's schools.

■ In 2004 Americans re-elected George W. Bush as President of the United States.

## VOCABULARY

**Matching** ■ Match the vocabulary word or phrase in Group B with the definition from Group A. You will not use all the words in Group B.

| Group A | Group B |
|---|---|
| _____ 1. These are dangerous weapons that can kill thousands of people. | A. inspectors |
| _____ 2. These people work for the United Nations and check for dangerous weapons. | B. ethanol |
| _____ 3. This results when a country imports more than it exports. | C. solar energy |
| _____ 4. This product is made from corn and can be used as fuel for cars. | D. European Union |
| _____ 5. This organization helps nations of Europe improve trade. | E. weapons of mass destruction |
| | F. trade deficit |

## USING INFORMATION

**Writing an Essay** ■ The United States fought against Iraq in 2003. Write one or more paragraphs in your social studies notebook explaining why the United States went to war against Iraq and what happened during and after the war. Start each paragraph with a topic sentence.

## COMPREHENSION CHECK

**Finish the Paragraph** ■ Use the words, names, and terms in the box to finish the paragraph. Next to each number, write the correct word you choose. The box has is an extra word, name, or term that you will not use.

| | |
|---|---|
| solar energy | wind energy |
| Iraq | NATO |
| trade deficit | Saddam Hussein |
| foreign oil | weapons of mass destruction |

In May 2003 the United States defeated **1**_____ in a war. The dictator, **2**_____ , had killed at least 300,000 of his own people. President Bush said that Iran and North Korea are trying to get **3**_____ . In recent years the United States has built up a huge **4**_____ , as it imports more goods than it exports. Americans will use less **5**_____ if they use **6**_____ to make electricity and **7**_____ from the sun to heat their homes.

## CRITICAL THINKING

**Fact or Opinion** ■ Write **F** on the blank next to each statement that is a fact. Write **O** on the blank if the statement is an opinion. If the statement gives both a fact and an opinion, write **FO**. Then write the part of the sentence that is an opinion.

_____ 1. In 2002 Congress voted for the United States to go to war against Iraq.

_____ 2. France and Germany did not support the war against Iraq, but they should have fought with the United States.

_____ 3. The United States must do everything it can to rebuild Iraq.

_____ 4. The United States should work harder to increase trade with China.

_____ 5. The No Child Left Behind Act was passed to help children improve in reading and math.

Study the time line on this page. You may want to read parts of Unit 5 again. Then use the words and dates in the box to finish the paragraphs. You will use one name twice.

**Iranians take 52 Americans as hostages.**
**1979**

**The Soviet Union breaks apart.**
**1991**

**Nineteen terrorists attack the World Trade Center and the Pentagon.**
**2001**

**The United States defeats Iraq in the Iraq War.**
**2003**

1980 — 1990 — 2000 — 2010

**1989**
The Berlin Wall is torn down.

**1991**
The United States defeats Iraq in the Persian Gulf War.

**1993**
The United States signs NAFTA.

**2002**
Congress approves the Department of Homeland Security.

**2005**
George W. Bush became President for a second term.

| | | |
|---|---|---|
| Homeland Security | *Columbia* | China |
| Egypt | Bosnia | George W. Bush |
| Soviet Union | intelligence | World Trade Center |
| nuclear missiles | Americans with | Berlin Wall |
| NAFTA | Disabilities | |
| hostages | Saddam Hussein | |

In 1979 President Jimmy Carter helped Israel and **1**_____ sign the first peace treaty between Israel and an Arab nation. That same year 52 Americans were taken as **2**_____ in Iran and were not freed until Ronald Reagan became President in January 1981. In 1987 Mikhail Gorbachev, the leader of the Soviet Union, and President Reagan signed the INF Treaty to eliminate many **3**_____ . In 1989 the **4**_____ was torn down and the Cold War ended.

To protect disabled Americans, Congress passed the **5**_____ Act in 1990. During the summer of 1990, an army from Iraq invaded Kuwait. In the Persian Gulf War that followed in 1991, the United States forced the Iraqi army to leave Kuwait. At the end of that year, Mikhail Gorbachev resigned, and the **6**_____ fell apart. It became Russia and 14 independent republics.

To improve trade with Canada and Mexico, the United States signed **7**_____ in 1993. The United States helped leaders from **8**_____ write a peace agreement in Dayton, Ohio. To improve trade with **9**_____ , the United States granted the Communist country PNTR.

After the 2000 election for President, the Supreme Court helped decide that **10**_____ would be the 43rd President of the United States.

On September 11, 2001, nineteen terrorists from the Middle East attacked the **11**_____ and the Pentagon and killed almost 3,000 people. To protect the nation from future attacks, Congress started the Department of **12**_____ in 2002.

American technology led to the invention of reusable spaceships called space shuttles. There were many successful flights. But in 2003 the **13**_____ space shuttle broke apart as it tried to return to Earth. All seven crew members died.

The United States captured Iraq's dictator, **14**_____ , after the Iraq War in 2003. In 2004 the 9/11 Commission said the FBI and the CIA must share **15**_____ information with each other. On January 20, 2005, **16**_____ became President for a second term.

# THE WORLD: PHYSICAL

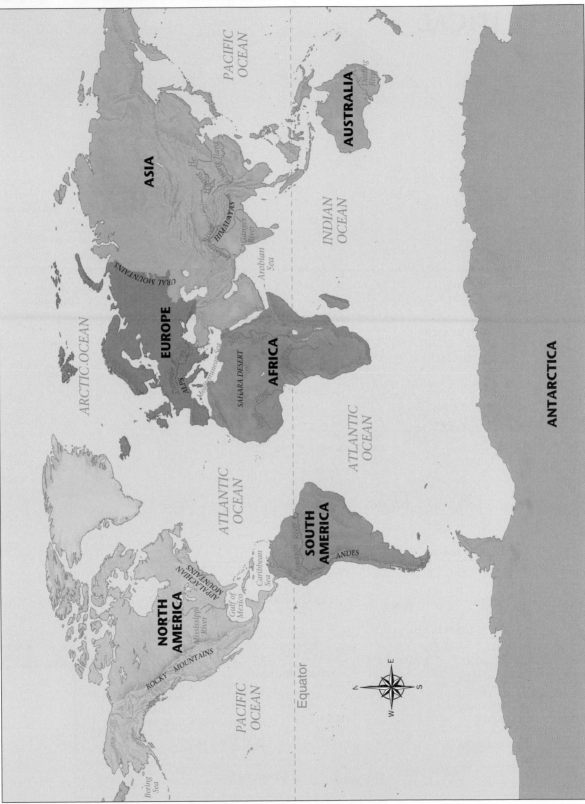

ARCTIC OCEAN

ASIA

He
Shang
Chang Jiang
HIMALAYAS
Ganges River
URAL MOUNTAINS
Arabian Sea
INDIAN OCEAN

AUSTRALIA
Darling River

PACIFIC OCEAN

EUROPE

ALPS
Danube
Mediterranean Sea
Niger River
SAHARA DESERT
River
AFRICA

ATLANTIC OCEAN

ANTARCTICA

NORTH AMERICA

ROCKY MOUNTAINS
Mississippi River
APPALACHIAN MOUNTAINS
Gulf of Mexico
Caribbean Sea

ATLANTIC OCEAN

SOUTH AMERICA
Amazon River
ANDES

Equator

PACIFIC OCEAN

Bering Sea

N
E
W
S

# THE WORLD: POLITICAL

RUSSIA

ALASKA (U.S.)

CANADA

PACIFIC OCEAN

UNITED STATES

MIDWAY ISLANDS (U.S.)

WAKE ISLAND (U.S.)

HAWAII (U.S.)

ATLANTIC OCEAN

MEXICO

Inset, below left

VENEZUELA
GUYANA
SURINAME
FRENCH (FR.)

GUATEMALA
EL SALVADOR

MARSHALL ISLANDS

COLOMBIA

Equator

GALÁPAGOS IS. (ECUA.)

ECUADOR

NAURU

WESTERN SAMOA

KIRIBATI

SOLOMON ISLANDS

TUVALU

TOKELAU (N.Z.)

PERU

BRAZIL

VANUATU

COOK IS. (N.Z.)

FRENCH POLYNESIA (FR.)

BOLIVIA

PARAGUAY

FIJI

TONGA

NEW CALEDONIA (FR.)

NIUE (N.Z.)

AMERICAN SAMOA (U.S.)

PACIFIC OCEAN

CHILE

URUGUAY

ARGENTINA

NEW ZEALAND

FALKLAN (U.K.)

## Caribbean Inset

Gulf of Mexico

U.S.

BAHAMAS

ATLANTIC OCEAN

MEXICO

CUBA

TURKS & CAICOS ISLANDS (U.K.)

PUERTO RICO (U.S.)

VIRGIN ISLANDS (U.K.)

CAYMAN IS. (U.K.)

DOMINICAN REPUBLIC

BELIZE

HAITI

ANTIGUA & BARBUDA

GUATEMALA

JAMAICA

VIRGIN IS. (U.S.)

GUADELOUPE (FR.)

HONDURAS

ST. KITTS & NEVIS

DOMINICA

MARTINIQUE (FR.)

Caribbean Sea

CURAÇAO (NETH.)

ST. LUCIA

BARBADOS

EL SALVADOR

NICARAGUA

ARUBA (NETH.)

GRENADA

ST. VINCENT & THE GRENADINES

BONAIRE (NETH.)

TRINIDAD & TOBAGO

COSTA RICA

Panama Canal

PACIFIC OCEAN

PANAMA

COLOMBIA

VENEZUELA

GUYANA

SVALBARD (NOR.)

ARCTIC OCEAN

Mediterranean Sea

**Inset, below right**

RUSSIA

KAZAKSTAN

MONGOLIA

UZBEKISTAN    KYRGYZSTAN

TURKMENISTAN    TAJIKISTAN

NORTH KOREA

SOUTH KOREA

JAPAN

IRAQ    IRAN    AFGHANISTAN    CHINA

BHUTAN

PACIFIC OCEAN

NORTHERN MARIANA ISLANDS (U.S.)

LGERIA    LIBYA    EGYPT    KUWAIT

BAHRAIN QATAR    PAKISTAN    NEPAL

INDIA

MYANMAR

TAIWAN

SAUDI ARABIA

UNITED ARAB EMIRATES

OMAN

BANGLADESH

LAOS

THAILAND

GUAM (U.S.)

ALI    NIGER    CHAD    ERITREA    YEMEN

8

11    NIGERIA

SUDAN    DJIBOUTI

15    ETHIOPIA

VIETNAM

CAMBODIA

PHILIPPINES

FEDERATED STATES OF MICRONESIA

9

10    12

RIAL    13    14    KENYA

NEA    RWANDA

MÉ &    BURUNDI

CIPE    16

CABINDA (ANG.)

SOMALIA    MALDIVES

SRI LANKA

BRUNEI

PALAU

UGANDA

TANZANIA    SEYCHELLES

MALAYSIA

SINGAPORE

INDONESIA

EAST TIMOR

PAPUA NEW GUINEA

SOLOMON ISLANDS

IC

MALAWI    COMOROS

ANGOLA    ZAMBIA

GAL

BIA    NAMIBIA    ZIMBABWE    MADAGASCAR

EA-BISSUA    BOTSWANA    MOZAMBIQUE    MAURITIUS

EA

A LEONE    SOUTH AFRICA    SWAZILAND

IA

D'IVOIRE    LESOTHO

INA FASO

NA

N

CROON

ON

BLIC OF THE CONGO

RAL AFRICAN

BLIC

CRATIC REPUBLIC

E CONGO

INDIAN OCEAN

AUSTRALIA

N

W    E

S

**Europe Inset**

FINLAND

NORWAY    SWEDEN    ESTONIA

NETHERLANDS    DENMARK    (RUSSIA)    LATVIA

LITHUANIA

RUSSIA

IRELAND    UNITED KINGDOM    GERMANY    POLAND    BELARUS

ATLANTIC OCEAN

BELGIUM

LUXEMBOURG    LIECH.    CZECH REPUBLIC    SLOVAKIA    UKRAINE

SWITZ.    AUSTRIA    HUNGARY    MOLDOVA

FRANCE    SAN MARINO    SLOVENIA    ROMANIA

CROATIA    SERBIA AND MONT.

ANDORRA    MONACO    BOSNIA AND HERZ.    BULGARIA    GEORGIA

PORTUGAL    SPAIN    VATICAN CITY    ALBANIA    MACEDONIA    ARMENIA

ITALY    GREECE    TURKEY    AZERBAIJAN

GIBRALTAR (U.K.)    IRAN

MALTA    CYPRUS    SYRIA

TUNISIA    Mediterranean Sea    LEBANON    IRAQ

MOROCCO    ALGERIA    ISRAEL    (WEST BANK)

LIBYA    EGYPT    JORDAN

255

# THE UNITED STATES: PHYSICAL

PACIFIC OCEAN

RUSSIA
Bering Sea
Bering Strait
ALASKA
Gulf of Alaska
PACIFIC OCEAN
ARCTIC OCEAN
CANADA

PACIFIC OCEAN
HAWAII

MEXICO

CALIFORNIA
SIERRA NEVADA
CASCADE RANGE
OREGON
WASHINGTON
NEVADA
IDAHO
ROCKY MOUNTAINS
ARIZONA
UTAH
WYOMING
MONTANA
NEW MEXICO
COLORADO
NEBRASKA
SOUTH DAKOTA
NORTH DAKOTA
Rio Grande
TEXAS
OKLAHOMA
KANSAS
MINNESOTA
Missouri River
IOWA
ARKANSAS
MISSOURI
WISCONSIN
Mississippi River
LOUISIANA
ILLINOIS
Lake Superior
MISSISSIPPI
INDIANA
MICHIGAN
Lake Michigan
ALABAMA
TENNESSEE
KENTUCKY
OHIO
Ohio River
Lake Huron
GEORGIA
SOUTH CAROLINA
NORTH CAROLINA
VIRGINIA
WEST VIRGINIA
PENNSYLVANIA
Lake Erie
Lake Ontario
NEW YORK
VERMONT
NEW HAMPSHIRE
APPALACHIAN MOUNTAINS
FLORIDA
Washington D.C.
MARYLAND
DELAWARE
NEW JERSEY
CONNECTICUT
RHODE ISLAND
MASS.
MAINE
CANADA

Gulf of Mexico
ATLANTIC OCEAN
CUBA
BAHAMAS

# THE UNITED STATES: POLITICAL

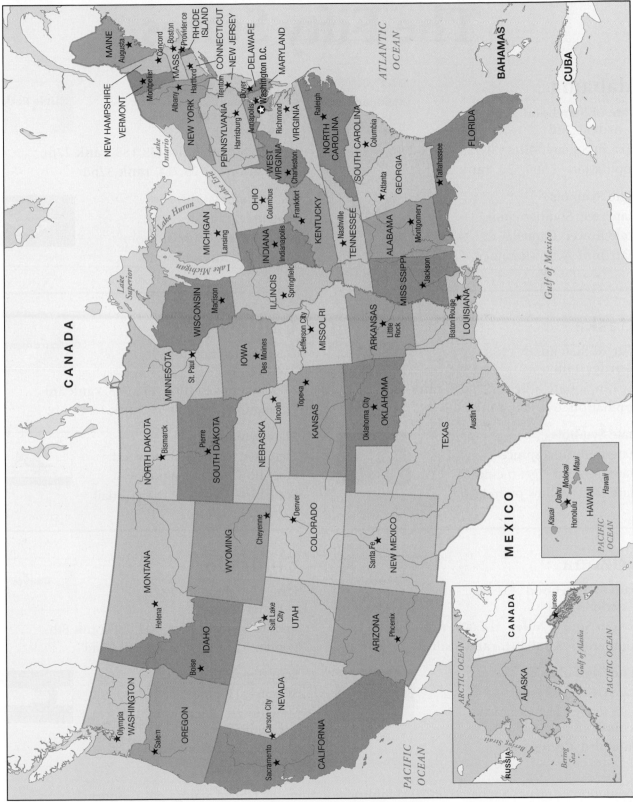

CANADA

MAINE
Augusta ★
Concord ★
Boston ★
Providence
RHODE ISLAND
CONNECTICUT
NEW JERSEY
DELAWARE
MARYLAND
MASS.
Montpelier ★
Hartford ★
Trenton ★
Dover ★
Washington D.C.
Albany ★
NEW HAMPSHIRE
VERMONT
NEW YORK
PENNSYLVANIA
Harrisburg ★
Annapolis ★
Richmond ★
VIRGINIA
Raleigh ★
NORTH CAROLINA
SOUTH CAROLINA
Columbia ★
ATLANTIC OCEAN
BAHAMAS
CUBA
FLORIDA
Tallahassee ★

Lake Ontario
Lake Erie
WEST VIRGINIA
Charleston ★
OHIO
Columbus ★
Frankfort ★
KENTUCKY
Nashville ★
TENNESSEE
Atlanta ★
GEORGIA
ALABAMA
Montgomery ★

Lake Huron
MICHIGAN
Lansing ★
INDIANA
Indianapolis ★
MISSISSIPPI
Jackson ★

Lake Superior
Lake Michigan
WISCONSIN
Madison ★
ILLINOIS
Springfield ★
MISSOURI
Jefferson City ★
ARKANSAS
Little Rock ★
Baton Rouge ★
LOUISIANA
Gulf of Mexico

IOWA
Des Moines ★
MINNESOTA
St. Paul ★

NORTH DAKOTA
Bismarck ★
SOUTH DAKOTA
Pierre ★
NEBRASKA
Lincoln ★
KANSAS
Topeka ★
OKLAHOMA
Oklahoma City ★
Austin ★
TEXAS

MONTANA
Helena ★
WYOMING
Cheyenne ★
Denver ★
COLORADO
Santa Fe ★
NEW MEXICO

IDAHO
Boise ★
Salt Lake City ★
UTAH
ARIZONA
Phoenix ★

WASHINGTON
Olympia ★
OREGON
Salem ★
Sacramento ★
NEVADA
Carson City ★
CALIFORNIA

PACIFIC OCEAN

MEXICO

Kauai
Oahu
Honolulu ★
Molokai
Maui
Hawaii
HAWAII
PACIFIC OCEAN

CANADA
Juneau ★
ALASKA
ARCTIC OCEAN
Gulf of Alaska
PACIFIC OCEAN
Bering Strait
Bering Sea
RUSSIA

257

# The Fifty States

## Alabama

Date of Statehood 1819,
 order 22nd
Area in Square Miles 51,718, **rank** 29th
Population 4,500,752, **rank** 23rd

**State Symbols**
State tree Southern pine
State flower Camellia
State bird Yellowhammer

## Alaska

Date of Statehood 1959,
 order 49th
Area in Square Miles 589,878, **rank** 1st
Population 648,818, **rank** 46th

**State Symbols**
State tree Sitka spruce
State flower Forget-me-not
State bird Willow ptarmigan

## Arizona

Date of Statehood 1912,
 order 48th
Area in Square Miles 114,007, **rank** 6th
Population 5,580,811, **rank** 18th

**State Symbols**
State tree Paloverde
State flower Saguaro cactus
 blossom
State bird Cactus wren

## Arkansas

Date of Statehood 1836,
 order 25th
Area in Square Miles 53,183, **rank** 27th
Population 2,725,714, **rank** 32nd

**State Symbols**
State tree Pine tree
State flower Apple blossom
State bird Mockingbird

## California

Date of Statehood 1850,
 order 31st
Area in Square Miles 158,648, **rank** 3rd
Population 35,484,453, **rank** 1st

**State Symbols**
State tree California redwood
State flower Golden poppy
State bird California valley quail

## Colorado

Date of Statehood 1876,
 order 38th
Area in Square Miles 104,091, **rank** 8th
Population 4,550,688, **rank** 22nd

**State Symbols**
State tree Blue spruce
State flower Rocky Mountain
 columbine
State bird Lark bunting

Population estimates are based on 2003 information from the United States Census Bureau.

# Connecticut

Date of Statehood  1788,
    order 5th
Area in Square Miles  5,006, rank 48th
Population  3,483,372, rank 29th

**State Symbols**

State tree  White oak
State flower  Mountain laurel
State bird  Robin

# Georgia

Date of Statehood  1788,
    order 4th
Area in Square Miles  58,930, rank 21st
Population  8,684,715, rank 9th

**State Symbols**

State tree  Live oak
State flower  Cherokee rose
State bird  Brown thrasher

# Delaware

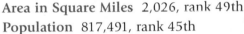

Date of Statehood  1787,
    order 1st
Area in Square Miles  2,026, rank 49th
Population  817,491, rank 45th

**State Symbols**

State tree  American holly
State flower  Peach blossom
State bird  Blue hen chicken

# Hawaii

Date of Statehood  1959,
    order 50th
Area in Square Miles  6,459, rank 47th
Population  1,257,608, rank 42nd

**State Symbols**

State tree  Kukui
State flower  Yellow hibiscus
State bird  Nene (Hawaiian goose)

# Florida

Date of Statehood  1845,
    order 27th
Area in Square Miles  58,681, rank 22nd
Population  17,019,068, rank 4th

**State Symbols**
State tree  Sabal palmetto palm
State flower  Orange blossom
State bird  Mockingbird

# Idaho

Date of Statehood  1890,
    order 43rd
Area in Square Miles  83,574, rank 13th
Population  1,366,332, rank 39th

**State Symbols**
State tree  White pine
State flower  Syringa
State bird  Mountain bluebird

# Illinois

Date of Statehood  1818,
   **order** 21st
Area in Square Miles  56,343, **rank** 24th
Population  12,653,544, **rank** 5th

## State Symbols
State tree  White oak
State flower  Native violet
State bird  Cardinal

# Indiana

Date of Statehood  1816,
   **order** 19th
Area in Square Miles  36,185, **rank** 38th
Population  6,195,643, **rank** 14th

## State Symbols
State tree  Tulip tree
State flower  Peony
State bird  Cardinal

# Iowa

Date of Statehood  1846,
   **order** 29th
Area in Square Miles  56,276, **rank** 25th
Population  2,944,062, **rank** 30th

## State Symbols
State tree  Oak
State flower  Wild rose
State bird  Eastern goldfinch

# Kansas

Date of Statehood  1861,
   **order** 34th
Area in Square Miles  82,282, **rank** 14th
Population  2,723,507, **rank** 33rd

## State Symbols
State tree  Cottonwood
State flower  Sunflower
State bird  Western meadowlark

# Kentucky

Date of Statehood  1792,
   **order** 15th
Area in Square Miles  40,395, **rank** 37th
Population  4,117,827, **rank** 26th

## State Symbols
State tree  Kentucky coffee tree
State flower  Goldenrod
State bird  Kentucky cardinal

# Louisiana

Date of Statehood  1812,
   **order** 18th
Area in Square Miles  47,752, **rank** 31st
Population  4,496,334, **rank** 24th

## State Symbols
State tree  Bald cypress
State flower  Magnolia
State bird  Brown pelican

# Maine

Date of Statehood  1820,
   **order** 23rd
Area in Square Miles  33,128, **rank** 39th
2003 pop estimate  1,305,728, **rank** 40th

**State Symbols**

State tree  White pine
State flower  White pine cone
   & tassel
State bird  Chickadee

---

# Maryland

Date of Statehood  1788,
   **order** 7th
Area in Square Miles  10,455, **rank** 42nd
Population  5,508,909, **rank** 19th

**State Symbols**

State tree  White oak
State flower  Black-eyed Susan
State bird  Baltimore oriole

---

# Massachusetts

Date of Statehood  1788,
   **order** 6th
Area in Square Miles  8,257, **rank** 45th
Population  6,433,422, **rank** 13th

**State Symbols**

State tree  American elm
State flower  Mayflower
   (trailing arbutus)
State bird  Chickadee

---

# Michigan

Date of Statehood  1837,
   **order** 26th
Area in Square Miles  58,513, **rank** 23rd
Population  10,079,985, **rank** 8th

**State Symbols**
State tree  White pine
State flower  Apple blossom
State bird  Robin

---

# Minnesota

Date of Statehood  1858,
   **order** 32nd
Area in Square Miles  84,397, **rank** 12th
Population  5,059,375, **rank** 21st

**State Symbols**

State tree  Norway pine
State flower  Pink and white lady's
   slipper
State bird  Common loon

---

# Mississippi

Date of Statehood  1817,
   **order** 20th
Area in Square Miles  47,716, **rank** 32nd
Population  2,881,281, **rank** 31st

**State Symbols**

State tree  Magnolia
State flower  Magnolia
State bird  Mockingbird

# Missouri

Date of Statehood  1821,
  **order** 24th
Area in Square Miles  69,686, **rank** 19th
Population  5,704,484, **rank** 17th

**State Symbols**
State tree  Flowering dogwood
State flower  Hawthorn
State bird  Bluebird

# Montana

Date of Statehood  1889,
  **order** 41st
Area in Square Miles  147,047, **rank** 4th
Population  917,621, **rank** 44th

**State Symbols**
State tree  Ponderosa pine
State flower  Bitterroot
State bird  Western meadowlark

# Nebraska

Date of Statehood  1867,
  **order** 37th
Area in Square Miles  77,359, **rank** 15th
Population  1,739,291, **rank** 38th

**State Symbols**
State tree  Cottonwood
State flower  Goldenrod
State bird  Western meadowlark

# Nevada

Date of Statehood  1864,
  **order** 36th
Area in Square Miles  110,561, **rank** 7th
Population  2,241,154, **rank** 35th

**State Symbols**
State tree  Single-leaf piñon &
  bristlecone pine
State flower  Sagebrush
State bird  Mountain bluebird

# New Hampshire

Date of Statehood  1788,
  **order** 9th
Area in Square Miles  9,283, **rank** 44th
Population  1,287,687, **rank** 41st

**State Symbols**
State tree  White birch
State flower  Purple lilac
State bird  Purple finch

# New Jersey

Date of Statehood  1787,
  **order** 3rd
Area in Square Miles  7,790, **rank** 46th
Population  8,638,396, **rank** 10th

**State Symbols**
State tree  Red oak
State flower  Purple violet
State bird  Eastern goldfinch

## New Mexico

Date of Statehood  1912,
   **order** 47th
**Area in Square Miles**  121,593, **rank** 5th
Population  1,874,614, **rank** 36th

**State Symbols**
**State tree**  Piñon
**State flower**  Yucca
**State bird**  Roadrunner

## New York

Date of Statehood  1788,
   **order** 11th
**Area in Square Miles**  49,112, **rank** 30th
Population  19,190,115, **rank** 3rd

**State Symbols**
**State tree**  Sugar maple
**State flower**  Rose
**State bird**  Bluebird

## North Carolina

Date of Statehood  1789,
   **order** 12th
**Area in Square Miles**  52,672, **rank** 28th
Population  8,407,248, **rank** 11th

**State Symbols**
**State tree**  Pine
**State flower**  Flowering dogwood
**State bird**  Cardinal

## North Dakota

Date of Statehood  1889,
   **order** 39th
**Area in Square Miles**  70,704, **rank** 17th
Population  633,837, **rank** 48th

**State Symbols**
**State tree**  American elm
**State flower**  Wild prairie rose
**State bird**  Western meadowlark

## Ohio

Date of Statehood  1803,
   **order** 17th
**Area in Square Miles**  41,328, **rank** 35th
Population  11,435,798, **rank** 7th

**State Symbols**
**State tree**  Buckeye
**State flower**  Scarlet carnation
**State bird**  Cardinal

## Oklahoma

Date of Statehood  1907,
   **order** 46th
**Area in Square Miles**  69,919, **rank** 18th
Population  3,511,532, **rank** 28th

**State Symbols**
**State tree**  Redbud
**State flower**  Mistletoe
**State bird**  Scissortailed flycatcher

## Oregon

Date of Statehood  1859,
   **order** 33rd
Area in Square Miles  97,052, **rank** 10th
Population  3,559,596, **rank** 27th

**State Symbols**
State tree  Douglas fir
State flower  Oregon grape
State bird  Western meadowlark

## South Carolina

Date of Statehood  1788,
   **order** 8th
Area in Square Miles  31,113, **rank** 40th
Population  4,147,152, **rank** 25th

**State Symbols**
State tree  Palmetto
State flower  Yellow jessamine
State bird  Carolina wren

## Pennsylvania

Date of Statehood  1787,
   **order** 2nd
Area in Square Miles  45,308, **rank** 33rd
Population  12,365,455, **rank** 6th

**State Symbols**
State tree  Hemlock
State flower  Mountain laurel
State bird  Ruffed grouse

## South Dakota

Date of Statehood  1889,
   **order** 40th
Area in Square Miles  77,122, **rank** 16th
Population  764,309, **rank** 46th

**State Symbols**
State tree  Black Hills spruce
State flower  American
   pasqueflower
State bird  Ring-necked pheasant

## Rhode Island

Date of Statehood  1790,
   **order** 13th
Area in Square Miles  1,213, **rank** 50th
Population  1,076,164, **rank** 43rd

**State Symbols**
State tree  Red maple
State flower  Violet
State bird  Rhode Island Red

## Tennessee

Date of Statehood  1796,
   **order** 16th
Area in Square Miles  42,146, **rank** 34th
Population  5,841,748, **rank** 16th

**State Symbols**
State tree  Tulip poplar
State flower  Iris
State bird  Mockingbird

# Texas

Date of Statehood  1845,
   order 28th
Area in Square Miles  266,874, **rank** 2nd
Population  22,118,509, **rank** 2nd

State Symbols
State tree  Pecan
State flower  Bluebonnet
State bird  Mockingbird

# Utah

Date of Statehood  1896,
   **order** 45th
Area in Square Miles  84,905, **rank** 11th
Population  2,351,467, **rank** 34th

State Symbols
State tree  Blue spruce
State flower  Sego lily
State bird  Seagull

# Vermont

Date of Statehood  1791,
   order 14th
Area in Square Miles  9,615, **rank** 43rd
Population  619,107, **rank** 49th

State Symbols
State tree  Sugar maple
State flower  Red clover
State bird  Hermit thrush

# Virginia

Date of Statehood  1788,
   order 10th
Area in Square Miles  40,598, **rank** 36th
Population  7,386,330, **rank** 12th

State Symbols
State tree  Flowering dogwood
State flower  Flowering dogwood
State bird  Cardinal

# Washington

Date of Statehood  1889,
   order 42nd
Area in Square Miles  68,126, **rank** 20th
Population  6,131,445, **rank** 15th

State Symbols
State tree  Western hemlock
State flower  Coast rhododendron
State bird  Willow goldfinch or wild canary

# West Virginia

Date of Statehood  1863,
   order 35th
Area in Square Miles  24,231, **rank** 41st
Population  1,810,354, **rank** 37th

State Symbols
State tree  Sugar maple
State flower  Rhododendron
State bird  Cardinal

# Wisconsin

Date of Statehood  1848,
   order 30th
Area in Square Miles  56,145, **rank** 26th
Population  5,472,299, **rank** 20th

State Symbols
State tree  Sugar maple
State flower  Wood violet
State bird  Robin

# Wyoming

Date of Statehood  1890,
   order 44th
Area in Square Miles  97,914, **rank** 9th
Population  501,242, **rank** 50th

State Symbols
State tree  Cottonwood
State flower  Indian paintbrush
State bird  Western meadowlark

# Territories and Possessions of the United States

## District of Columbia

Status  federal district
Area in Square Miles  68
Population  563,384

Symbols
Tree  Scarlet oak
Flower  American beauty rose
Bird  Wood thrush

## American Virgin Islands

Status  territory
Area in Square Miles  151
Population  124,778

Symbols
Tree  n.a.
Flower  Yellow elder
Bird  Yellow breast

## Puerto Rico

Status  commonwealth
Area in Square Miles  3,515
Population  3,878,532

Symbols
Tree  Ceiba
Flower  Maga
Bird  Reinita

## Guam

Status  territory
Area in Square Miles  209
Population  163,941

Symbols
Tree  Ifit (Intsiabijuga)
Flower  Puti Tai Nobio
  (Bougainvillea)
Bird  Toto (Fruit dove)

## Northern Marianas

Status  commonwealth
Area in Square Miles  184
Population  78,252

Symbols
Tree  n.a.
Flower  n.a.
Bird  n.a.

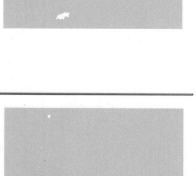

## American Samoa

Status  territory
Area in Square Miles  77
Population  57,902

Symbols
Tree  Ava
Flower  Paogo
Bird  n.a.

n.a. = not applicable/not available

# The Presidents
## of the United States of America

**George Washington**
**1789–1797**
**Born:** 1732 in Westmoreland County, Virginia
**Died:** 1799
**Elected from:** Virginia
**Party:** none
**Vice President:** John Adams

**John Adams**
**1797–1801**
**Born:** 1735 in Braintree (now Quincy), Massachusetts
**Died:** 1826
**Elected from:** Massachusetts
**Party:** Federalist
**Vice President:** Thomas Jefferson

**Thomas Jefferson**
**1801–1809**
**Born:** 1743 in Goochland (now Albemarle) County, Virginia
**Died:** 1826
**Elected from:** Virginia
**Party:** Democratic-Republican
**Vice Presidents:** Aaron Burr, George Clinton

**James Madison**
**1809–1817**
**Born:** 1751 in Port Conway, Virginia
**Died:** 1836
**Elected from:** Virginia
**Party:** Democratic-Republican
**Vice Presidents:** George Clinton, Elbridge Gerry

**James Monroe**
**1817–1825**
**Born:** 1758 in Westmoreland County, Virginia
**Died:** 1831
**Elected from:** Virginia
**Party:** Democratic-Republican
**Vice President:** Daniel D. Tompkins

**John Quincy Adams**
**1825–1829**
**Born:** 1767 in Braintree (now Quincy), Massachusetts
**Died:** 1848
**Elected from:** Massachusetts
**Party:** Democratic-Republican
**Vice President:** John C. Calhoun

## Andrew Jackson
**1829–1837**
**Born:** 1767 in Waxhaw, South Carolina
**Died:** 1845
**Elected from:** Tennessee
**Party:** Democratic
**Vice Presidents:** John C. Calhoun, Martin Van Buren

## Martin Van Buren
**1837–1841**
**Born:** 1782 in Kinderhook, New York
**Died:** 1862
**Elected from:** New York
**Party:** Democratic
**Vice President:** Richard M. Johnson

## William Henry Harrison
**1841**
**Born:** 1773 in Berkeley, Virginia
**Died:** 1841
**Elected from:** Ohio
**Party:** Whig
**Vice President:** John Tyler

## John Tyler
**1841–1845**
**Born:** 1790 in Charles City County, Virginia
**Died:** 1862
**Elected as V.P. from:** Virginia
**Party:** Whig
**Vice President:** None

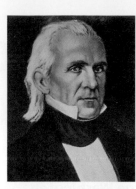

## James K. Polk
**1845–1849**
**Born:** 1795 in Mecklenburg County, North Carolina
**Died:** 1849
**Elected from:** Tennessee
**Party:** Democratic
**Vice President:** George M. Dallas

## Zachary Taylor
**1849–1850**
**Born:** 1784 in Orange County, Virginia
**Died:** 1850
**Elected from:** Louisiana
**Party:** Whig
**Vice President:** Millard Fillmore

## Millard Fillmore
**1850–1853**
**Born:** 1800 in Cayuga County, New York
**Died:** 1874
Elected as V.P. from: New York
**Party:** Whig
**Vice President:** None

## Franklin Pierce
**1853–1857**
**Born:** 1804 in Hilsboro, New Hampshire
**Died:** 1869
**Elected from:** New Hampshire
**Party:** Democratic
**Vice President:** William R. King

### James Buchanan
### 1857–1861

**Born:** 1791 in Stony Batter, Pennsylvania
**Died:** 1868
**Elected from:** Pennsylvania
**Party:** Democratic
**Vice President:** John C. Breckinridge

### Abraham Lincoln
### 1861–1865

**Born:** 1809 near Hodgenville, Kentucky
**Died:** 1865
**Elected from:** Illinois
**Party:** Republican
**Vice Presidents:** Hannibal Hamlin, Andrew Johnson

### Andrew Johnson
### 1865–1869

**Born:** 1808 in Raleigh, North Carolina
**Died:** 1875
**Elected as V.P. from:** Tennessee
**Party:** Democratic
**Vice President:** None

### Ulysses S. Grant
### 1869–1877

**Born:** 1822 in Point Pleasant, Ohio
**Died:** 1885
**Elected from:** Illinois
**Party:** Republican
**Vice Presidents:** Schuyler Colfax, Henry Wilson

### Rutherford B. Hayes
### 1877–1881

**Born:** 1822 in Delaware, Ohio
**Died:** 1893
**Elected from:** Ohio
**Party:** Republican
**Vice President:** William A. Wheeler

### James A. Garfield
### 1881

**Born:** 1831 in Orange, Ohio
**Died:** 1881
**Elected from:** Ohio
**Party:** Republican
**Vice President:** Chester A. Arthur

### Chester A. Arthur
### 1881–1885

**Born:** 1830 in Fairfield, Vermont
**Died:** 1886
**Elected as V.P. from:** New York
**Party:** Republican
**Vice President:** None

### Grover Cleveland
### 1885–1889

**Born:** 1837 in Caldwell, New Jersey
**Died:** 1908
**Elected from:** New York
**Party:** Democratic
**Vice President:** Thomas A. Hendricks

### Benjamin Harrison
### 1889–1893
**Born:** 1833 in North Bend, Ohio
**Died:** 1901
**Elected from:** Indiana
**Party:** Republican
**Vice President:** Levi P. Morton

### William Howard Taft
### 1909–1913
**Born:** 1857 in Cincinnati, Ohio
**Died:** 1931
**Elected from:** Ohio
**Party:** Republican
**Vice President:** James S. Sherman

### Grover Cleveland
### 1893–1897
**Born:** 1837 in Caldwell, New Jersey
**Died:** 1908
**Elected from:** New York
**Party:** Democratic
**Vice President:** Adlai E. Stevenson

### Woodrow Wilson
### 1913–1921
**Born:** 1856 in Staunton, Virginia
**Died:** 1924
**Elected from:** New Jersey
**Party:** Democratic
**Vice President:** Thomas R. Marshall

### William McKinley
### 1897–1901
**Born:** 1843 in Niles, Ohio
**Died:** 1901
**Elected from:** Ohio
**Party:** Republican
**Vice Presidents:** Garret A. Hobart, Theodore Roosevelt

### Warren G. Harding
### 1921–1923
**Born:** 1865 in Corsica (now Blooming Grove), Ohio
**Died:** 1923
**Elected from:** Ohio
**Party:** Republican
**Vice President:** Calvin Coolidge

### Theodore Roosevelt
### 1901–1909
**Born:** 1858 in New York City, New York
**Died:** 1919
**Elected as V.P. from:** New York
**Party:** Republican
**Vice President:** Charles W. Fairbanks

### Calvin Coolidge
### 1923–1929
**Born:** 1872 in Plymouth Notch, Vermont
**Died:** 1933
**Elected as V.P. from:** Massachusetts
**Party:** Republican
**Vice President:** Charles G. Dawes

### Herbert Hoover
### 1929–1933
**Born:** 1874 in West
Branch, Iowa
**Died:** 1964
**Elected from:** California
**Party:** Republican
**Vice President:** Charles
Curtis

### Franklin D. Roosevelt
### 1933–1945
**Born:** 1882 in Hyde Park,
New York
**Died:** 1945
**Elected from:** New York
**Party:** Democratic
**Vice Presidents:** John N.
Garner, Henry A. Wallace,
Harry S. Truman

### Harry S Truman
### 1945–1953
**Born:** 1884 in Lamar,
Missouri
**Died:** 1972
Elected as V.P. from:
Missouri
**Party:** Democratic
**Vice President:** Alben W.
Barkley

### Dwight D. Eisenhower
### 1953–1961
**Born:** 1890 in Denison,
Texas
**Died:** 1969
**Elected from:** New York
**Party:** Republican
**Vice President:** Richard M.
Nixon

### John F. Kennedy
### 1961–1963
**Born:** 1917 in Brookline,
Massachusetts
**Died:** 1963
**Elected from:**
Massachusetts
**Party:** Democratic
**Vice President:** Lyndon B.
Johnson

### Lyndon B. Johnson
### 1963–1969
**Born:** 1908 in Stonewall,
Texas
**Died:** 1973
**Elected from:** Texas
**Party:** Democratic
**Vice President:** Hubert H.
Humphrey

### Richard M. Nixon
### 1969–1974
**Born:** 1913 in Yorba Linda,
California
**Died:** 1994
**Elected from:** New York
**Party:** Republican
**Vice President:** Spiro T.
Agnew, Gerald R. Ford

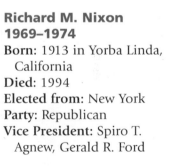

### Gerald R. Ford
### 1974–1977
**Born:** 1913 in Omaha,
Nebraska
**Party:** Republican
**Vice President:** Nelson A.
Rockefeller

### Jimmy Carter
### 1977–1981
**Born:** 1924 in Plains, Georgia
**Elected from:** Georgia
**Party:** Democratic
**Vice President:** Walter F. Mondale

### William J. Clinton
### 1993–2001
**Born:** 1946 in Hope, Arkansas
**Elected from:** Arkansas
**Party:** Democratic
**Vice President:** Albert Gore, Jr.

### Ronald Reagan
### 1981–1989
**Born:** 1911 in Tampico, Illinois
**Died:** 2004
**Elected from:** California
**Party:** Republican
**Vice President:** George Bush

### George W. Bush
### 2001–
**Born:** 1946 in New Haven, Connecticut
**Elected from:** Texas
**Party:** Republican
**Vice President:** Richard Cheney

### George H.W. Bush
### 1989–1993
**Born:** 1924 in Milton, Connecticut
**Elected from:** Texas
**Party:** Republican
**Vice President:** J. Danforth Quayle

# GLOSSARY

**acid rain** (page 208) Acid rain is rain mixed with air pollution, which causes damage to the environment.

**addicted** (page 217) To be addicted means to not be able to stop using something.

**affirmative action** (page 160) Affirmative action programs require colleges and businesses to set aside a certain number of places for minorities.

**aggression** (page 120) Aggression is the use of military force.

**AIDS** (page 205) AIDS, or acquired immune deficiency syndrome, is a deadly disease caused by the HIV virus.

**aircraft carrier** (page 132) An aircraft carrier is a large ship that has a long, flat deck on which planes can land.

**alliance** (page 81) An alliance is an agreement between two or more nations to work together.

**al Qaeda** (page 235) Al Qaeda is an organization founded by Osama bin Laden that has been involved in attacks against civilian and military targets around the world.

**anarchist** (page 95) An anarchist is a person who does not believe in any form of government.

**annex** (page 61) To annex is to add or attach to something larger.

**anti-Semitism** (page 120) Anti-Semitism is the hatred of Jews.

**apartheid** (page 205) Apartheid was the system in South Africa that kept different racial groups separated.

**appeasement** (page 121) Appeasement is the policy of giving into an enemy's demands to maintain peace.

**arbitration** (page 39) Arbitration is a process that helps two groups come to an agreement.

**arms race** (page 148) The arms race is a competition between countries to build the largest military forces.

**assassin** (page 81) An assassin is a person who kills someone for political reasons.

**assembly line** (page 96) An assembly line is a line of factory workers and machines used to put together a product.

**atomic bomb** (page 132) An atomic bomb is an explosive weapon that causes great destruction.

**Axis nations** (page 120) Germany, Italy, and Japan formed an alliance in the 1930s called the Axis.

**balanced budget** (page 219) A balanced budget is a budget in which the money taken in is equal to the money spent.

**ballots** (page 233) Ballot are pieces of paper, cards, or other objects used in voting.

**barbed wire** (page 17) Barbed wire is twisted strands of wire that has barbs, or sharp points, along it. Barbed wire is used to make fences.

**barrack** (page 129) A barrack is a building used to house people temporarily.

**Berlin Airlift** (page 148) The Berlin Airlift was a mission by the United States and Great Britain to deliver supplies to West Berlin by plane when the Soviet Union would not allow supplies to come in by land.

**Bicentennial** (page 178) The Bicentennial was the 200th birthday of the United States, celebrated on July 4, 1976.

**big stick diplomacy** (page 74) Big stick diplomacy was President Theodore Roosevelt's foreign policy. It said that the United States would use military force to settle problems.

**blitzkrieg** (page 121) A blitzkrieg is a quick military attack.

**Buddhism** (page 168) Buddhism is a religion based on the teachings of Buddha.

**budget** (page 219) A budget is a plan for spending money.

**budget deficit** (page 219) A budget deficit occurs when a country spends more than it takes in with taxes and other fees.

**budget surplus** (page 219) A budget surplus means there is more than enough money to pay for everything in the budget.

**camera phone** (page 227) A camera phone is a type of cell phone that takes pictures that can be sent to other camera phones or computers anywhere in the world.

**campaign** (page 5) To campaign means to take part in activities to gain support for a cause.

**Camp David Accords** (page 192) The Camp David Accords was a peace treaty signed by Israel and Egypt in 1979.

**capital** (page 24) Capital is money that is used to earn more money.

**capitalism** (page 25) Capitalism is a type of economic system that allows people to own businesses and keep the money the businesses earn.

**carpetbagger** (page 7) Carpetbagger was the name Southerners gave to a person from the North who came to the South during Reconstruction to become rich.

**casualty** (page 169) A casualty is a person who is injured or killed during a war.

**cease-fire** (page 172) A cease-fire is an agreement to stop fighting.

**cell phone** (page 227) A cell phone is a type of hand-held radio used for communication.

**Central Intelligence Agency** (page 179) The Central Intelligence Agency, or CIA, is a government agency that gathers political, economic, and military information about other nations.

**civil disobedience** (page 158) A person commits civil disobedience when he or she peacefully refuses to obey certain laws that are considered unfair.

**civilian** (page 122) A civilian is a person who is not in the military.

**Civil Rights Act** (page 5) A Civil Rights Act is a law that protects the rights of people.

**civil rights movement** (page 154) The civil rights movement was the struggle to win equal rights for African Americans.

**civil service** (page 47) Civil service jobs are jobs in the federal government.

**coalition** (page 202) A coalition is a temporary alliance.

**Cold War** (page 144) The Cold War was a political and economic struggle between the United States and the Soviet Union that lasted from 1945 until about 1989.

**collective bargaining** (page 39) Collective bargaining is a process that helps two groups come to an agreement.

**commonwealth** (page 64) A commonwealth is a territory, state, or nation that rules itself.

**Communist** (page 83) A Communist is someone who believes in the system of government called communism.

**competition** (page 25) Competition is when two or more businesses try to sell similar goods or services to the same people.

**concentration camp** (page 120) A concentration camp was a place during World War II where Jews and other people were kept as prisoners by the Nazis. Millions of prisoners were killed in concentration camps.

**conservation** (page 50) Conservation is the protection and wise use of Earth's natural resources.

**conserve** (page 247) To conserve means to save.

**containment** (page 146) Containment was President Harry Truman's policy to keep communism from spreading.

**contra** (page 195) The contras were Nicaraguan rebels who opposed the Sandinistas.

**corollary** (page 74) A corollary is an idea that follows up another idea. The Roosevelt Corollary builds upon the ideas of the Monroe Doctrine.

**corporation** (page 26) A corporation is a type of business.

**counterculture** (page 181) A counter-culture is made up of a group of people who do not agree with the traditional beliefs of their society.

**debris** (page 235) Debris is the pieces left from something broken down or destroyed.

**defense industry** (page 128) The defense industry is made up of businesses that produce weapons and other equipment for fighting wars.

**deficit** (page 197) A deficit is when a government spends more money than it takes in.

**Department of Homeland Security** (page 237) This department is responsible for keeping United States citizens safe from terrorist attacks, natural disasters, and other emergencies.

**depression** (page 47) A depression is a time when business activity is slow and many people are unemployed.

**descendant** (page 62) A descendant is a person that comes from a certain ancestor.

**destroyer** (page 122) A destroyer is a type of warship.

**détente** (page 182) Détente was a time of peaceful relationship between the United States and the Soviet Union.

**discrimination** (page 155) Discrimination is the unfair treatment of a person because he or she belongs to a certain religious or racial group.

**DNA** (page 227) DNA is a molecule found in every cell that contains information necessary for life processes.

**dogfight** (page 82) A dogfight is a battle that takes place in the air between enemy planes.

**dollar diplomacy** (page 74) Dollar diplomacy was President Taft's policy toward Latin America. It encouraged the growth of American businesses there.

**domino theory** (page 168) The domino theory was the belief that if one country in Southeast Asia became a Communist nation, then all the other nations would become Communist as well.

**drug abuse** (page 217) Drug abuse is using a drug in a way that it was not intended to be used.

**due process** (page 6) Due process is a lawful way to give everyone the same rights and treatment.

**electoral vote** (page 232) The electoral vote is the votes cast by the electoral college. To become President of the United

States, a candidate must win the electoral vote.

**electronic mail** (page 227) Electronic mail, or e-mail, is a type of message sent between computers.

**embassy** (page 172) An embassy is the official home and office of an ambassador to a foreign country.

**emissions** (page 225) Emissions are substances sent into the air that cause damage to the environment.

**energy crisis** (page 182) An energy crisis occurs when a nation does not have enough energy to meet the normal needs of all of its citizens.

**environmental pollution** (page 225) Environmental pollution is when the earth is harmed through human activities.

**escalate** (page 169) To escalate means to increase.

**ethanol** (page 247) Ethanol is a chemical found in alcoholic drinks that can also be used as a fuel.

**ethnic group** (page 80) An ethnic group is a group of people of the same culture, of the same religion, or from the same country.

**European Union** (page 246) This is a group of 25 European nations that work together for peace and trade.

**evacuate** (page 233) To evacuate is to remove people from a place of danger.

**execute** (page 96) To execute is to kill a person, by order of the government, as punishment for breaking the law.

**expansionism** (page 60) Expansionism is the desire to gain more land.

**facilities** (page 155) A facility is a place created to serve a particular purpose, such as a school or a hospital.

**famine** (page 205) A famine is a severe food shortage.

**Fascist** (page 119) A Fascist is a member of the Fascist party. Fascist governments build powerful armies and are led by dictators.

**Federal Bureau of Investigation** (page 237) The Federal Bureau of Investigation is one of the country's main intelligence services which gathers and studies intelligence in the United States.

**federation** (page 207) A federation is a union formed by agreement between states, nations, or other groups.

**foreign oil** (page 247) Oil, or petroleum, is used to make gasoline, kerosene, and fuel oils. Foreign oil is petroleum purchased from other nations.

**freedman** (page 5) A freedman was a slave who was set free.

**free enterprise** (page 25) Free enterprise is the economic system that allows people to operate businesses in competition with other businesses. It is so called because the businesses generally operate free from government rules.

**gas chamber** (page 131) A gas chamber was a room that was filled up with poison gas to kill people.

**ghetto** (page 37) A ghetto is a neighborhood in a city where people from the same country or of the same religion live because they are discriminated against.

**glasnost** (page 198) Glasnost was the increase in personal freedoms in the Soviet Union during the 1980s.

**global warming** (page 226) Global warming is a rise in the earth's temperature.

**gold standard** (page 46) The gold standard was an economic idea in which all paper money was backed by gold from the United States Treasury.

**Good Neighbor Policy** (page 75) The Good Neighbor Policy was a policy toward Latin America during the 1930s. It said that the United States would not use military force there.

**grandfather clause** (page 9) A grandfather clause is a part of a law that allows someone to be excused from the law.

**guerrilla war** (page 170) A guerrilla war is a war that is fought by soldiers called guerrillas who do not fight openly and make surprise attacks.

**hijack** (page 233) To hijack is to steal a vehicle or force its operators (such as the pilot of a jet) to go where the hijacker demands.

**hippie** (page 181) A hippie was a person in the 1960s and 1970s who did not believe in the established culture.

**HIV virus** (page 217) The HIV virus is the virus that causes AIDS.

**Holocaust** (page 131) The Holocaust was the mass murder of Jews and other people during World War II.

**Hooverville** (page 108) A Hooverville was an area of a city where poor, homeless people built shacks to live in during the Great Depression. Hoovervilles were named after President Hoover.

**hostage** (page 195) A hostage is a person who is held as a prisoner until demands made by the captors are met.

**human rights** (page 194) Human rights are the rights to personal freedom and safety.

**illegal alien** (page 208) An illegal alien is an immigrant who enters a country without permission.

**impeach** (page 6) To impeach is to charge a government leader with a crime.

**import** (page 207) To import is to bring in goods from other nations.

**inflation** (page 46) Inflation is a sharp, quick rise in prices.

**injunction** (page 40) An injunction is an order given by a court that forbids a person from doing something.

**inspectors** (page 244) Inspectors are people who view and examine in an official way.

**insurance** (page 110) Insurance is protection against property loss or damage.

**integration** (page 155) Integration is the act of making something open to people of all races.

**intelligence** (page 237) Intelligence is secret information about another country or possible enemies.

**Internet** (page 226) The Internet is a system that links millions of computers.

**internment camp** (page 129) An internment camp was a place where Japanese Americans living on the West Coast were sent and held as prisoners by the government during World War II.

**invest** (page 106) To invest is to buy something or to put money into a business in order to make more money.

**investigation** (page 183) An investigation is the act of looking into a specific subject carefully to get information.

**iron curtain** (page 146) The iron curtain was a term that described the political division between Eastern and Western Europe during the Cold War.

**Islam** (page 204) Islam is a religion based on the teachings of Muhammad. People who follow Islam are called Muslims.

**isolationism** (page 122) Isolationism is a policy in which a nation avoids getting involved with the economic and political problems of other nations.

**isolationist** (page 61) An isolationist nation is a nation that avoids economic or political dealings with other countries.

**isthmus** (page 72) An isthmus is a narrow strip of land that connects two larger pieces of land.

**Ku Klux Klan** (page 8) The Ku Klux Klan, or KKK, was a secret organization started by Southerners after the Civil War. The KKK attacked, frightened, and killed African Americans to stop them from using the rights they had won.

**laissez-faire** (page 29) Laissez-faire is the idea that the government should not try to control business.

**liberate** (page 131) To liberate means to set free.

**literacy test** (page 10) A literacy test was a reading test a voter had to pass in order to vote. Literacy means the ability to read and write.

**malaria** (page 73) Malaria is a deadly disease that causes chills, fever, and sweating. People get malaria from the bite of an infected mosquito.

**management** (page 38) Management is made up of the person or persons who are in charge of a business.

**McCarthyism** (page 150) McCarthyism, named for Senator Joseph McCarthy, is the policy of falsely accusing people of working against the government.

**Medicare** (page 180) Medicare is a federal health care program that provides medical care for older Americans.

**merchant ship** (page 83) A merchant ship is a ship that carries goods.

**microchip** (page 226) A microchip is a tiny device that stores or processes information in a computer.

**microsurgery** (page 226) Microsurgery is surgery that is done with microscopes and specially built, small instruments.

**migrant farm worker** (page 108) A migrant farm worker is a person who goes from farm to farm looking for work.

**militarism** (page 80) Militarism is the build up of large, powerful armies and navies.

**minority** (page 112) A minority is a group of people that is thought to be different than the larger group it is a part of because of race or religion.

**missile** (page 179) A missile is a weapon that is shot at a target.

**monopoly** (page 27) A monopoly is when one company controls an entire industry.

**muckraker** (page 48) A muckraker is a writer who exposes political and social wrongdoings in business and in government. Muckrakers got their name because they raked up the muck, or dirt, in American life.

**multicultural** (page 214) Multicultural means made up of different cultures.

**Muslim** (page 204) A Muslim is a person who follows the religion of Islam.

**NAFTA** (page 208) NAFTA, or the North American Free Trade Agreement, is a trade agreement between the United States, Canada, and Mexico.

**NASA** (page 179) NASA, the National Aeronautics and Space Administration, is the United States' space agency.

**National Grange** (page 45) The National Grange is an organization that promotes laws that are helpful to farmers.

**nationalism** (page 80) Nationalism is a feeling of deep love and loyalty for one's nation.

**nativism** (page 95) Nativism is a fear of foreigners.

**natural resource** (page 24) A natural resource is a material found in nature that can be used by people. Iron, coal, water, and trees are natural resources.

**naval** (page 62) Naval means having to do with a navy.

**Nazi** (page 119) A Nazi is a member of the Nazi party. The Nazi party in Germany believed in nationalism and blamed other people, particularly Jews, for their country's problems.

**negotiate** (page 172) To negotiate is to talk to reach an agreement.

**No Child Left Behind Act** (page 246) This is an act signed by President Bush in 2001 to improve education for students from kindergarten through high school.

**nonaggression pact** (page 121) A non-aggression pact is an agreement between two countries to not attack each other during a war.

**nonviolent resistance** (page 158) Nonviolent resistance uses peaceful methods, such as boycotts, sit-ins, and marches, to end unfair laws.

**Northern Alliance** (page 236) The Northern Alliance was an organization of different groups whose goal was to remove the Taliban from power in Afghanistan.

**oath** (page 4) An oath is a promise.

**Open Door Policy** (page 65) The Open Door Policy was the American idea in the early 1900s that all nations should be allowed to use China's ports.

**open range** (page 16) The open range was unfenced, grassy land on which cattle grazed, or fed.

**orbit** (page 225) To orbit is to circle around an object, especially a sun, planet, or other object in space.

**overthrow** (page 204) To overthrow is to remove from power.

**pacifism** (page 136) Pacifism is the belief that wars are wrong and that disputes should be settled peacefully.

**pardon** (page 183) To pardon is to forgive a person for possible crimes.

**partnership** (page 25) A partnership is when two or more people own and run a business together.

**Peace Corps** (page 178) The Peace Corps is an organization made up of volunteers who go to developing countries to teach people how to improve health care, farming, and education.

**pension** (page 110) A pension is a sum of money paid regularly to a person after he or she has retired from a job.

**perestroika** (page 197) Perestroika was the opening up of the Soviet economy during the 1980s.

**persecuted** (page 120) To persecute is to harm someone because of their beliefs.

**personal digital assistant** (page 227) A personal digital assistant is a hand-held computer with which you can keep track of appointments, addresses, and phone numbers.

**peso** (page 208) The peso is the unit of money used in Mexico.

**PNTR** (page 207) PNTR, or Permanent Normal Trade Relations, is a trade status given to certain countries. Countries with PNTR pay lower tarrifs on goods.

**poison gas** (page 82) Poison gas is a deadly chemical used in war.

**polio** (page 113) Polio is a disease that is caused by a virus. It leads to paralysis and mainly affects children.

**poll tax** (page 9) A poll tax is a tax people pay when they vote.

**popular vote** (page 232) The popular vote is the votes cast by the people.

**poverty** (page 19) Poverty means being poor, or having little money.

**poverty line** (page 217) The poverty line is an amount of money that the federal government uses to determine whether or not a person is poor.

**privatization** (page 219) Privatization is the act of allowing private companies to run government programs.

**Prohibition** (page 93) Prohibition was the time period from 1919 until 1933 when it was illegal to manufacture, sell, drink, or ship alcoholic beverages.

**propaganda** (page 84) Propaganda is ideas or information that is deliberately spread to try to influence how people think and act.

**prosperity** (page 95) Prosperity is success, wealth, or good fortune in life.

**public office** (page 6) A public office is an elected or appointed job in the government.

**quota system** (page 37) The quota system in the United States limited the number of immigrants from different countries who could move to this country.

**race riot** (page 160) A race riot is a violent disturbance caused by the frustration that one race feels at being treated unfairly.

**racism** (page 95) Racism is a person's belief that he or she is better than other people who are not of the same race.

**Radical Republican** (page 4) A Radical Republican was a member of a group in Congress who wanted to punish the South for starting the Civil War.

**ration** (page 129) To ration is to limit the amount of items allowed.

**reaper** (page 15) A reaper is a machine that harvests crops.

**Reconstruction** (page 4) Reconstruction was the period after the Civil War when the Southern states rejoined the Union.

**recount** (page 233) Recount means to count again.

**recovery** (page 110) A recovery is a return to normal conditions.

**recycle** (page 129) To recycle means to make an item fit to be used again.

**Red Scare** (page 95) The Red Scare was a panic that occurred in 1919 when Americans feared that Communists might win control of the United States. It is so called because red was a symbol of communism.

**refinery** (page 28) A refinery is a place where oil is cleaned and turned into other products.

**refuel** (page 62) To refuel means to take on a fresh supply of fuel.

**refugee** (page 179) A refugee is a person who left his or her country for safety.

**reservation** (page 17) A reservation is a piece of land set aside by the federal government as a place for Native Americans.

**riot** (page 38) A riot is a violent disturbance created by a large number of people.

**rovers** (page 225) Rovers are machines used to explore the surface of other planets.

**sanctions** (page 205) A sanction is a method used by nations to force a country to change.

**Sandinista** (page 195) A Sandinista is a member of a group of people who ruled Nicaragua.

**satellite** (page 150) A satellite is an object that orbits a planet.

**scalawag** (page 7) Scalawag was the name used by Southern Democrats for white Southern Republicans who worked in Reconstruction governments.

**scandal** (page 94) A scandal occurs when a person does something that leads him or her to be publicly embarrassed.

**segregation** (page 9) Segregation means separating people because of their race.

**settlement house** (page 48) A settlement house provides poor people with services such as English classes, summer camp for children, and day care for the children of mothers who work.

**shah** (page 194) The shah was the name given for the rulers of Iran.

**share** (page 26) A share is one of the equal parts of ownership into which a business is divided. A share is sold to a specific person or group.

**sharecropper** (page 8) A sharecropper was a poor farmer who rented farmland from a landowner and paid rent with a share of the crops.

**sit-in** (page 158) A sit-in is a peaceful way to protest unfair laws. People seat themselves in a place that follows these unfair laws and refuse to leave until their demands are listened to.

**solar energy** (page 247) Solar energy is energy from the sun's rays.

**Solidarity** (page 198) Solidarity was a labor union that helped end communism in Poland.

**sphere of influence** (page 65) A sphere of influence is an area of a nation that is controlled by a foreign nation.

**spike** (page 16) A spike is a large, heavy nail that is used to join railroad tracks.

**stable government** (page 70) A stable government is a government that does not change frequently.

**stagflation** (page 183) Stagflation is when inflation combines with unemployment to create a stagnant, or slow, economy.

**stock** (page 26) A person owns stock when he or she owns one or more shares in a business.

**stock market** (page 106) A stock market is a place where stocks are traded.

**Strategic Defense Initiative** (page 197) The Strategic Defensive Initiative was a plan for a defense system that would use satellites to shoot down nuclear missiles fired at the United States. It is also called Star Wars.

**strategy** (page 129) A strategy is a plan for winning a war.

**submarine** (page 82) A submarine is a ship that can travel underwater.

**suffrage** (page 48) Suffrage is the right to vote.

**superpower** (page 144) A superpower is a powerful nation, such as the United States, whose actions and policies affect many other countries.

**supply-side economics** (page 199) Supply-side economics is the idea that the economy will improve if the amount of goods produced increases.

**Taliban** (page 235) The Taliban is an Islamic movement that ruled most of Afghanistan from 1996–2001. Even after losing power, the Taliban stayed active in Afghanistan.

**technology** (page 15) Technology is the use of science for practical puposes, such as industry and farming

**tenement** (page 36) A tenement is an apartment building that is usually run-down and crowded, and which has unhealthy living conditions.

**terrorism** (page 196) Terrorism is the use of dangerous, violent acts against innocent people to force an enemy to give in to terrorists' demands.

**third party** (page 50) A third party is a political party other than the two major parties.

**torpedo** (page 84) A torpedo is a missile that is launched underwater from a ship or a submarine and is designed to blow up when it hits its target.

**totalitarian** (page 119) Totalitarian governments are led by dictators that have total power over the people they rule.

**trade deficit** (page 246) A trade deficit occurs when a country imports more goods than it exports.

**transcontinental** (page 15) Transcontinental means across a continent. The transcontinental railroad goes from the Atlantic Ocean to the Pacific Ocean.

**trench warfare** (page 82) Trench warfare was used to fight World War I. Trenches were long ditches dug in the earth in which soldiers hid and attacked the enemy.

**truce** (page 149) A truce is an agreement between enemies to stop fighting

**trust** (page 27) A trust is formed when a group of companies join together under the same leadership so that they can control an industry.

**trustbuster** (page 49) A trustbuster is a person who tries to break up and punish business trusts.

**tutoring** (page 246) Tutoring is teaching another person, usually one tutor to one student.

**unskilled labor** (page 35) Unskilled labor means workers who have few skills.

**urban** (page 98) Urban means having to do with a city.

**vaccine** (page 218) A vaccine is a medicine given to protect against a disease.

**veteran** (page 109) A veteran is a person who has been in the armed forces.

**Vietnamization** (page 171) Vietnamization was a program to train South Vietnam's soldiers to fight the Communists by themselves.

**weapons of mass destruction** (page 243) Weapons of mass destruction include nuclear, chemical, or biological weapons that can kill a large number of people in a short time.

**Western Hemisphere** (page 70) The Western Hemisphere is the western half of the earth. It includes North America and South America.

**wind energy** (page 247) Wind energy is gathered from flowing air by windmills or wind turbines.

**withdrawal** (page 171) Withdrawal is the act of removing, as in troops from a battle.

**world power** (page 60) A world power is a major country whose actions affect other countries of the world.

**World Trade Organization** (page 245) The World Trade Organization (WTO) deals with the rules of trade between nations.

**yellow journalism** (page 62) Yellow journalism is exciting but untrue stories printed by a newspaper to attract more readers and sell more papers.

**Zionism** (page 136) Zionism is the belief that Jews should have their own country in Palestine, or present-day Israel.

# INDEX

King, Martin Luther, Jr., 158–159, 160, 161, 171
Kissinger, Henry, 172
Knights of Labor, 38
Korean War, 149
Kosovo, 206
Ku Klux Klan, 9, 95–96

**L**

Labor unions, 37–40, 41, 76, 198
Laden, Osama bin, 235, 236
Laissez-faire, 29, 108
Latin America, 70–71, 74–75, 95, 113, 150, 178, 179, 195–196, 197
Lazarus, Emma, 36
League of Nations, 86, 87, 118
Lend-Lease Act, 123
Lenin, V.I., 83
Liliuokalani, (Queen), 62, 66
Lindbergh, Charles, 98
Lodge, Henry Cabot, 86
*Lusitania*, 84, 88–89

**M**

MacArthur, Douglas, 109, 132, 146–147, 149
*Maine*, 63
Mandela, Nelson, 205
Mao Zedong, 149
Marshall, George C., 146
Marshall Plan, 146, 151
Martí, Jose, 62
Marx, Karl, 83
Mbeki, Thabo, 205
McCarthy, Joseph, 150
McCoy, Elijah, 26
McKinley, William, 47, 49, 63, 66, 76
Meat Inspection Act, 50

Mexican Revolution, 75
Middle East, 83, 86, 182, 192–195, 197, 202–203, 205–206
Middle East wars, 182, 192–193
Midway Islands, 62, 132
Migrant farm workers, 108–109, 181
Monroe Doctrine, 71, 74
Morgan, Garrett, 85–86, 97
Morgan, J.P., 30
Muckrakers, 48–49
Murrow, Edward R., 134–135, 150
Muslim, 206, 235
Mussolini, Benito, 119, 130

**N**

NASA, 179, 224–225
National Association for the Advancement of Colored People (NAACP), 41, 156
National debt, 219
National Grange, 45, 46
Nationalism, 80, 119
Nationist China, 149
Native Americans, 17–19, 20, 85, 182
Natural resources, 24, 25, 50, 61, 226
Nazis, 119–120, 131–133
Neutrality Act, 122
New Deal, 109–113
New Frontier, 178–179
New York City, 233, 239, 240
Nimitz, Chester W., 132
Nixon, Richard, 171, 172, 178, 182–183
North American Free Trade Agreement (NAFTA), 208

North Atlantic Treaty Organization (NATO), 148, 151
Novello, Antonia, 248

**O**

Open Door Policy, 65
Owens, Jesse, 125

**P**

Pacific Railway Act, 15–16
Palestine, 205–206
Panama Canal, 72–74, 76, 194
Parks, Rosa, 157–158, 161
Pattillo Beals, Melba, 163
Pearl Harbor, 62, 113, 124, 129
Perry, Matthew C., 61
Pershing, John J., 75, 85
Persian Gulf War, 202–203, 209, 243
Philippines, 62, 63, 64, 65, 72, 132
Platt Amendment, 64, 72
Plessy, Homer, 10
PNTR, 207
Poland, 36, 121, 130, 131, 146, 198
Populist party, 46–47
Powell, Colin, 202, 209
Prejudice, 37, 96, 99, 129, 223
Problems in America, 216–219, 246–247
Progressive Movement, 48–50, 94
Progressive party, 50
Prohibition, 93
Puerto Rico, 62, 64, 65, 71–72
Pullman, George, 40

Pure Food and Drug Act, 49
Putin, Vladimir, 204

## R

Rabin, Yitzhak, 205
Racism, 95–96, 99, 223
Railroads, 15–16, 17, 25, 26, 27, 28, 29, 40, 45–46
Reagan, Ronald, 195, 196, 197–198, 199, 209
Reconstruction, 4–10
Reconstruction Act, 6
Red Cloud, (Chief), 20
Red Scare, 95, 149
Reform movement(s), 45, 47–50
Reservations, 17–18, 19
Roaring Twenties, 97
Robeson, Paul, 99
Rockefeller, John D., 27–28
Rodriguez, Arturo, 181
Roosevelt, Eleanor, 111–113
Roosevelt, Franklin D., 75, 109–113, 122–124, 129, 131, 132, 136, 145, 151
Roosevelt, Theodore, 49, 50, 53, 63–64, 73, 74, 76, 113
Russia. *See also* Soviet Union. 36, 61, 76, 80, 81, 82, 83, 85, 144, 204
Ruth, Babe, 98

## S

Sacco and Vanzetti trial, 96
Scalawags, 7, 8
Schwartzkopf, H. Norman, 202, 209
Securities and Exchange Commission, 110
Segregation, 10, 41, 151, 154–158, 160, 161, 162, 163

Selective Service Act, 84
Senate, 6–7, 8, 86, 87, 150, 183, 194, 223
September 11 attacks, 233, 234, 237, 238, 239
Serbia, 81, 206–207
Seward, William Henry, 61
Sherman Antitrust Act, 29, 49
Sinclair, Upton, 49, 52
Sitting Bull, 18–19, 20
Smith, Alfred, 95
Social Security, 110–111, 112, 215, 219
Soviet Union. *See also* Russia. 99, 118–119, 121–123, 130–131, 133, 144–150, 179–180, 182, 194, 197–199, 203–204
Space missions, 179, 224–225
Spain, 62–63, 64, 73
Spanish-American War, 62–64, 65, 71, 72, 76
Stalin, Joseph, 119, 121, 129, 131, 145, 148
Stanton, Elizabeth Cady, 51
Stock market, 106–107
Supreme Court, 10, 29, 45–46, 111, 154–157, 158, 160, 183, 233

## T

Taft, William Howard, 50, 74–75
Taliban, 235–236
Taxes, 10, 47, 50, 72, 84, 110, 112, 123, 160, 199
Technology in America, 228
Tennessee Valley Authority (TVA), 110
Tenure of Office Act, 6

Terrorism, 196–197, 206, 218
Tiananmen Square, 207
Tilden, Samuel, 9
Tojo, Hideki, 119, 120
Tonkin Gulf Resolution, 169, 172
Treaty of Paris, 64
Treaty of Versailles, 86, 87, 118, 119, 120
Truman, Harry S, 131, 132, 146–149, 151, 179
Truman Doctrine, 146, 168

## U

United Nations, 131, 133, 144, 149, 202

## V

Vietnam War, 167–173, 174, 180–181, 207, 209
Villa, Pancho, 75, 85
Voting Rights Act, 160

## W

War Powers Act, 173
Warsaw Pact, 148
Washington, Booker T., 11, 41
Wilson, Woodrow, 50, 75, 83, 86, 87
Women's suffrage, 48, 51, 94
World War I, 80–87, 93–95, 118, 120, 121
World War II, 113, 118–125, 128–135, 148, 151

## Y

Yeltsin, Boris, 204
Yugoslavia, 206–207